MEMORIES OF
MARIE

Reflections on the Life and Work of
Marie Clay

COMPILED BY JENNY CLAY

Thank you to the very many people who have contributed to this book with information, photos, articles and memories of Marie.

www.pearsoned.co.nz

Your comments on this book are welcome at
feedback@pearsoned.co.nz

Pearson Education New Zealand
a division of Pearson New Zealand Ltd
67 Apollo Drive, Rosedale, North Shore 0632, New Zealand

Associated companies throughout the world

First published by Pearson Education New Zealand 2009
NZ ISBN 978-1-4425-1844-5

Produced by Pearson Education New Zealand
Printed in Malaysia (CTP-VVP)

Library of Congress Cataloguing-in-Publication Data
CIP data is on file with the Library of Congress
ISBN-13: 978-0-325-02675-6
ISBN-10: 0-325-02675-0

United States: Heinemann, 361 Hanover Street, Portsmouth, NH 03801-3912.

Acknowledgements
Some of the photographs in this book are from Marie Clay's family photograph collection. In
addition, Jenny Clay wishes to acknowledge and thank the many people and organisations who
have provided photographs for this book; in particular, National Reading Recovery, New Zealand;
Reading Recovery Council of North America; Lynette Bradley; Elonda Stevens; Barbara Watson; Peg
Gwyther; Gwen Graham; Audrey Weldon-Johnson; Margaret Griffin; Heather Bell; Linda Gambrell;
Seok Moi Ng; Joy Cowley; and Carl Braun.

Chapter opening page photographs
Page 11 – Young Marie Irwin on the Wellington coast in 1931.

Page 51 – Marie Clay in 1974 in the University of Auckland grounds by Old Government House.

Page 78 – New Zealand Tutors and Trainers at the 1993 Tutor Development week.

Page 93 – Dame Marie Clay and Sir Paul Reeves (Governor General) at her investiture in 1987.

*Page 104 – Julia Douëtil and Jean Prance with Marie Clay. Jean Prance (on the right) went to New Zealand to
train as a Reading Recovery Tutor in 1989, and began the first teacher course in Surrey in 1990.*

Page 119 – Marie Clay, President of the International Reading Association 1992–93.

Page 137 – Marie Clay giving her acceptance speech at the Dana Foundation Awards in 1993.

Page 189 – Marie Clay with some of her published books in 1982.

Page 233 – Marie Clay in Kansas, 2004.

Cover
Cover design: Helen Andrewes
Cover image: iStock photograph by José Luis Gutierrez

All royalties from sales of this book will go to The Marie Clay Literacy Trust.

Contents

The Institute of Education, University of London

International Reading Association

The USA and Canada

Language, Writings and Translation

Marie's Legacy

Introduction

The project of bringing together a memorial book on my mother, Marie Clay, came about initially from an international response in cards and letters to her death. Graham McEwan, her editor and the chairperson of her Literacy Trust, and I discussed the idea.

In the initial stages I talked to a few people in Auckland who had worked with or been students of Marie, and I contacted others to write pieces for the book, including Dorothy Butler, who wrote *Reading Begins at Home* with Marie, and Warwick Elley, who like Marie is one of the New Zealanders listed in the Reading Hall of Fame. Internationally I asked Courtney Cazden, Professor Emerita of Harvard, and Marie's friends at Texas Woman's University to write for the book.

I knew that I needed to contact more people further afield and I sought the assistance of Mary Anne Doyle, an editorial consultant on the Marie Clay Literacy Trust in the United States, and the Chair of the Executive Board of the International Reading Recovery Trainers Organisation, and Barbara Watson, who helped to establish Reading Recovery in New Zealand and overseas, to suggest relevant people to invite to write for the memorial book. I also searched the Internet for email addresses of people Marie had worked with at universities around the world. Many of the people I approached said they felt honoured to be asked to write for such a book. What an amazing legacy to have this response. To bring together the diversity sometimes seemed to me an overwhelming task. It was also an opportunity to work through a grieving process with her friends, associates and colleagues.

'I am history,' Marie said in her talk 'Simply by sailing in a new direction you could enlarge the world' in 2004. She lived through a time of enormous change through the twentieth century and into the twenty-first, from a time of typewriters to word processors, computers and email; through an economic depression, a world war, a time of prosperity and times of constant restructuring. There were adjustments through her life in terms of career and family. She was someone who used challenges and disappointments to increase the expectations she had of herself. She was a world traveller from the age of 25, when with the assistance of a Fulbright scholarship she set off to study in the United States. In the accounts of Marie's life before I was born, I have often used her notes made at different stages, or the first-hand accounts of others. I have also interspersed some of her letters in the later period, and therefore parts of the book have been written with her assistance.

Marie was diagnosed with advanced cancer in January 2007 at Auckland Hospital, after she was admitted to have liquid drained from a lung. The doctors decided the primary source was pancreatic cancer and that she had a short time left to live. Marie told few people this information. She dealt with it privately, and was concerned least it affect the work and funding of Reading Recovery internationally. Over the next three months she was mainly cared for in her own home by her son, Alan, her brother, Robert Irwin, and myself. Her grandchildren, Michael, Ida and Manuka, came from overseas to see her, from Australia and Europe.

In Mercy Hospice during Marie's final two weeks she said to a nurse during one of my visits, 'My daughter asks so many questions.' This trait, by others' accounts, I have inherited from her. I hope in putting together this book I have asked some of the right ones.

Marie Clay's ideas in developmental psychology, in language and literacy have influenced academics around the world; students have been challenged and assisted by Marie; children in many countries have been helped in their learning; and decades of teachers have been touched and affected in their work by her. Many of Marie's books remain in print and continue to be used internationally.

From her hospice bed, Marie said she wished her colleagues to continue with the work, the work in literacy which was fundamentally important to her. At the front of her book *By Different Paths to Common Outcomes*, Marie has a dedication to the people who contributed to her life: 'to all my teachers — family, colleagues, teachers, and young learners — for they have all immensely increased my view of what is possible.'

From the Beginning

Early Life

Marie's parents met in the choir of the Kent Terrace Presbyterian Church in Wellington, where they were married in January 1923. Her father, Donald Leolin Irwin, was an accountant and her mother, Mildred Blanche Godier, a teacher of music and singing. They were known in the family by their middle names, Leo and Blanche. Three years after their marriage, Marie Mildred Irwin was born on 3 January 1926. Leo would call her 'Marie with those starry eyes' from a nineteenth-century poem 'Baby' by George MacDonald: 'Where did you get those eyes so blue? Out of the sky as I came through.'

As a preschooler she accompanied her parents and a group of singers and performers from Kent Terrace Presbyterian Church to entertain at institutions like the Berhampore Children's Orphanage. On one occasion they went to a women's prison, Mt Crawford, where Marie was meant to sing Christopher Robin songs but insisted instead on singing: 'Jesus bids us shine with a clear, pure light, like a little candle burning in the night. In this world of darkness, we must shine. You in your small corner, and I in mine.'

Marie remembered a strong Wellington earthquake when she was three. Her London-born mother, immobilised by fear, called out to Marie. She didn't respond. Her explanation later failed to impress her mother: 'I was watching my doll's pram go round and round and round all by itself! How amazing!' She mused, 'What

Wedding photo of the marriage of Leo Irwin to Blanche Godier.
Back row: (left to right) Annie Margaret and Robert Irwin (Leo's parents), Cyril Irwin (his brother), Donald Leolin Irwin, Mildred Blanche Godier, Hannah Godier (Blanche's mother), and Harold Godier (her brother).
Front row: Leo's three sisters and two of Blanche's friends: (left to right) Eileen Riwaka Irwin, Dora May Abbott, Evangeline (Eve) Irwin, Eileen Lord, and Ethel Irwin.

else is possible?' It was a question she continued to ask throughout her life, as she explored what had not been tried before.

Annie Margaret Munro, her Scottish grandmother, known as Maggie, was a strong influence in Marie's life. Maggie had eight children to her school teacher husband, Robert Irwin, and dominated her family. Robert Irwin's parents were Irish, having emigrated from Ballygawley to Timaru in the South Island. When they met, Robert was teaching at Rangitata, north of Timaru, and Maggie was a pupil teacher at Kingsdown school. They married in 1896. By 1906 they had moved to Lyell in the Buller Gorge, where Robert was

Blanche holds baby Marie, visiting Marie's great-uncle Archibald and his wife, Ada, in Napier.

the headmaster and Annie Margaret was the assistant mistress. In the middle of that year Maggie had their fourth child, Lyell Ross Irwin. Their children often took one of their names from their place of birth: when they moved to Riwaka and to Havelock, the children born at this time were called Eileen Riwaka and Archibald Havelock Irwin. Robert and Maggie later relocated their large family to Nelson so the two eldest boys, Cyril and Leo, could go to Nelson College. In 1924 they moved to Wanganui. This was closer to their eldest son, Cyril Irwin, who was in a health sanatorium in Waipukurau and had tuberculosis. Cyril died a year later. Robert was headmaster of Queens Park School in Wanganui from 1924 until 1927.

While Marie Irwin was growing up, Robert and Maggie were still living on Durie Hill in the 'garden suburb' of Wanganui. Marie's early birthdays were spent at her grandparents' house. She remembered it as a long trip with her father in

the car from Wellington. The car had a 'dicky seat' and there were often flat tyres, and sometimes the water in the engine boiled over.

The back garden of the house was full of vegetables and had a chicken coop. Marie's grandfather Robert let her do the gardening with him and pick the violets at the side of the path. Grandpa Robert wrote poetry, some of which was published in the local newspaper. Marie remembered a story of her grandfather chasing a chicken around the garden, 'but Grandma had

Marie's grandparents, Robert and Maggie Irwin, with their eight children.
Back row: (left to right) Ross, Leo, Ethel, Cyril, and Archibald.
Front row: (left to right) Gordon on Robert's knee, Eileen, and Maggie with baby Eve.

Reading begins at home. Robert Irwin, Marie's grandfather, reads to his younger children. From left to right: Archibald, Gordon on Robert's knee, Ross, and Eileen.

to wring his neck' as Grandpa was too soft-hearted. When Marie ran a sewing machine needle through her finger, it was Grandma Maggie that 'set her free'. Marie's aunts and uncles came and went. Uncle Gordon was shut away doing schoolwork and later became a doctor. Her favourite aunt, Eve, was only ten years older than her and took Marie out on excursions.

When Marie tried to play the organ at the Durie Hill house, she discovered her limitations as a four year old. She could pull out the stops or fiddle with the keys, or get down and push the pedals, but she couldn't do everything at the same time. At the combined wedding of Ethel and Eileen Irwin, Marie's eldest aunts, to Dunlop Brown and Cecil Cornwall respectively, her mother Blanche played the organ. Marie was a four-year-old flower girl 'in a powder blue georgette frock frilled to the ankles'.

Marie's parents separated when she was five and a half. This made her very conscious of children whose lives didn't go to plan. They had just moved to a house where they lived on the bottom floor and another family lived upstairs. On the day her father left, Marie had fallen down and taken the knee out of her long woollen stockings. She thought her mother would be furious as the stockings were brand new, but Blanche didn't say anything. Leo boarded

Marie, the performer.

with a very big family and other boarders in a large house surrounded by bush and gardens. Marie was close to her father, and after the separation she stayed with him every second weekend.

In 1932 her grandfather Robert died. The family story was he died of a broken heart after his son Archibald was lost at sea in 1931. Archibald had been studying science at university and teaching. He was a talented scholar and yachtsman. He'd finished his final exams and sailed with experienced mates on a yacht called the

Leo and Marie with the 'starry eyes'.

Windward to the Chatham Islands. The *Windward* set off for the return to Wellington at the beginning of January but it disappeared off the Wellington coast and was never found.

Grandma Maggie, now a widow, came to stay with Blanche and Marie while she was settling Eve into university and teachers college. The seven-year-old Marie didn't appreciate their vegetarian diet started by a Wanganui doctor. She was unimpressed by the vegetable and lettuce sandwiches provided for her school lunches during their stay.

Marie sometimes went down to the road around 5 o'clock at night from her mother's house to wait for the milkman with his horse and cart. If she found good grass she was allowed to feed his horse. Next door was a friend called Marjory. One day when Marie was visiting, she noticed the earphones Marjory's father was wearing. He asked whether she would like to listen to the radio, and she wondered what this was.

The young reader.

When she put the headphones on she could hear a man's voice talking. It was 1933 and this was the first radio Marie had ever heard.

During the thirties Leo built a bach at Otaki Forks for his second brother with tuberculosis, Lyell Ross Irwin. Ross had been advised by doctors to live in isolation with his family. Marie spent many hours playing on her own in the bush at the lower reaches of the Rimutaka ranges at Otaki Forks while her father built the small bach, and later during their visits with Ross, his wife and their young son. It was from this time she gained the image she later used in talks of making paths in the bush, paths that were likely to be overgrown by the next visit.

Marie's school friends didn't know she had two separate homes. In those days the assumption was that children from split homes would not succeed. She wanted to become living proof that this was not the case. This made her determined to succeed and motivated her to try to find solutions to problems. As she moved with

Marie Irwin at primary school in 1932 (middle row, third from the right).

her mother around Wellington she became familiar with children at her schools that had tough lives and problems to overcome.

Marie helped around the house. Her mother was often sick and had been since she was a young girl. Blanche was born in September 1898 in Walthamstow, England, to William and Hannah Godier, 14 years after her brother, Harold. The Godiers, according to Marie's genealogy research, were originally Huguenots, and probably silk weavers, who came over to England from France. Blanche and Harold were the only two survivors of what could have been a large family. Eleven other children died before the age of five, and Blanche had been one of twins. She was hospitalised with rheumatic fever at six years of age. Blanche taught herself to read books during her long illnesses, and learned to play music. Her older brother, Harold, played and taught the organ and piano. William Godier died in 1906 after being ill with tuberculosis. In the same year his son, William Harold, was diagnosed with the early stages of tuberculosis. He left his job as a clerk at the Port of London Authority to immigrate to New Zealand as a health cure. Two years later his mother, Hannah, and sister, Blanche, joined him.

After arriving in New Zealand, Harold obtained a position as the organist and choir master at the Trinity Methodist Church in Newtown, Wellington. He met the minister of the Newtown Congregational Church, the Reverend Evans and his wife, Kate. Kate Evans was Kate Edger before her marriage, the first woman to graduate from the University of New Zealand. When she was living with her husband on Mt Victoria with three young sons, Kate ran her own private school in the family home. Marie believed that Blanche went to Kate's private school for young ladies in exchange for Kate Evans receiving free organ tuition from Harold.

By 1911 Harold Godier was the organist at the Kent Terrace Presbyterian Church in Wellington. Blanche Godier became one of the soprano members of the Kent Terrace Church choir in 1915, and Leo Irwin joined the choir three years later. His boss at the Farmers' Institute, J.W. Jack, was very involved in this church. Leo's older brother Cyril joined the choir briefly before his diagnosis and departure for a sanatorium in Masterton. The courting couple, Leo and Blanche, spent holidays with the Irwin family in Nelson, where Robert Irwin was teaching.

Blanche's ambition prior to marriage was to study opera at the Melbourne Conservatorium of Music. She was a skilled pianist, singer and accompanist, and later a teacher of piano and singing. She had an interest in Theosophy and Esperanto while Marie was growing up, and attended talks around Wellington. Blanche was also interested in the rights of women and women having careers in previously male-dominated areas, such as in journalism. Marie suspected Kate Edger had a direct influence on Blanche and an indirect influence on herself. Marie said, 'I never doubted that women could work and have minds of their own.'

While on a group opera tour of Eastern Europe in 2006, Marie remembered her Wadestown years, during a performance of Richard Wagner's *Tannhauser* in Dresden. Marie said in her tour notes, 'Tapping in to old memories I cannot tell where I gained my familiarity. I think the overture must have been on an old HMV record in the 1930s, together with the huge chorus … This belongs to my

Wadestown years 1935–1936 in Harold Godier's living room with his prominent record player, and the HMV dog.'

For two years Marie and her mother lived at 129 Wadestown Road with Blanche's brother, Harold Godier, his wife, Dora May (née Abbott), and their daughter, Cherry, who was six years younger than Marie. 'These were years when family members played pieces and then transposed them, or played the pieces as a different composer would have written them. Harold did this, so did my mother, and cousin Cherry was beginning to join them.' Cherry became a music

teacher after raising a family. Marie didn't feel she had what was needed to play the piano well, after unsuccessful piano lessons with her mother, and then another teacher had passed her on to a senior pupil. She did sing, recite and perform on many occasions, and had a beautiful singing voice, although rarely used later in life.

There were duets in the Wadestown drawing room where Blanche sang soprano and her sister-in-law Dora May sang contralto. The others would join in. Marie also remembered her mother had 'played Maid Marian in the local Robin Hood musical' in Wadestown 'and wore her own long hair, reconstructed', hair so long Blanche had been able to sit on it. Marie did her first serious writing at Wadestown Primary School, editing a classroom newspaper.

Blanche as Maid Marian in Robin Hood, St Luke's Hall, Wadestown, September 1933.

Marie's father was managing an office of Rubber Distributers at this time. The warehouse appeared to the young Marie to be full of gumboots and hose pipes. She was afraid of the lift because it seemed to stop between floors. It took her a while to realise the doors opened on different sides to let people in and out. When Marie was eight, Leo Irwin submitted his thesis on 'The Development of Electric Power in New Zealand' for a Masters in Commerce. His Masters was awarded by the University of New Zealand, setting an academic example Marie later followed.

At the end of 1936 her parents' divorce went through, and Leo married Chad (Claribel Cletis Thomson) the following year. Blanche wished to explore life in Sydney, and so Marie went to stay with Leo and Chad in their small apartment. When her mother suggested that Marie join her in Sydney, Marie steadfastly refused as she'd found a school she was happy in. People often adjusted to where Marie was in her life, and Blanche returned to Wellington to be with her. Chad gave birth to

Marie holds her little brother, Robert.

Robert in 1939 and Lorraine in 1942, Marie's half brother and sister. Marie was happy to have siblings although distant in age. Lorraine still has a doll that Marie designed and made clothes for.

After going to many primary schools, Marie Irwin attended one secondary school for four years, Wellington East Girls College, on a windswept piece of land on the city side of Mt Victoria above the Hataitai traffic tunnel. When Marie enrolled in 1939, her father Leo couldn't see any point in her learning Latin, so she started class in 3 Modern, not 3 Latin. Her repertoire of subjects included sewing and cooking. She believed this helped her later reputation for pavlovas, with the enforced diligent beating of egg whites; and her dressmaking skills helped her to sew her own clothes, often elegant numbers, for many years. At the end of the Form 3 (Year 9), she was first in her class in drawing and received a book prize, *Thy Servant the Dog* by Rudyard Kipling. She enjoyed drawing and would have gone to the Technical High School to learn Commercial Art if her father had permitted it.

In September of 1939, the Second World War was declared. The Red Cross asked for help and the Wellington East girls responded, Marie among them. They made hussifs — little sewing kits with scissors, threads, and safety pins slotted in — for the armed forces; they sewed tapes onto a strip of khaki drill, attaching spare buttons and flannel patches for pins and needles. In a talk at a Wellington East Girls College prizegiving in 1986, Marie recalled that during a fourth form French lesson, the teacher lost control and Marie's whole class moved to the window to watch the barque *Pamir* in full sail going out of the harbour. The sailing ship was headed for England with much needed stores and would travel through the battle zones of the Atlantic.

The Wellington Boys College was down the hill from Wellington East Girls School, separated by a boundary fence. The only contact allowed with the boys was supervised during ballroom dancing classes held in the Wellington East Assembly Hall. In 1942, Marie's final year at the school, the American troops arrived in Wellington in response to the threat of a Japanese invasion. The troops were seen by school staff as more of a threat than

Marie Irwin in school uniform in the Wellington East Girls College grounds.

the Japanese and created severe anxiety for them. The schoolmistress at morning assemblies referred to purity, self-respect and womanhood. There were warnings to the girls about talking to the American marines in the streets.

Marie remembered fire, earthquake and air-raid drills when the girls rushed under the school into the Mt Victoria tunnel and assembled there. For 'the war effort' the girls knitted balaclavas and mittens, and raised money with sweet stalls, until sugar was rationed in early 1942; and they held concerts. To assist in one concert Marie decided to take her mother's six green Venetian glass goblets along,

Marie leading the netball team.

after she'd discovered how musical they were when filled with water at differing levels and tapped. She gave a satisfying accompaniment to the improvised class band, and arrived home with only two intact goblets. Blanche was not impressed.

Marie enjoyed secondary school, feeling it made up for difficulties in her home life. She played netball and was awarded prizes each year. In Form 5 (Year 11) she was first in her class for languages, and first equal in science and mathematics. She had been barred from involvement in a Gilbert and Sullivan show that year as she was sitting the University Entrance exam. She worked hard and gained University Entrance in 1941 after three years of high school as well as School Certificate in seven subjects. She remembered running along the corridor, late for class, and just missing a collision with the deputy principal, whose arms were piled high with books, by ducking under the sleeves of her gown. 'And we were thinking of making you a prefect,' the deputy principal said.

They still did.

MARIE AT SECONDARY SCHOOL
Dr Geraldine McDonald

Geraldine McDonald (née Player) and Marie Irwin were prefects together in the sixth form. Geraldine McDonald became a lecturer at Wellington College of Education before writing a doctoral thesis on the language and thought of Maori and non-Maori children. Her Masters thesis was the study of the effect of Playcentre on building a sense of community. When she was appointed to the New Zealand Council of Educational Research (NZCER) in 1973, she set up the Early Childhood Unit. In 1977 she was appointed Assistant Director of NZCER.

Marie Irwin and I (Geraldine Player) were both pupils of Wellington East Girls College. The school had been built to cater for girls from the eastern suburbs of Wellington. The building had a very imposing façade. The main entrance was approached by steps which led to marble stairs leading to the offices of the principal and staff. The girls were not allowed to enter this area. Beyond this grandeur the architecture tended to tail off. There were two blocks arranged in a T with two floors of classrooms off concrete corridors. On the third side there was an assembly hall. The library was a small area under the entrance to the school. I suspect that some original plans had been tempered by the economic depression of the 1930s and then, in the 1940s, when both Marie and I attended, by the war. The only construction work I can remember was some bomb shelters dug into the croquet lawn in case the Japanese had their eye on the school. There was no swimming pool and the swimming sports entailed a long walk to the seawater baths at Oriental Bay.

Prefect photo 1942, Wellington East Girls College, with Marie Irwin (back row far right) and Geraldine Player (third from right).

Marie and I were together in the sixth form in 1942. She was clever and efficient. We were both appointed prefects. Appointment was by the staff, and those of us being considered for office were interviewed by the principal in her office. One of the standard questions was our attitude to boys. There was quite a lot about avoiding boys at Wellington East Girls. The school had a boundary shared with Wellington College. Our school was on a hillside above a traffic tunnel while the boys were way down below on the flat. Possibly some daring lads had once scaled the hill in their lunch hour but I cannot recall any such incident. To guard against such an eventuality there was a strip of land about 6 feet wide inside the boundary fence. As prefects we were expected to see that no girls entered this area and we took turns to patrol it, usually in a howling northerly, while third formers dodged around in the bushes to annoy us.

The school offered a range of courses but its main interest was in scholarship and examination passes. The teachers, virtually all unmarried women, wore academic gowns. We wore gym tunics with hems which were required to be a set number of inches from the ground when we were kneeling. One of the pleasures of the school was the cultural activity it offered. There was a weekly lunch-time gathering, at which one week girls presented speeches, prepared and impromptu, while on the following week plays were performed. Virtually the whole school turned up for these events. There were also light-hearted contests. One favourite involved hanging a curtain across the stage of the assembly hall. The curtain did not reach the ground. Girls then stood behind it with bare legs displayed from the knees down and a teacher judged who had the best legs. I was talking to Marie many years later and reminiscing about our school days. She said she had never forgotten that in one of these contests, it was decided that she had the best legs, and how grateful she felt to the teacher who had chosen her. I can remember the occasion and that indeed Marie's legs were shapely.

I saw very little of Marie after we left school because we lived in different cities but she was New Zealand examiner for my doctoral thesis ('Aspects of the Language and Thought of Four-year-old Maori Children'). Marie had to fly to Wellington for the oral examination. The weather was atrocious and the plane finally landed more than an hour past schedule. I was waiting anxiously for her arrival and wondered whether her judgement would be affected by the flight, but no. She passed my work, and she approved of the fact that I had concluded that meaning was far more important for understanding than verbal form. This fitted in with Marie's own findings of the importance of meaning in learning to read.

I followed Marie's international reputation with interest and was always pleased to remember that we were once prefects together at Wellington East Girls College.

In her final year at Wellington East Girls, Marie got her Higher Leaving Certificate and a copy of *Letters and Art in New Zealand* by E.H. McCormick, her book prize for 'English, History, Crafts, Drawing, and Geography'. She looked at career options. Her suggestion of being a journalist was dismissed by a teacher, perhaps because she didn't think Marie could write! She was a year under age for her choice of training as an occupational therapist, and so Marie Irwin began teacher training, following the path of her grandfather Robert, and her aunts, Ethel and Eve.

She had a small allowance as a trainee teacher. This enabled her to study at the university, the Wellington campus of the University of New Zealand, which became Victoria University. Growing up during the depression and coming from basically a one-parent household, Marie was used to having little in the way of financial resources. She walked daily from Courtenay Place to the university 'not for physical fitness but to save the tram fare from my monthly allowance of 5 pounds 11 shillings and 5 pence'. She believed her savings helped her to get to the University of Minnesota seven years later. The politics of war and peace pervaded her university

Walking to university along the Wellington streets.

activities. Daily lives were focused on the news from many countries. Courses in history and political science introduced her to federal and parliamentary systems and confirmed her liberalism. In New Zealand universities, psychology as a subject was still evolving out of philosophy departments, but Marie's Psychology 1 course in 1944 was taught by Sir Thomas Hunter, who in 1912 had set up the first psychology laboratory in the southern hemisphere.

As most of the men were away at war, Marie learned an unusual skill for a woman while at Wellington Teachers College; she learned how to coach rugby, an essential part of the curriculum for boys in the South Pacific. For the same reason she said she sang tenor in the Teachers College choir. She served on the training college social committee from 1943 to 1944 and washed dishes after the bobhops each Friday night.

Marie and friends from the university netball team.

Marie and her mother lived with Madame Bligh, a ballroom dancing teacher, for many of the years that she was at Wellington East Girls and

Victoria University. Madame Rosina Hope Bligh had a two-storey house in Waitoa Road in Hataitai by the bus tunnel. She taught ballroom dancing downstairs, and had tenants in other parts of the house. A young girl, Barbara Squire, lived around the corner from the house along Hinau Road. She studied singing with Blanche and participated in pantomimes

Her friends hold Marie high.

organised by Madame Bligh. Barbara remembers Madame Bligh as a regal lady, whose studio was approached down a dark flight of stairs not far from the area where Blanche and Marie lived, or by an outside door on the east side. Barbara's father gave Madame Bligh's daughter, Joyce, away in marriage to Alan Shearer. Barbara learned dancing steps in studio classes to a wind-up gramophone, which her family inherited when Rosina Bligh died in 1952. Marie was reminded of her 'dancing years' over a meal in Warsaw, on the 2006 European tour, when being entertained with songs of the thirties and forties.

Blanche and Marie had small rooms on the top floor of the house, and a little kitchen with a gas-ring. Into her bed-sitter Blanche fitted her piano. Barbara Squire and her friend Joan Harris shared singing lessons there on Saturday mornings. They presented vocal items at the Wellington Esperanto Club with the accompaniment of Blanche Godier on the piano. Barbara remembers Marie studying by the window in the sun or sitting on her bed, her legs tucked under her, surrounded by books. During her holidays Marie worked in the railway cafeteria in

Blanche Godier with her daughter, Marie.

Wellington, where she served tea in the Crown Lynn railway mugs.

While at Wellington Training College Marie Irwin had primary school teaching sections at Kelburn Normal, Clyde Quay and Terrace Model School. In her second year at training college she had coached a ten year old who couldn't read, at one of the lower socio-economic schools in Wellington. She didn't believe there were any services in New Zealand for his particular needs. In writing about this time she said that in USA 'Marion Monroe, Grace Fernald and Arthur Gates were beginning to document some new ideas which introduced us to remedial reading; and in England Cyril Burt and Fred Schonell were devising assessments for diagnosing reading difficulties.'

Marie had set her heart on a third-year arts and crafts specialisation at Wellington Teachers Training College. She missed out by one place. In response she threw herself into her university studies. There were celebrations in the Wellington streets in 1945 when peace was declared. Marie had graduated as a teacher and was in her probationary teaching year at Hataitai School, when the 'lads' returned. During 1946 she took leave for full-time study to complete her Bachelor of Arts degree. At the end of the year she was awarded the Senior Scholarship in Education from the University of New Zealand.

She embarked on papers for her Masters of Education degree while teaching at Thorndon Primary School. Although Marie already had a busy schedule, she was also involved in costume design for amateur dramatic productions at the university. She was given two books, *Romance at the English Theatre* by Donald Brook and *Contemporary Ballet* by Audrey Williamson, for her participation in the 1947 'Extravaganza'. Extravaganzas had a high profile at Victoria campus around the war years. Marie described the Mozart opera that she attended in Berlin in 2006 as 'four hours long, reminiscent of a university Extravaganza'.

After finishing at Wellington Teachers College, rather than going on country service, Marie had taken city positions teaching children in Junior Special Class, pupils who were selected as being of low intelligence, at Thorndon and Newtown schools. While she was teaching she wrote a thesis, 'The Teaching of Reading in New Zealand Special Classes', on those who made some remarkable progress in learning to read. In her writing she consulted the doctoral dissertation of Helen M. Robinson whose arguments came 'from a complex statistical analysis of the multiple causation of reading difficulties'. Robinson became co-founder of the International Reading Association with Albert B. Harris. In 1949 Marie Irwin graduated with both a Diploma of Education and a Master of Arts with Honours in Education.

Marie began to work for the Psychological Services of the Department of Education during 1949. She had applied in 1947 for a bursary for a training course as an educational psychologist under Ralph Winterbourn. The first trial training course had produced two male educational psychologists, and this was the second course advertised. She was interviewed and two weeks later turned down. The explanation given was 'that as a woman likely to marry and have children, I was too much of a risk' (of not using the training).

In August of 1949 Marie was appointed to the Department of Education as a psychological assistant to Miss A.R. Sheat, the Supervisor of Special Classes in Auckland, where she worked for a year. Marie then worked from August 1950 as a psychological assistant to the Department in Wellington, selecting special class entrants for the Taranaki, Hawkes Bay, Wellington and Nelson education boards under the guidance of Mr. J. Caughley, Supervisor of Psychological Services. In her 'spare time' she was involved in costume and stage design in repertory theatre in both cities.

Marie started to look for opportunities overseas for post-graduate study. Professor Fred Schonell accepted her for his course in England, but before she could take this up he obtained a position at the University of Queensland. Marie Irwin turned her attention to Senator Fulbright's plan to use war surplus funds in several countries

Marie Irwin applies to study overseas. One of the photos Audrey Weldon received.

to get foreigners to the USA to study. Marie applied for and won a Fulbright Scholarship to the University of Minnesota. To be able to afford to go, she also applied for a supplementary grant through the Institute of International Education, a partner organisation of the Fulbright programme. References were forwarded that had been submitted for her United States Government travel grant. The references were from: Colin L. Bailey, her Professor of Education at Victoria University College; Mr. V.H. Thwaites, the headmaster of Thorndon School, where she had taught for two and a half years; Miss A.R. Sheat, the Supervisor of Special Classes for the Department of Education in Auckland; and Mr. J.C. Caughley, the Supervisor of Psychological Services in the Department of Education in Wellington. They were all supportive of her application.

Marie Irwin travelled to America on the ship *Ceramic* in 1951, her first opportunity to go overseas. She found catching a one-class ship to the Panama Canal and disembarking at Balboa a shock, having never been to another country before. She took a train to Panama City and a plane flight to Miami, the first flight of very many in her life. On the two-and-a-half-day train trek to Chicago she was surprised by the flatness of the land. After her final train journey from Chicago to Minneapolis, Marie was met on 20 September by 'her American sister', Audrey Weldon, and her family.

The Weldon family, Mrs Helen Weldon and her daughters, Bernadine and Audrey, welcome Marie into their home in Minnesota in September 1951.

Audrey had joined the University of Minnesota in her third year after two years at Bethel College, a small Baptist college. In her family memoir book, *Time and Chance Happen to Us All*, Audrey says, 'The Foreign Sister Program interested me because I needed to feel more connected to the university and make it my school.' It was a system for adjusting visiting Fulbright students to the universities. Audrey chose Marie

Marie was enchanted with her bedroom in the Weldons' home, and was reading the London Illustrated *magazine when this photo was taken.*

as her 'foreign sister' from the photos submitted from New Zealand. Marie was welcomed into the Weldon household by Audrey, her parents and her younger sister, Bernadine. The first Sunday after Marie's arrival she discovered the coloured local newspaper, the *Saint Paul Dispatch-Pioneer Press* so unlike the black and white newspapers of home, and was delighted.

There were 500 overseas students in a university student population of 25,000. There had only ever been one other New Zealand student at the University of Minnesota, and that person had studied agriculture. When Marie moved from the Weldon household into Chi Omega Sorority House, she regarded the 'free room' as the sorority's good deed for the year. As a foreign student and, at 25 years, much older than the other students, she was the only graduate in the undergraduate club. In her later report to the NZ Fulbright Association, Marie said, 'The living conditions were very comfortable and the companionship of the twenty house-girls and fifty members all-told was very welcome. It was understood that as a graduate student I would have a bigger workload than the sorority girls who were all undergraduates and I was given every consideration. At the same time I was included in any activity I wished. Much of the success of the arrangement was due to the kindness of the housemother, who acted as a counsellor for the girls.' Marie later remembered from the Sorority House 'the good cook and wonderful housemother with special supper snacks around exam time'. The cook was called Martha and the house mother Mrs Chris. Audrey was often invited to join them for events and meals because Marie Irwin was her 'foreign sister'.

After her arrival Marie had a set-back. She found the courses in special education that she'd planned to take at the College of Education no longer existed. She discovered an alternative at the Institute of Child Welfare and was allowed to study there for a quarter year before taking the qualifying exam. Although the approach to examining material was very different to New Zealand, she continued for two further quarters with 'A' grades.

There were 10 foreign students at the Institute of Child Welfare of the University of Minnesota during her time there. In her Fulbright report Marie said, 'Foreign students have problems in common on an American campus and tend to draw together. At first there was a noticeable cliquing of British Commonwealth students, but gradually we found we had more to learn from the Asian and European students about conditions in their countries. Those who were English speaking could assist them with their cultural and language difficulties. I spent numerous evenings in discussions on education with students from many parts of the world, and made staunch friends of Dutch, Norwegian, and American students who were school psychologists in their own countries.' Among the foreign students was Maria Janssen, a Fulbright scholar from Holland, who became a lifelong friend. Maria was seven years older than Marie, as her education had been broken up by the war. She was a psychologist back home in Holland. Marie and Maria would meet throughout their lives in Europe, America and England at conferences and homes.

In October 1951 there was an early winter blizzard in Minnesota. Snow wouldn't usually have come until November or December and it was a new experience for Marie. In her typed notes 'A Personal View of History' she said, 'I remember the cold of watching ice hockey, ploughing through snow in the early morning to the childcare centre for my practical work, and falling down on the ice in ten-minute desperate dashes' between lectures, and 'fantastic lectures in some subjects'.

Marie's main courses of study were in developmental psychology and clinical child development, on how most children develop and learn, and how those who have difficulty can be helped, and she took a minor in reading difficulties. Marie was under

Audrey Weldon and Marie Irwin in the Minnesota snow in October.

the supervision of Guy Bond, a student of Arthur Gates, during her teaching of children with reading difficulties. Her major was in developmental child psychology. John Anderson was influential for Marie. He trained at Yale University and was the Director at the Institute of Child Welfare. A saying of his that remained with her was, 'Sin in science is not using a better way of answering your questions when it is available to you.'

At the University of Minnesota, Marie learned techniques that she used later on in her career. In a class on reading they 'reviewed current research and each student presented a critique of a research, providing classmates with practice in finding the flaws in one's arguments'. Marie wanted to give the class some material from outside the USA and selected 'a smoothly designed five-group teaching

Marie's sketch for the costume of Jade Pure from her designs for the stage production of The Land of the Dragon.

intervention conducted by Fred Schonell and published in the *British Journal of Educational Psychology*', which compared different interventions, the main research finding surprising her classmates. She was involved in working on clinical programmes and teaching 'for our lecturers and classmates behind a one-way screen, turning in detailed case studies for assessments'.

Marie had enrolled in one paper in children's theatre, pursuing her interest in drama. Among her coursework she did a detailed analysis and design for a children's production of *The Land of the Dragon* by Madge Miller (1946), a stylised Chinese play. A character called Road Wanderer travels with his pet dragon, and rescues Princess Jade from captivity and her impending marriage.

In her article 'International Perspectives on the Reading Recovery Program' in the *Handbook of Research on Teaching Literacy through the Communicative and Visual Arts* (Lapp, 1997), Marie mentioned doing this paper in 1951 for personal interest. She said, 'I still have my production script for a Chinese play with full stage design and costumes for three dragons, an interest never allowed to flourish.'

Prior to leaving New Zealand, Marie had met Warwick Clay in Wanganui, where he was an engineer with the Wanganui Harbour Board. Marie was visiting schools as a psychological assistant with the Department of Education, and she stayed at the private hotel where Warwick was living. Warwick had studied to be a civil engineer at night school when his father indicated the family did not have the money for him to attend university full-time. He'd done well at Takapuna Grammar School, and had worked as a cadet at the Auckland Harbour Board while studying with the Institute of Civil Engineering. When he was 20 he trained as an officer in the New Zealand Navy. As his ship was embarking across the Pacific Ocean, the Second World War ended and the ship was recalled. He'd worked as an engineer in Timaru and Taumarunui, before being appointed to the Wanganui Harbour Board.

Warwick, like Marie, was interested in travelling overseas. He went part of the way of her journey on the same ship, the *Ceramic*, but continued on to England. They kept in contact. After travelling in the United Kingdom, Warwick followed Marie to Minnesota, arriving before Christmas in 1951. He'd been appointed to an assistantship at the Hydraulic Laboratory of the University of Minnesota, and worked there part-time during his stay in Minneapolis. In between studies and work, they caught Greyhound buses and toured around many of the states.

Warwick Clay arrives in Minnesota before Christmas. Marie Irwin, Mrs Chris (Ruby Christiansen), and Warwick Clay at Chi Omega House, December 1951.

During Easter of 1952 Warwick proposed, a year after they'd met. The 26-year-old Marie accepted. Marie chose to be married in Minnesota away from the separated family situation. Her parents came together in Wellington to discuss this and,

Marie's bridesmaid helps her prepare for her wedding.

although not happy with her decision, they accepted it. Grandma Maggie voiced regret when she heard about the marriage saying, 'I always hoped she would make something of herself.'

Marie completed an assignment, for the children's theatre department, the night before the wedding. Warwick Clay and Marie Irwin were married in Andrew Riverside Presbyterian Church in Minnesota, on 14 June 1952.

Marie surprised the minister by having a woman give her away, Mrs Chris, the housemother. The wedding was attended by her American sister's family, friends at the university and her sorority, all of whom wished the couple well. As Marie had finished her Fulbright studies, she and Warwick departed immediately for Niagara Falls.

Marie wrote in a letter from Chicago years later of old memories that surfaced: '... married in the morning in Minneapolis, Warwick and I travelled by Greyhound bus as far as Chicago and spent the night here. Next day we visited the city's new showpiece, the Merchandise place — a bit like an early version of today's big shopping malls. In the afternoon we went on to the town of Niagara where I couldn't really view the falls because I had no passport and couldn't cross into Canada ... another story.'

Warwick and Marie continued on their honeymoon to England and Europe. They met another honeymoon couple in Scotland, Will and Gwen Graham. Gwen wrote down her memories of this time:

Warwick and Marie on board ship on their honeymoon.

'In 1952, I left my teaching job in Western New York State to go to England to be married. Will was in the United States Air Force as a weatherman. We were married July 21st in London and went to England's Lake District for our honeymoon. One day we took a sightseeing tour to Edinburgh, Scotland. We were standing in line at the entrance to Holyrood Palace and Warwick and Marie were in front of us. We struck up a conversation, and soon found out we both were on our honeymoon.

Upon learning that we were to be living in London, they asked if we knew of an inexpensive place where they could stay while touring the city. We could not think of any at the moment, but would give it some thought and maybe could come up with something during the day. We would see them on the bus back to London and would fill them in then if we thought of a place, and ... during the day Will and I did come up with an idea. Would they like to stay with us? We had a two-bedroom house in Ealing ... right close to the bus stop and not far from the 'tube' (underground train). The area surrounding our house on Creighton Road had been heavily bombed during World War II, so it was fairly new. Sugar, butter and meat were still on ration. Because the base was quite a distance from where we were living, I managed to live as my British neighbours did. (Once in a while the butcher would give me a little extra.)

They accepted. We went shopping together after making up a week's menu.

The plan was for Will to report to his base each day in Ruislip, Warwick and Marie would go sightseeing, and I would be off on my own jaunts. We met again about 5 or 6 in the evening and Marie and I would make dinner. We all did dishes together and when done with that, we played bridge to the wee hours. We had a wonderful time together. I remember showing our wedding movies to them and several couples from the Air Force base. The women sat on the stairs and the men watched as they stood around the punch bowl eating snacks! It was an evening I will always remember.

Our house was what we in America call a 'row house'. There were about 12 side by side with a common wall between, all were two storey of light-colored brick and had small front flower gardens with a gated entrance. Before they left we promised that we would visit them in New Zealand.'

Gwen and Will Graham threw a party at the Ealing house to show their wedding movies. Gwen is at the bottom of the stairs, and Marie is halfway up on the right.

Marie and Warwick travelled through Europe for six weeks and returned to New Zealand by boat through the Suez canal. They settled in Wanganui, where Marie's grandparents had lived, and Warwick resumed his previous work as an engineer with the Wanganui Harbour Board. He made a proud purchase of a new Ford Consul, a car that remained with the family for 11 years.

After her return, Marie wrote in a report for the NZ Fulbright organisation about her time in America: 'The scientific, experimental approach to research adhered to by the Institute of Child Welfare … was in keeping with my training and background.' She said that most of the people who she had lived with had not been outside the state of Minnesota, so for some she put New Zealand on the map. Comparisons were made between local conditions and those in New Zealand and 'other Commonwealth countries' when she visited schools, during class discussion groups, and on visits to American homes. 'I was a guest in about a dozen private homes, and frequently at the home of my "American sister". She still shows a keen interest in New Zealand and as a new graduate to teaching she has recently adopted a Scottish exchange teacher on her staff and has invited her to her home.' Marie also gave five talks to groups within the university. 'A Kindergarten Mothers' Club proved to be my most curious audience.'

Marie would have liked to have done her Masters at Minnesota University rather than in New Zealand, and then return to complete a doctorate on New Zealand material, but she had gained 'a wealth of valuable experiences overseas' and was very grateful 'to all the associations and the individual persons who made it possible'. She 'was able to get specialised training not available in New Zealand and to delve into … material not accessible here. I sincerely hope that I have now a better understanding of people, places and politics in the USA' she continued, 'and I did manage to travel through 37 of the 48 states' during her stay of less than a year 'and thus gained a fairly comprehensive view. I think that New Zealand holds a more important place in the minds of my American friends now, and continued correspondence should keep this interest alive.'

Warwick and Marie lived at Castlecliff in Wanganui, and Marie taught children in standard three and four at Castlecliff School. Marie noted: 'I was teaching nine- and ten-year-old children in a coastal town. It was an ordinary classroom except for the fact that the local school inspectors had heard of my ventures abroad and, from time to time, my head teacher had to enrol a child in this age group who had more difficulties in learning than most children. This did tend to bias the population in this age group a little.

'Fame and confusion descended on me when he found that I had a "reading scheme" adapted to the newly introduced group teaching then sweeping through New Zealand schools. I had four groups engaged in different activities and children rotated around these activities on four days of the week and with recreational reading activity on Fridays. Book reading, word study, comprehension, and children finding all these things hard, turned me into a whirling dervish with both instructional and control problems.

'Usually I was encouraging and supportive but occasionally I felt the time was ripe for an increase in my demands for better quality work. I clearly remember the boy who, on such an occasion, treated me to a flow of swearing that enlarged my personal vocabulary by leaps and bounds,' she said with characteristic humour. 'He learnt to read and seemed genuinely apologetic when later I left the district. It was, I understood, unusual to have such a systematic plan for learning to read in the upper classes and I had to make my first public speech on reading to the parent and school meeting ... I was a bundle of nerves. I got through it promising myself that one had to start somewhere and it would get better ...'

Warwick and Marie's first child, their son Alan, was born in Wanganui in November 1954. He was proudly taken to visit with his great-grandmother, Annie Margaret Irwin.

Marie had decided she wanted to seek work opportunities in a bigger city, and the family relocated to Auckland. Warwick worked for the Auckland Metropolitan Drainage Board, which was later taken over by the Auckland Regional Authority. His work provided a house at low rental at Abingdon Place

Visiting with the new baby. Warwick Clay, Leo Irwin, Marie with baby Alan, Chad Irwin, Lorraine (Marie's sister), and Maggie Irwin (Marie's grandmother).

in Glendowie. Marie did some relieving at Tamaki Primary School. She also obtained work as a part-time psychologist with the Psychological Service in schools.

The couple searched for affordable land to buy in Auckland, which had a view of the sea that Warwick wanted. They found a scrub-covered section looking across the sea towards Rangitoto Island at Murrays Bay on the North Shore on a street without sewerage or water. Warwick designed the house, which was built for them. Later, when services were put on and the water tanks removed from under the house, he put in a large playroom and a second garage.

In the early days, journeys to work in the city were by ferry, as the Auckland Harbour Bridge was yet to be built; it opened in 1959. Jenny, their daughter, was born towards the end of 1956. The night she was born the maternity hospitals were full and Marie's obstetrician was attending the opera. After they'd driven around several hospitals, Marie managed to get into Narrow Neck Hospital in Devonport, then leased by the Auckland Hospital Board from the Naval Base. Shortly after midnight a matron delivered the baby. At that time new mothers were allowed up to two weeks in the maternity ward, but Marie returned home after a week with the baby girl, to be ready for her son's birthday party.

The following year, Marie's mother Blanche went on a boat trip to England and Europe, a working holiday helping a family in London, visiting with friends and attending shows in England and Europe. On the boat she met a widower, Neil MacMillan. He became her second husband after they returned to New Zealand.

Marie's father, Donald Leo Irwin, was involved in the Wellington Chamber Music Society, and helped to establish the New Zealand Federation of Music Societies. At the inaugural meeting in 1950, he was appointed to the executive committee as their Secretary-Treasurer. In a history of the Music Federation of New Zealand, *Into a New Key* by John Mansfield Thomson, 'Don Irwin' is described as 'a highly successful public accountant, although not always easy to work with, he was dedicated, and his office in the DIC building in Lambton Quay became the head office of the Federation'. Leo instigated some of the tours from overseas for the Music Federation, such as the tour by Hungarian cellist Gabor Retjo and pianist Yaltah Menuhin in 1952, an artistic and financial success. During the fifties Leo formed a company, Delta Trading Company Ltd, which started importing and eventually manufacturing Deutsche Gramophone Records under licence in New Zealand, the first country to do so. He was part owner and managing director of the business. He had a lifelong interest in classical music and the spoken arts, and regularly sent his daughter and grandchildren records.

The Clay family would sometimes visit with Leo and Chad Irwin at their

Robert Irwin, Marie's brother, marries Judy Campbell.
Left to right: Marie Clay, Leo Irwin, Judy and Robert, Chad, and Lorraine Irwin.

Leo Irwin with his daughter, Marie, and grandchildren, Alan and Jenny.

holiday section at Kinloch at Lake Taupo in January school holidays, and pitch a tent close to their caravan. They attended the weddings of Marie's younger brother and sister, Robert Irwin to Judy Campbell, and Lorraine Irwin to Rick Christie, in Wellington during the sixties.

Marie with her young children, Jenny and Alan.

At Murrays Bay in Auckland with two preschoolers, Marie taught remedial reading at the kitchen table overlooking the Rangitoto Channel. She resumed work in 1958 as a part-time psychologist, though at a more senior level with the Department of Education. She and Lorna McLay, who later became the first counsellor at the University of Auckland, had applied for the same job with the Psychological Service. At a Suffrage Centennial event in 1993, a 'Women in Psychology Dinner' for women who had pioneered psychology in New Zealand, she said, 'We both [Lorna and Marie] went for the same job and we became a team doing the senior psychologist's job, both of us with babies. I don't know if we were ready for it, but we did our best, even if the babysitting was hard to organise.' Marie also took her children along to the local Mairangi Bay Playcentre, where she was on a roster of supervising parents.

Lorna McLay referred one of two 10 and 11 year old boys to Marie for remedial reading who, subsequent to a slow start, Marie thought made astonishing progress. After a few months of individual 'remedial reading' lessons, the two boys 'suddenly shot up through three class levels in a matter of months. Theories of reading [of the day] did not explain these rapid gains.' Marie also searched through psychological theories. 'From detailed records of my teaching these boys I could see changes in reading and writing behaviours, but these did not lead to obvious explanations for the sudden success … It was as if, together, we had slowly unpicked a massive tangle of false assumptions, and at some point in this process the learners took over. They went by a route I could not explain and clocked up massive gains in the reading of more and more difficult texts.' She decided a pilot study would be helpful, once she had found ways to observe and record what young readers did and said as they interacted with print.

The boy referred by 'Mrs McLay' was called Ron. His mother, Gwen, would collect him each week from Torbay Primary School to take him for an hour of one-to-one tuition with Marie at Murrays Bay. He remembered climbing the stairs of the house to work at the kitchen table and looking out over the gulf. Ron was fanatical about boats, belonging to the Torbay Boat Club and sailing at the weekends. Although not successful in the school, in that context he was highly successful. A book that he vividly remembers Marie having him read was a nautical almanac, a book belonging to Warwick from his naval days. It must have been one of the advanced texts, a specialist and 'complex book for grown-ups', which gave information such the description of anchoring and parking a ship. He believes Marie was very clever in picking on a subject that he was so intensely interested in.

His teacher at school was reading at the same time to the class from *Swallows and Amazons* by Arthur Ransome, based around children's sailing adventures. Ron was familiar with the sailing terminology, and he became hooked on reading.

'I read through all the *Swallows and Amazons* books,' he said, 'and read all about people cruising their yachts around the world.'

As a young adult this is what he did, sailing other people's yachts. He also had a talent in art. While on a boat-building apprenticeship and attending classes at Technical College in Auckland, he designed a boat a fellow student built. The boat performed very well. When he was sailing for an American based in San Francisco, a yacht designer gave him a job on the basis of his amateur drawings. Ron Holland's boats won major prizes, and he very quickly became an internationally renowned yacht designer. On holidays back in Auckland from the States he would ring his old reading teacher at Murrays Bay, feeling a sense of appreciation. He sent Marie copies of articles that he wrote about his travels, showing that he could not only read but he could also write. These articles were published in a New Zealand yachting magazine. Later when he set up his business in Ireland, and Marie moved from Murrays Bay, they lost contact. In the late seventies Marie clipped an article from the local paper about Ron Holland's international success, as one of the foremost boat designers in the world. She wrote at the top '1958'.

Marie began teaching developmental psychology at the University of Auckland in the early sixties in the Education Department, on the basis of her work for the Psychological Service in schools. Professor Ralph Winterbourn was the Head of Department. He had received his doctorate in educational psychology from the University of London in the 1930s, where Marie received an honorary doctorate in 2002. Clarence E. Beeby, who had been the Director-General of Education, said in *Biography of an Idea* that Ralph Winterbourn was New Zealand's 'leading authority on vocational guidance and the man who [helped Beeby to] start the psychological service in the Department of Education.'

In a talk to staff in 1986, Marie reflected on her career at the University of Auckland: 'My first encounter with Education staff was at the end of 1959 when, as a prospective temporary full-time lecturer, I was invited to the end-of-the-year staff dinner-dance.' Dave Barney, a lecturer in the department, and his wife Audrey 'were the only ones I knew. Des Minogue [a senior lecturer] must have asked me to dance (how brave he was) because what I remember was being startled by the 'interview' that went with the waltz. "And what are you going to teach? Do you have some experience in that? Really! Well, we're glad you are going to join us." '

Jenny encourages as Marie types her lectures at Murrays Bay.

'I am glad that a misunderstanding got me here in 1960,' Marie also said. 'Psychological Service offered me to Ralph for the start of the Diploma of Educational Psychology course. No one told Ralph I was a part-timer in the Psychological Service with children aged three and five years. For the next five years or so colleagues helped me manage a full-time appointment by allowing me first pick of my lecture hours, a gesture they seemed to treat as just fair.' After 'two years as a Temporary and aged 36 years I slipped into a full-time position at the bottom of the lecturers scale and began a PhD.' Marie had a close friend, Eleanor England, who had a family in the same neighbourhood of Murrays Bay. In the early days Alan and Jenny often went to their place after school. Marie established Developmental Psychology courses above Stage 1 in the Department, where she said her 'academic interest lay … after my postgraduate year at the University of Minnesota'.

The assistance she was given by her colleagues when her children were young was sometimes echoed in the assistance Marie gave to others. This letter was received from Bernadette Hillyer after Marie's death. Bernadette trained under Marie as an educational psychologist: 'For me, Marie … transformed my life. I had suffered a terrible loss — that of a daughter in an accident when she was with me. I felt totally responsible but having other children I knew I had to pull myself together. Marie made that possible by encouraging me, a total stranger, pregnant and with a two-year-old daughter, to enrol in her relatively new and forward-thinking programme, even though for the first year I could only attend labs. I got notes of lectures from a member of class. After that first year I progressed to lecture attendance, Marie regularly allowing me to bring my now three year old to the lectures and occasionally (towards the end of my time with her) the new baby.

'Not only was she inspiring to every class member but she was very understanding and a marvellously warm woman. I went on to graduate with a Diploma of Educational Psychology and finally to operate a Psychological Service Office in Takapuna.'

Marie studied for her doctorate between 1963 and 1966, while working full-time at the university. At six schools she recorded the diverse responses of five year olds learning to read and write in her weekly observations of 100 children in classrooms during their first year at school. Each child was five years old at entry to school and at the end of the observations, when they were retested, each was six years old. Marie observed what the children learned to do in reading and writing, how they began, how their behaviour changed over time and fitted together in complex patterns.

During the family summer camping trip holidays, Marie worked on the research results.

CAR CAMPING TRIPS
Jenny Clay

'Settle down
    in the back
No more
    horse play'

but there were
    never horses
apart from
the white ones
we looked for
    after the black dog

and kept
    our fingers
crossed
    in between.

Marie works on her research study results during the summer holidays.

Marie prepares the lunch, and Jenny and Alan play by the Consul car, while camping.

Helen M. Robinson was one of the supervisors for Marie's doctorate, '*Emergent Reading Behaviour*', and Ralph Winterbourn, her head of department, was another. Helen Robinson became the first president of the International Reading Association and one of the four original members of the Reading Hall of Fame. Marie and Warwick Elley later joined them in the Reading Hall of Fame. Marie completed her doctorate in 1966, the year her father Leo died. Her mother accompanied her when she was capped for her doctorate the following year.

Marie Clay is capped for her doctorate in May 1967, accompanied by her mother, Blanche.

Marie once told Geraldine McDonald that as soon as her doctoral thesis was through, such was the interest, that she received mail about it every day. Geraldine said, 'The *New Zealand Journal of Educational Studies* was first published in 1966. It was entirely male. Not only the editor, the editorial board, and members of a large advisory council but all the contributors were men. However, in the first issue of the second volume, an article by Marie appeared. It was based on her PhD thesis and it was the first article by a woman to appear in the journal: "The reading behaviour of five-year-old children: A research report", *NZJES* 2, 1: 11–31, 1967.'

In 1968, a trip by the family to Europe was based around Marie's presentation at the Second World Congress in Reading at Copenhagen, where Billie Askew said her major professor at the University of Arizona in the sixties, Ruth Strang, introduced Marie Clay and her research to the world. At the conference Marie was impressed by the talk given by Helen Robinson, her doctoral examiner. She met Ralph Staiger, the past executive director of the IRA, who talked about UNESCO, and Mogens Jansen of Denmark, who introduced her 'to new cultural and language issues in reading'. Marie felt privileged when she was invited to have lunch with Helen Robinson and the other co-founder of the International Reading Association, Albert Harris.

After Europe, Marie and Jenny went on to Canada and the United States, and Warwick and Alan went to Egypt and Japan. Marie revisited friends in Minnesota: Audrey Weldon, now the wife of Roy Johnson; her sister Bernadine, who had a family of five children; Mrs Chris, who had been the sorority housemother during Marie's days at Chi Omega; and Martha the cook. She had met up with Maria Janssen in Amsterdam, where there was a conference on the 'Interaction of Theory and Practice in Psychology', and they met again at the conference of the American Psychological Association in San Francisco. Marie Clay was the official delegate of the New Zealand Psychological Association.

About Marie Clay

Dorothy Butler
Children's literacy advocate, author and educator

It was in the mid-sixties that I first became conscious of Marie Clay and her work. A teacher whom I knew well and respected greatly, Ruth Evans, of Takapuna Primary School, told me that a PhD student was doing research at her school. Ruth was at that time senior teacher of junior classes and as this research concerned the way in which children acquired reading skills, from their entry to school at five, she felt deeply involved. After all, *her* children were part of the research! My good friend Val Shaw was teaching in the junior classes at Takapuna at that time, and also told me about the research. Clearly, Marie Clay, 'the PhD student was receiving wide attention'.

No one could have known, of course, that her work and the books she would write on the subject — and beyond — would ultimately attract worldwide attention. Less still that she would be president of

Dorothy Butler and Marie Clay with the first edition of Reading Begins at Home.

the International Reading Association, or occupy the chair as professor of the Department of Education at the University of Auckland — the first woman to attain this position in any department, at that university.

At this time, I was in the planning stage of my children's book business. I had intended to return to secondary school teaching, for which I was trained, when my children were all launched into the school world, but had hesitated for various reasons. My Playcentre experience had confirmed my belief that the earliest years in a child's life were the most important of all, in terms of emotional and cognitive development. In particular, I had developed an intense interest in the way children acquire language and reading skills. My youngest children were at that time five and six. Whereas I had merely expected the older children to learn to read (as had happened), I had by now become intrigued with the process. I was watching these two, very different little girls, closely.

When an opportunity came to hear Marie Clay speak, I was there in the audience, listening to every word. What she said made good sense to me, gave me pointers to look for, and much to think about. I determined to return to university, as time allowed; I had included one stage of Education in my degree 20 years before, and would go on, I decided.

This I did, completing stages 2 and 3 of Education, while my bookshop and my children grew. I was pleased when Marie brought a distinguished American professor to the shop. I could see that she was anxious to prove that New Zealand was holding its head up (or starting to!) in its provision of services for the young. After this, I met Marie at various functions, where often I would be providing a book display. She was always interested and we invariably found something to talk about, and, of course, Marie loved children's books.

My next and closer contact with her came when one of my grandchildren, Cushla Yeoman, first child of my daughter Patricia and her husband Stephen, was born with multiple handicaps. Marie, always interested in children and their development, became involved with the family at this time.

In September 1972, Marie arranged for Cushla, aged nine months, to be tested in the baby's own home by a psychologist from the University of Auckland, and she tested the baby herself at the university at 17 months. Cushla's interaction with picture books was of particular interest to Marie, as she knew of the work that her parents had been doing with her since early babyhood.

As expected, Cushla showed 'a clear developmental lag in gross motor scores' (six months as against her actual age of 17 months). And yet, to quote the report:

> Book behaviour, trained by adults in her family, was very advanced. She peered at the book at close quarters, scanned the pictures with her eyes, uttered appropriate sounds for some pictures without prompting (s, sailor; m, mouse; p, pig; f, fish) and turned the pages — a fine motor coordination task.

Marie appended the following note: 'I checked this carefully, because it was inconsistent with the rest of the record.'

It should be noted that Marie's characteristic approach to both baby and parent was that of an 'ordinary' friendly New Zealander: never an austere professional. This, of course, will have characterised her research at Takapuna Primary School; in fact, Ruth Evans had told me of Marie's acceptance by both children and staff in exactly this role. There was never any stiffness in Marie's manner — and an attractive tendency to laugh always endeared her.

When I consulted Marie about the possibility of using Patricia's records of Cushla's development through picture books for an 'original investigation' for a Diploma in Education, she was uncertain: Would I be able to be objective enough, as the subject was my grandchild? However, she agreed, and I began.

The fact that this account ultimately became a book, published by Hodder and Stoughton in England in 1979, astonished me, and clearly delighted Marie; in fact, she agreed to the publisher's request that she write an introduction to the book, producing a statement which still moves me, as I read it. I think Marie was as pleased as I was when the book (shortlisted that year for the top New Zealand award) went into American and then Japanese editions, and beyond, and has remained in print through all these years.

When David Heap, of Heinemann Publishers, approached me about co-authoring a book with Marie Clay, I imagined that this was the publisher's idea. However, I learned later that it was Marie's. This was to be a book about preschoolers. It would be aimed at helping parents help their very young children towards reading. I remember asking, 'Does Marie really need me?' and being told that both she and the publishers wanted both our names on the book: mine, I suspected, to engender the 'this is a book for ordinary parents' feeling, and Marie's to add the assurance of real scholarship.

In the event, we enjoyed the project enormously. I remember Marie making essential points while I scribbled madly. I had access to a considerable number of small children, and had always written down their remarks — funny, interesting and profound, as children often are — and Marie was anxious to include many of these, if they were relevant. 'Plenty of anecdotes — people love them!'

I had never contemplated writing *with* someone else, and neither had Marie, but having agreed to do so, we entered into the undertaking with enthusiasm. 'How do other people do this sort of thing?' we asked one another and the editor assigned to us, a most obliging and likeable young man, but no helpful answer emerged.

And so we bumbled along. It seemed sensible to decide on headings, and we felt that a 'paragraph' approach would be less daunting to inexperienced readers than solid pages of text. We decided that there would certainly be parents out there who, despite our prescription for a rich and satisfying life, full of experiences that would lead their children to reading, still wanted to *do* something!

I had already devised a reading game using a 'sentence' approach, and Marie approved of this so we included it; we devised a chapter of parents' questions, providing, we hoped, helpful answers; and also included a list of books for parents to extend their knowledge, and a list by age group — from birth to school entry of books for children. Black and white illustrations throughout were provided by Peter Dent, and we engineered permission for an enchanting illustration by Shirley Hughes of a crawling baby disembowelling a bookcase (from her picture book *Helpers*) for the front cover, and we were there.

Writing a book together is rather like, I suspect, the experience of being adrift on the ocean in a small boat with only one other occupant. You simply have to get along; and finding that you have a great deal in common and laugh at the same things, as Marie and I always had, makes it all possible. And so we turned our book loose on the world, and resumed our very separate but equally demanding lives. The year was 1979.

We were pleased to receive good reviews, and even more pleased to hear that *Reading Begins at Home* had been bought by an American publisher. In New Zealand, like the vast majority of published books, it survived a few years although it was, unlike most, reprinted once (in 1982). In America, however, *Reading Begins at Home* established itself firmly as a useful book for both parents and teachers — and kept on selling.

Every time a new edition appeared and we each received a copy, Marie and I would exclaim and wonder at the phenomenon: 'Won't the illustrations be a bit out of date by now?' We didn't have to worry about the booklists, as the US publisher arranged for an American authority to update them. Still …

Our 'little book' has endured in America to this day, and will continue. In November of 2006 Graham McEwan, Marie's editor and good friend, brought her to see me at my home in Karekare. Marie at that time was very frail, but still resolutely planning a new series of books: 'For teachers — but I want the first one to be for parents. I want you to revise *Reading Begins at Home*. It will be your book this time.'

Marie's voice was a strong as ever. We talked animatedly, over a cup of tea, about reading and books and children; Graham told me later that Marie had been more buoyant than he had seen her for some time; that on the way home, she talked almost excitedly about her planned books.

I put all other work aside, and worked on the planned revision of *Reading Begins at Home*. Marie and I talked frequently on the phone, I with suggestions, and Marie as discerning as ever. I worked steadily; I wanted Marie to read the final manuscript. It was finished, and being typed, when Graham rang to tell me that Marie had died.

At the private family funeral, to which I was invited, Graham told me that he knew Marie had trusted me. We both think that Marie would be happy to have her name on the book. And so it is: Dorothy Butler with Marie Clay.

Marie and I were born less than a year apart. We went to primary schools in different cities but, in the custom of the day, read the same books, learned the same songs. Our families lived through the Depression and the war as we grew up. We both became teachers, somehow managed university degrees, were in time Playcentre mothers, both then following our separate but allied paths.

Marie had a superbly functioning mind. With her energy and application, it took her to the top in her field. But her quality of 'earthiness', her experience of real children, living in the real world with parents both responsible and fallible, gave her a strength, a sureness, which was her own. I, and the rest of the world, feel her loss.

Marie Clay's Contribution to the Teaching of Reading

Warwick Elley
Emeritus Professor of Education, University of Canterbury

Few New Zealanders can claim to have put New Zealand on the world stage in the way that Dame Marie Clay did. In my view she fits comfortably alongside such illustrious Kiwis as Ernest Rutherford, Edmund Hillary, Kiri Te Kanawa and Peter Jackson. All these people have drawn the world's attention to New Zealand for their outstanding skills or character. Marie achieved such pre-eminent status by virtue of her deep understanding of the beginning reading problems of young children, and subsequently, by devoting her life's work to spreading her message to thousands of children in many countries.

According to recent American reports, her world-renowned Reading Recovery intervention has enabled over one and a half million American children to overcome their stumbling blocks in learning to read. They were using the Reading Recovery intervention that Marie developed, here in Auckland schools. Not surprisingly, when Marie died in April 2007, many educators in the US heaped praise on her enormous contribution to the lives of so many, on her extraordinary insights into the way children tackle the reading process, her concern for the struggling reader, her original scholarship, all combined with a relentless curiosity and a natural Kiwi modesty. Countless educators in countries as diverse as Australia and Bermuda, Canada and Spain, England and Denmark sing the praises of her remarkable Kiwi export. Judged by Reading Recovery alone, Marie's contribution justified her status as an eminent New Zealander.

Furthermore, Marie was the first, and still the only, non-North American to be elevated to the top of the International Reading Association (IRA), and serve as its President, during the early 1990s. During her presidency, a position she fulfilled remarkably well, Marie travelled the globe, promoting the cause of literacy for all, and she proved an excellent ambassador for reading, and for New Zealand. It is no wonder that she received countless honours, in this country and overseas, for her distinctive contribution to the cause of quality teaching and worldwide literacy. It is no wonder

Marie Clay with the 'New Zealander of the Year' medal, 1994.

that she was knighted in 1987, and granted the honour of being the inaugural holder of the title of New Zealander of the Year in 1994. Overseas, she was the first New Zealander to receive the International Citation of Merit, which is awarded by the IRA to only one outstanding educator each year, for services to reading, and she was the first Kiwi to be elected by that organisation to the Reading Hall of Fame, the prestigious group of outstanding reading educators from all countries of the world. New Zealand has long enjoyed a strong international reputation in the teaching of reading, and Marie played a large part in contributing to it.

My personal contacts
My first contacts with Marie took place at the University of Auckland in the early 1960s, when we were both ambitious young lecturers in the Department of Education. We had both enjoyed periods in North America, undertaking graduate research in education, and we shared a consuming interest in generating research which would make a real difference to our understanding of how children learn — she in beginning reading, and developmental psychology, and I in language learning and assessment. Marie was still collecting data for her PhD research, for a study that was to have an enormous influence on the way we view children's reading. I still recall discussions we had on her research design: 'Surely you should have had some clear hypotheses to test!' I said. Fortunately, she did not take my advice that time. We talked about those unusual tests she was using, the best ways to analyse her results, and the like. Marie would disappear from the Department often, to interview her 100 little five-year-old subjects, in five different primary schools round Auckland, and some of us had to provide extra support at busy times. But it was well worth it. For this study became a landmark in the history of New Zealand reading instruction. Many of the insights she gained and reported in that PhD research have become part of the traditional wisdom of skilled reading teachers throughout this country, and elsewhere.

What is my evidence for such sweeping generalisations? Here is one telling argument. Recently I undertook a project to study the strategies and beliefs of the most successful reading teachers in Years 1 and 2, in New Zealand schools. These were teachers whose children had achieved well above expectation for their decile level, in a nationwide survey of reading achievement that we conducted at the beginning of Year 3 (Elley, 2004). Many of the features common to these effective teachers were predictable — mature, enthusiastic staff, well-stocked book corners, balanced programmes, supportive principals, ample provision for struggling readers — but one feature that I did not expect was the number of these classroom teachers who had been trained in Reading Recovery, and applied its philosophy, not just to the strugglers, but to all the children in their classrooms. Most of these teachers conducted frequent close monitoring by means of Running Records, and followed up their findings conscientiously. This level of close observation, followed by tailored instruction for each individual, was surely a legacy of the work of Marie Clay. Reading Recovery has helped the 20 per cent or so in this country who experience initial difficulties, but its impact is clearly extending to mainstream children as well.

When Marie and I worked together in the 1960s, our Head of Department was Professor Ralph Winterbourn. Ralph had taught me as a graduate student, supervised my MA research, employed me from my prairie outpost in Canada, and was a regular source of support and wisdom. I was ever grateful for his leadership and help. It is to his credit that he also supervised Marie's thesis research, and gave her the kind of flexible support that enabled her to follow her intuitions and produce such a significant body of research.

After 1965, my career took me away from Auckland, and Marie and I met more often at overseas reading conferences — in Singapore, Darwin, Atlanta, San Diego, Suva, Toronto — than in New Zealand. However, I followed her work with considerable interest, and incorporated much of it in the university courses I taught. I also used some of her tests in my evaluations of language programmes in the South Pacific and among Northland Maori children. When New Zealand performed well in the first international survey of reading achievement in 1970, Marie and I were closely involved in the reporting and interpreting of results to others. Later, while serving as secretary of the newly formed Wellington Council of the NZ Reading Association, I was able to persuade her to bring her reading message to Wellington teachers in the early 1970s. Her talk on how we could — and should — reduce reading failure to 2 per cent brought out a record crowd, and was received with acclamation. Of course, we never did attain that lofty goal in this country, but without her efforts the level of failure would have surely been much greater. Indeed, if her Reading Recovery intervention had been adopted in every New Zealand school, and followed up with a 'Third Wave' for the 1–2 per cent of children who fail to reach the 'discontinuation' stage, we could well have set a fine example to the rest of the world. But the priorities of scholars and those of politicians are often out of phase.

At some time in 1975, Marie persuaded me to take over from her as National Coordinator of the Reading Association in New Zealand. My qualifications for accepting such an office paled in comparison with hers, and I was naturally reluctant. But when Marie was determined, she usually succeeded. As secretary of the Wellington Reading Association, I had helped organise the 4th New Zealand Reading Conference, and with the resources of the New Zealand Council for Educational Research behind me, she must have seen me as a soft touch for the job. Anyway, I learned from her experience and advice, and in the process of travelling the country on reading business I grew in enthusiasm for the International Reading Association, and for working to raise literacy levels throughout the country. For that enriching experience, I had Marie to thank.

When the gavel of the National IRA Coordinator was transferred to me, at the Hamilton Reading Conference, in 1975, I was asked to introduce Marie to the audience in the final plenary address, and as on several other occasions I found it an appropriate challenge to do this in the form of a light-hearted verse (see opposite page). The name 'Clay' is rich in potential for frivolity on such occasions. Unlike some of my colleagues, faced with such a possibly embarrassing situation, she did not complain. Indeed she recently informed me that she had reread the verse to a National Conference of the Reading Recovery Teachers in the US, a few months before she died. I was suitably flattered.

ODE TO MARIE CLAY

We are gathered here today,
To sit at the soft feet of Clay.
To hear her expand
And learn at first hand
About teaching to read the Clay-Way

Marie's aim is to cut reading failure
By closer attention to behaviour
To study mistakes
That each reader makes.
Of the slow-reading child she's the saviour.

We owe Marie our deep-felt affection
For her research has changed the direction
Of teachers' endeavour
From now and for ever,
We'll focus on each self-correction.

The effects of her work have been stunning.
And if you'll excuse me for punning
When she comes to a meeting
We run out of seating
She's broken several 'records-running' (or running records).

In the chair, she's efficient and brisk.
And she lectures on reading and WISC
And on children and tests.
Her good name now rests
For identifying children at risk.

In her duties, she travels the land,
Her talks are consistently grand.
A theory she's built,
Not on rocks, or on silt,
But on solid foundations of SAND.

And now I present Marie Clay,
The spokesperson for our IRA.
What we are needing
Is more about reading.
We're most keen to hear what you say.

Soon after Marie handed over the leadership of the IRA, she was instrumental in sending down to Wellington two gurus of the reading world, American visitors Ken and Yetta Goodman. I met them at Wellington Airport on a bleak Sunday afternoon in midwinter. The strong wind was blowing straight up from the South Pole, it seemed. As I shunted them into the terminal, I apologised for the weather, saying it was not at all typical. 'Oh,' said Ken sceptically, 'that's not what Marie told us.' Forgetting that Marie had lived in Wellington, I insisted that this cold snap was unusual, and that Marie was being unfair. Wellington's climate was not unlike that of Oregon or Washington State, I claimed. 'Does it ever snow here?' asked Yetta. 'No!' said I confidently. 'Occasionally on the hills, but not in the city.'

I steered them onto other topics, and installed them in a city hotel. Next morning we awoke to find two inches of snow on Wellington streets — the first for about 10 years. Not surprisingly, from then on, the Goodmans always had more confidence in Marie's word than mine.

The International Reading Association (IRA)

Marie was one of the first in New Zealand to see the potential of the International Reading Association for this country. She attended its second World Congress on Reading, which was held in Copenhagen in 1968, and the third one, in Sydney in 1970, and found both conferences very stimulating. Her own research on five year olds and her original measures of reading behaviour (Concepts About Print, Running Records, Writing Vocabulary) attracted the attention of researchers and teachers in many countries and she was soon deluged with invitations to speak. Once Reading Recovery became established in USA, it was unthinkable for any large IRA conference to go ahead without Marie as a plenary speaker. And she usually took a cadre of New Zealand educators with her, and was instrumental in bringing many other reading researchers and leaders to this country to offer us further inspiration.

The Association claims nearly 90,000 reading educators and book lovers as members, and fosters reading in many countries. It produces regular books, journals and newsletters, it sponsors large numbers of seminars and conferences, and is a source of inspiration and ideas for teachers and students worldwide. During the 1980s, Marie was elected to serve on the Board of Directors of the IRA, and in 1990, she was chosen to be its President. This was no mean feat. She had to overcome the natural tendency for the American-dominated Board and membership to choose one of their own. She then had to learn to cope with the political debates and local issues of the US, where the IRA headquarters are located. But all accounts are that she was an excellent president and ambassador for the reading cause. No other non-American has yet been acceptable for this position.

Marie's workload

It was a source of wonder to many as to how she managed to keep up her hectic schedule of speaking, teaching, consulting and researching, and churning out some 32 books and over 70 articles. Such a workload can only be imagined by some of us lesser mortals. Of course, she did have a reputation for efficiency, and she often had to say 'No', or 'Not in the next six months'.

I was a little surprised but in retrospect I admired her decision to give up her position as the first female Head of Department at Auckland University after two years. The responsibility was too great at a time when her research was at its peak, and she was sensible and courageous enough to see that she could not manage both tasks as well as she would like. Over 10 years later she took up the mantle of Head of Department again, between 1986 and 1988, and led her Department competently through a period of expansion, officially retiring from the University of Auckland in 1991.

For one as committed to such lofty causes as she was, retirement was not a period of relaxation and rest. It was just a change of direction. Numerous overseas universities clamoured to offer her awards and accommodation, and she took many opportunities to travel and spread the impact of Reading Recovery even further. There were conferences to attend, lectures to give, more books to write, Tutors to train, battles to fight with rival reading groups. From time to time, I sought her advice on research and consulting matters, and she was invariably helpful and generous with her time.

Teaching the world to read

One conviction I shared with Marie was the desire to contribute in some small way towards worldwide literacy. In 1970 she wrote: 'Personally, I feel that New Zealand has a responsibility beyond its own shores for the teaching of reading, and that the International Reading Association can focus our attention on what our contribution might be.'

Marie had just attended her second IRA World Congress on Reading, in Sydney, and came back enthused with the notion that New Zealand had avoided many of the mistakes of other countries, that we had something valuable to offer. I realised what she meant when I spent nearly six years in the South Pacific exploring the

reading problems of children in Fiji, Niue and other island nations. While teaching at the University of the South Pacific, I was fortunate to be able to spend much time in schools around the region. We uncovered some strange assumptions in the existing English programmes. We found many bored, unmotivated pupils, and much room for improvement. Using Kiwi-style strategies, with abundant quantities of New Zealand story books, and with advice from Marie and those she had taught, we were able to boost the literacy levels of many South Pacific children, in English reading, vocabulary, writing

Warwick Elley and Marie Clay at the South Pacific Conference on Reading, Suva, January 1995.

and oral language. For me, this 'Book Flood' work is continuing, with the help of many committed educators and book publishers — in South Africa, Sri Lanka, South-East Asia and several island nations in the South Pacific. For Marie, the extension of her valuable work will be carried on by others.

Both Marie and I spoke at several South Pacific and Asian conferences, with complementary messages. We were both honoured with invitations from the Singapore Ministry to give the annual Ruth Wong Memorial lecture, she in 1985, and I in 1998. Ruth Wong was the Marie Clay of Singapore. And we were both invited to give plenary addresses at the South Pacific Conference on Reading, on the same occasion, in Suva, Fiji, in January 1995. Marie spoke on the topic of 'Becoming Literate in a Multicultural World'. One memorable anecdote she recounted was the story about a little Indian boy called Ashok (reprinted in her book *By Different Paths to Common Outcomes*). He tried so hard to master the reading process, but he was confused. No teacher had ever realised why he persisted in saying 'apple' whenever he saw an 'a', and 'bird' when he saw a 'b'. Of course, his alphabet book had formed this link in his mind, but it would take an observant teacher to see what was happening, and this was Marie's trademark. Watch and learn what the child is responding to. This is a message still to be learnt by so many teachers with Ashoks in their class. There is no substitute for close observation.

Another distinctive contribution, less heralded in her reading work, was surely her pioneering research on the reciprocal links between young children's reading and writing (Clay, 1975). In the course of her PhD research in the 1960s, Marie studied the writing efforts of her five year olds. She gradually began to realise how important these early apparently nonsensical creations were for the children's development. They created opportunities for 'learning how letters, sounds and spellings are formed, how some words resemble other words, and how sentences, narratives and reports are constructed' (Clay 1998, p. 131). Furthermore, in a situation where diversity always reigns, children's writing efforts give teachers a wonderful insight into each child's current needs. As Marie so often repeated, no single prescriptive programme will enable all children to gain inner control over the reading process. All systems have their risks. The use of writing to assist teachers identify those risks was a welcome supplement to running records and the other valuable tools she developed. Classroom teachers have so many reasons to be grateful to this outstanding New Zealander.

References

Clay, M.M. 1975. *What Did I Write?* Auckland: Heinemann.

———. 1998. *By Different Paths to Common Outcomes.* New York: Stenhouse Publishers.

Elley, W.B. 2004. Effective Reading Programmes in the Junior School. *Set: Research Information for Teachers*, No.1: 2–6.

Border Crossings

Ann Ballantyne
Reading Recovery Trainer

I think of Marie Clay whenever I board an aeroplane; she travelled so often, so far and so well. About to embark on yet another journey of discovery or familiarisation she would tuck herself neatly into the economy class seat, a pile of papers on her lap, a recent novel in her handbag (in case there was time), a small whisky perhaps, and then fall quickly asleep. She was purposeful and disciplined. Even the whisky had a purpose, to encourage the sleep that was a necessary preparation for tomorrow's agenda. Perhaps there would be a familiar face to greet her on the other side of the world — increasingly this must have been so — and there might even be time to visit a museum, attend the theatre or track down some family history. For the most part though, Marie travelled for academic and/or educational purposes and the next day's agenda would probably require her to 'mix it' with new ideas, new people and new challenges — at an IRA meeting, Reading Recovery conference or university seminar. Canadian educator and admirer David Booth has used the wonderfully rich and compact image of an 'ice-breaker' to describe Marie's work and persona. What that image brings to mind for me is a strong sense of Marie's directedness (ice-breakers presumably don't just hang about in Antarctic waters waiting for some thing to happen) and also the social aspect, the way that she would talk with anyone and everyone, and always about important things.

Perhaps it is only when someone has left us that we really turn our minds to the question of how they could be who they were and do what they have done. What made it possible for Marie to cross borders with such apparent ease and to work so brilliantly with new ideas and new people in new territories, both literal and figurative? I can't answer this question, of course, but recent rereadings of Marie's work and some conversations I've had with her about her academic life suggest two factors: a strong sense of where she wanted to go and massive practice. Like many 'Reading Recovery' people, I met Marie fairly late in her career when she was already a seasoned traveller. It is natural, in these circumstances, to assume that Marie always found it easy to open doors and explore new territory. Intellectually, yes, this was probably the case. One has only to read the Masters thesis that she wrote in her early twenties to recognise her active, question-generating, problem-solving mind, already hard at work on the question of how to improve learning conditions for students. Soon after she completed her MA, Marie took up a Fulbright scholarship to study for a year in the USA. I never heard her comment on the bitter cold Minnesota winter or recall the distress she might have felt when she discovered that the courses she meant to take were not available. Instead

Marie would talk about the exciting new field of study that opened up for her at the Minnesota Institute of Child Development and the new questions these studies raised about the borderlands between typical and atypical development, average progress and special needs students.

Marie's academic career was replete with border crossings — she worked across different disciplines, studied a variety of age groups and carried out a range of important leadership roles in the research and education communities, locally and internationally. To navigate in this way across boundaries and between worlds requires a special ability to be able see things from different perspectives without losing the overall sense of direction; we might call this 'statesmanship' if the term did not have such a gender bias. These qualities were acknowledged when Marie was nominated as one of four 'evaluators' to consider the impact of a massive restructuring of the New Zealand education system; and, in an international context, when she was elected to be President of the International Reading Association — a challenging and highly political task that she is said to have performed extraordinarily well.

It would be wrong to assume that it was always easy for Marie to shoulder these very public roles and responsibilities — not least because it understates the extent of her achievement and the depth of her commitment. In relation to her doctoral research in the early 1960s, Marie once commented that she found it difficult to approach the schools and ask them to take part — that that sort of thing was hard for her do — and she appreciated the school inspectors who helped to smooth the way. When, soon after she had completed her doctorate, the opportunity arose to speak to school principals about her findings, Marie was nervous about speaking to such an 'august' group. The critical thing, of course, is that Marie did not let this put her off; she did speak to the group and was quite fierce about what she thought needed to be done to ensure that all children could get off to a good start at school. She continued to speak to groups in New Zealand and around the world, no doubt growing in confidence all the while and setting a wonderful example for all of us. Where did she find the courage and stamina to do all of this? I think it came from an absolute clarity of purpose and from the depth of her commitment to making the world a better place for young learners.

References

Clay, M.M. 1967. A challenge to some educational concepts from recent research on Auckland school entrants. Extension Course Lectures. Auckland: Headmasters Association.

Elley, W.B. 2007. Marie Clay's international contribution to literacy. *Reading Forum, NZ.*

Irwin, M.M. 1948. Teaching of Reading to Special Class Children. Unpublished Master of Arts thesis. Wellington: Victoria College, The University of New Zealand.

The University of
Auckland

The Journey to Professor

Marie Clay became a senior lecturer in the Department of Education in 1968, the year after she was awarded her doctorate. In 1970, Professor Tony McNaughton, one of only two professors in the department, encouraged her to apply for an associate professorship. Marie asked Helen Robinson, a supervisor of her doctorate and the co-founder of the International Reading Association, to be one of her external referees 'of high repute' in her 'specialist area'. In writing to her, Marie mentioned that the courses she taught were in developmental psychology, at undergraduate and postgraduate level. She had set up the postgraduate Diploma in Educational Psychology course, through which the school psychologists were trained. She specified her problem as being that her recent research work was in reading, which was not taught at the university but only at 'the separate Teachers Colleges', and therefore to 'plead strength in this area it must be as a researcher'. At the end of her letter, Marie said she was looking forward to attending the Third World Congress in Reading, with a New Zealand contingent of 15, in Sydney.

Marie's first application to become an associate professor was unsuccessful. Like previous setbacks, this did not deter her. Tony McNaughton continued to be supportive. He made suggestions regarding publishing further research material, diversifying her research base, and increasing her profile at the university, and pointed out that she could reapply in two years. Marie Clay did reapply in 1972. This time she was successful, and was promoted to associate professor.

Ralph Winterbourn was due to retire as head of the Education Department at the end of 1974, and the position of 'Professor and Head of the Education Department' was advertised during the year. As well as being experienced in university teaching within the disciplines of education, such as philosophy, history and psychology, the candidates were to be 'active in research and have a substantial record of research publications'. The staff research currently in progress in the department was listed. Associate Professor Marie Clay was active in over a third of it; research such as 'early language development in children, including cross-cultural studies', 'aspects of preschool education', 'studies of children of incomplete families', and 'studies of adolescent values'.

Marie decided to apply for the position. Dr Barnham, Professor of Education at the University of Otago, when replying to her request to be a referee, commented that he was surprised that her list of referees were all from outside her department and university. Colin Maiden was the Vice-Chancellor of the University of Auckland. He remembers chairing the Appointments Committee of Senate in 1974 'when we were interviewing shortlisted applicants … The two best candidates were from within the Department of Education, Tony McNaughton and Marie Clay, and the Committee had difficulty selecting between these two applicants.'

On 17 September 1974, D.W. Pullar, the Registrar at the University of Auckland, sent Marie Clay a letter saying:

'I have pleasure in formally conveying to you the Council's offer of the position of Professor and Head of the Department of Education from 1 February 1975 ... The Council very much hopes that you will accept the offer and I understand you have already indicated to the Vice-Chancellor that you are happy to do so.

All here are delighted with the Council's decision and join me in sending warm congratulations to Auckland's first woman Professor. The Vice-Chancellor has asked me to add his personal good wishes.

'Marie became the University's first woman professor in its 81 years of existence. Professor Marie Clay was Head of the Department of Education for several years and I found her a pleasure to work with,' Colin Maiden, the former Vice-Chancellor, said. 'She knew about education, was well organised and had a good sense of humour ... I recommended that she replace Professor Barney Sampson, in 1976, as assistant Vice-Chancellor (Student Accommodation and Welfare) and Professor Clay made a major contribution to the well-being of students at the University of Auckland ... She chaired the Student Accommodation and Welfare Committee of Council, which determined policy in the areas of student health, counselling, physical recreation, accommodation and careers and appointments. She got on well with both students and staff and brought a good commonsense approach to accommodation and welfare matters. During this period I worked closely with her and developed great admiration for her abilities and achievements.'

The next two years proved very busy ones, with the administration and negotiation involved in running the Department of Education added to Marie Clay's roles of teacher, writer and researcher. When she stood down from Head of Department in 1977 to have more time for her research, her colleague Professor Tony McNaughton took over the position. She was later persuaded to take the reins for two more years from 1986 to 1988.

Her achievement in becoming the first woman professor at the University of Auckland during the seventies made history.

MARIE CLAY, PROFESSOR OF EDUCATION
Anne Lloyd

Extracts from an article in Thursday *magazine, 5 June 1975. Reprinted with permission of the* New Zealand Herald.

On the door of Marie Clay's office it says clearly, *Prof. Marie Clay*. When you look closely you see that the *Assoc.* before the *Prof.* has been whited out. Nothing like economy and lack of fuss. Marie Clay herself is not a person who likes fuss.

She is Auckland University's first woman professor; there aren't more than a handful in the country, but she doesn't like fuss and isn't enthralled at the thought of an interview and publicity. She has too many other things to do … But she fits in the interview between a staff meeting and a lecture, in what should have been a lunch break. You suspect if it hadn't been for the interview she would have been working, not lunching, anyway. She says she's always busy, always has been.

'I sometimes wonder if I don't know how to say no. Since I accepted the professorship I still do the same lectures, plus administrative duties and running the department, and regrettably all this is stealing time from research and writing.' She grins good-naturedly and shakes her head. She obviously loves work.

When she first started teaching at the university in 1960 she had one child at playcentre and one at school.

'My husband is a civil engineer so his hours didn't allow him to help out with the children. We live on the North Shore and some days I'd cross the bridge six times. It's not convenient, but if you're well-organised it can be done.

'I had a really good friend who became a second mum to the children — I think it's important that they have a stable situation. I took it slowly at first. I applied for a temporary job to see if it would work out and after two years, when I found it did, I applied for a permanent job. I won't make any bones about it not being easy. There were stresses and strains. But if you don't like this then you don't do it …'

'When I had my family in the middle fifties, I did some teaching of remedial reading to pupils at home. My whole thinking was challenged by this experience. Our books didn't explain why children didn't read. We were lacking in information on the early stages of reading. I asked the question: "Is it possible to find out more about the early stages of reading, and can we see reading difficulties early on?" Previously this area had been left alone. When a child was seven or eight and not learning to read at the average rate he had been called a slow starter. There was a fear, and an understandable one about pressuring children too early,' says Professor Clay.

'I did a four-year programme for my PhD in which I examined 100 children from when they started school at five until their sixth birthday. I recorded what they were doing and saying in reading and writing. I described then the transitions that they underwent during their first year of reading. No one had done that before that I knew of, and certainly no one had done it here. My hope was that such a description would help teachers to observe more sensitively what is happening and therefore pick up little misconceptions sooner.'

Dr Clay also produced a diagnostic survey for teachers to use on their sixth birthday.

'We call it the six-year-old net, because we're hoping to catch in this net children who are having difficulty, so that they can be helped. Before this happened, along with fear of pressuring children went the attitude, "Oh, it'll come right, there's no real need to look at reading problems till the child is seven or eight." My work has overturned that concept.'

What research is she working on at the moment?

'It's really a matter of fitting it in,' Marie Clay says. 'The job here seems to be squeezing out time for research and writing. If there are any gaps anywhere I spend them writing.

'I do have a lot of work here and I do spend my vacations attending overseas conferences...

'If there is one thing I've learned from my work it's that in education — in everything that happens in school, in the community, at home — there are no absolute truths. Unless, of course, it's that you can be sure if something is right for one child it will be wrong for another. We want to get rid of the thinking that there is one "right" system of education. We should be looking for a way of providing variety for all the different kinds of people there are. Perhaps a stimulating thing to happen to a child would be a swap between a "free expression" kind of system and a more conventional approach and vice versa. That would be a challenge to ... Excuse me.'

She answers the phone that has been ringing for a few seconds. '... Yes, I know we must talk about the books, but I have a lecture in a few minutes.'

She looks at me. I nod and gather my things to leave.

Before I close the door Professor Clay is deeply and happily immersed in yet another conversation about education.

Marie and Warwick had pursued their separate interests within their marriage, which had difficulties. By the end of 1976 Marie had stopped trying to resolve the difficulties. She purchased a townhouse and left Warwick. Both children were by this time grown up, Jenny at university and Alan overseas. Warwick was initially disturbed by the final break-up, but a few years later he met Janet Lambert at a singles club, a younger partner who had children from a previous marriage, and in 1984 they married. They remained together, much of the time travelling around the world on his yacht, until his death in July 2007.

Jenny and Marie outside the townhouse in 1977.

Viviane Robinson Talks About Marie Clay as Mentor

Professor, Faculty of Education, The University of Auckland

Viviane Robinson said at the memorial for Marie Clay at the Maidment Theatre at the University of Auckland: 'In the old days, I'm talking sixties and seventies here, there was little talk of mentors and mentoring ... yet Marie Clay was in today's terms a consummate mentor of her graduate students and I was one of the beneficiaries.'

Marie was one of her education lecturers when Viviane was completing her Bachelor of Arts in education and psychology at the university. In planning for her Masters degree, Viviane was concerned 'to find that all the graduate courses in both education and psychology described the world through a variety of academic lenses, but that none were directly concerned with intervening to change it'. Viviane, as a young graduate student, wished to change things and not to simply describe them. She went to talk to Marie, who taught developmental psychology, and argued, 'How can we advocate for children, and address important problems of practice, if intervention is not a key focus of our graduate study?'

To her surprise, over the summer Marie rose to the challenge by planning such a course and implementing it the following year. The course was called 'Deviant Development', a term which would not be used these days, and was about intervening in order to change behaviour. About a dozen people enrolled in the graduate seminar course including Stuart McNaughton, Ted Wotherspoon and Viviane Robinson. The students chose a topic (Viviane's was autism), wrote a big research paper and presented the material to the class, and in the exam covered about three topics.

Viviane was impressed with how flexible Marie had been in developing the course from a student's idea and providing the resources and support. She regarded this as the beginning of Marie's mentoring of her.

Viviane praised Marie for coaching graduate students to write for different audiences, 'an essential skill for academics in education. Writing for teachers and policy makers required engagement with their world, their concerns and their language. Authentic engagement with teachers required spending time in schools and classrooms. Writing for an international or national academic audience required a different identity', a theoretical conversation where 'New Zealand issues and concerns had to be located within a relevant international academic debate'. When Viviane's early attempts at international publications were rejected, Marie taught her 'how to explain the New Zealand educational context to an audience that had barely heard of our country, let alone of the issues I was addressing'.

Marie Clay 'modelled participation in many worlds and helped me to navigate their different languages, politics and expectations.'

Viviane Robinson completed her Masters thesis in the early seventies. Her supervisor was Ted Glynn, a young lecturer who had studied behavioural analysis for his doctorate at Kansas University. Viviane felt that she was expected to do all or part of her doctoral study at one of the best overseas universities. Marie Clay and Ted Glynn encouraged her along this path. Both had benefited from overseas study, Ted at Kansas and Marie on a Fulbright scholarship at Minnesota University. The system of applying to do an overseas doctorate before the days of the Internet and email was laborious. Viviane researched in the library collection of overseas university calendars, sent airmail letters to admission offices asking for material, waited for replies, and then sent her personal statement and grades. She sent copies of her Masters thesis to the universities in America that she had shortlisted, and was accepted at several. They were impressed by the quality of research involved in the thesis, as education Masters degrees in the United States tended to be taught as papers. Viviane eventually chose to do her doctorate at Harvard.

During 1972, when she was applying for overseas universities, Viviane was also working for Marie on a research project on the second stage of a study of the children of separated parents. An earlier research grant from the University of Auckland had enabled a census-type survey to be conducted at the end of 1970. In the first part of the study, 'returns were obtained from 94 per cent of the primary schools in the Auckland metropolitan area'. This provided a plot of the incidence in families of children not living with two natural parents, and looked at school attainment and adjustment. Throughout New Zealand the 1971 national census showed less than 5 per cent 'of all households had one parent permanently absent through death, separation or divorce'.

The second stage of the project was funded by a Nuffield Foundation grant, and supplemented by the University of Auckland, for a trained research worker to conduct a 'study focused on the behavioural reactions of children at the time of separation, the custody and access rulings made by the courts, and the way these are worked out in practice'. Marie chose to hire Viviane for this position. It was the first major research project that Viviane had undertaken, and she felt this was a generous opportunity to participate in her research.

Government agencies did not allow their lists of separated families to be used in approaching people for the research. The people who were interviewed, therefore, were members of solo parents organisations, who had volunteered to participate. These were likely to be more extroverted people and unlikely to have been recently separated. This meant the sample was missing the more withdrawn parents, the 'resolutely' independent ones, and the recently separated.

The custodial parents ranged from Manukau to the North Shore. Viviane interviewed them, travelling often at night across Auckland in her mother's car. Her family were supportive as she came from a background of service and teaching. The interviews were conducted between February and August 1972. In the main, the women had custody of the children, and the final interview sample consisted of 69 parents, 62 mothers and 7 fathers, with custody of 161 children who were under 13 at the time of separation. Questions were asked, for example, about 'children's behaviour before separation and whether there were any changes after separation'. Viviane felt the 'year of field work interviewing parents with custody of their children left me with a, fortunately temporary, dislike of men and of marriage — attitudes that I overcame with a combination of more knowledge about sampling bias and meeting some nice men'.

Marie gave Viviane her first job. When Viviane was completing her doctorate at Harvard, she'd applied for positions back in New Zealand. She'd been accepted for a postdoctoral fellowship in Dunedin, and at the same time she was applying for a lectureship at the University of Auckland. Stuart McNaughton had also been shortlisted for this lectureship. He was an exact contemporary of Viviane's and had just finished his doctorate, partly at the University of Auckland with one year at Kansas University. In the end, both were appointed to the University of Auckland to start in 1976.

Marie had been appointed a full professor and head of department in 1975. Viviane went to talk to Marie, her new head of department of education, in Alten Road about what she wanted her to teach. In the initial stages Viviane thought she needed 'six weeks to prepare my first lecture and I think Marie agreed. The support side of Marie's mentoring was definitely winning over the challenge side at that time. I eventually became more productive.'

Stuart McNaughton and Viviane Robinson attended the first New Zealand Association for Research in Education (NZARE) conference in 1979. Dr C.E. Beeby,

Participants at an Early Childhood Research Conference, Massey University, February 1977.
Back row from left: Jim Hefford, Louis Gurr, John Kirkland, Liz Straton, Donald McAlpine, Alan Hall, Michael Cooper, Anne Bray, Dorothy Howie.
Middle row: Marie Bell, Fay Panckhurst, Linda Hall, Joan Brockett, Anne Meade, Peter Dinniss, Anne Smith, Maris O'Rourke, Penny Jamieson, David Mitchell.
Seated: David Barney, Alison St George, Margery Renwick, Beverley Morris, John Watson, Marie Clay, Geraldine McDonald, Dave Fergusson.

who had been the Director-General of Education and the first director of New Zealand Council for Educational Research, gave an address at the conference dinner. Geraldine McDonald chaired a group which planned this first NZARE conference. Geraldine said: 'Keith Pickens of NZCER and I decided to survey the state of the art at the first conference and we invited people to prepare a paper on various areas of education. We invited Marie to survey child development. She made a thoroughly professional job of this and her paper "Research on Child Development in New Zealand" appeared in the NZARE (1980) *Research in Education in New Zealand: The State of the Art*, Delta Research Monograph Number 3, pages 17 to 41.'

In the Education Department Viviane taught the Diploma of Educational Psychology students about intervention. This covered theories of change, strategies for intervention, what consultation meant, and how to enter a system. 'Psychologists are constantly going into other people's houses figuratively and literally, going into schools and other people's homes.' The course dealt with strategies to 'help those responsible for children to make the changes they need'.

Viviane continued her work towards the book on *Children of Parents who Separate* after her return from Harvard. She wrote up the results of the interviews, worked on a literature review, and was listed as the co-author with Marie when the book was published in 1978 by the New Zealand Council for Educational Research.

The following year Viviane participated in a series of extension lectures of the Auckland Primary Principals Association held at the Auckland Museum. She spoke about the results in her talk, 'The Children of Separated Parents: Testing Some Assumptions'. In this she stated children with separated parents may differ in numerous ways apart from the number of parents in the household, such as 'the extent to which their fathers have been involved in their upbringing; their exposure to parental conflict; the socio-economic circumstances; ... the number of shifts of home and school they have experienced; probability that mother works; number of and extent of childcare arrangements', and that all of these things could impact on school attainment and social adjustment.

Having more male teachers was, and is, seen as providing 'surrogate "father figures" to father-absent boys ... promoting a masculine identity' and 'providing the discipline that mother cannot, or will not, provide'. Viviane expressed a couple of thoughts on this: 'The development of a secure masculine identity in boys is associated with paternal interest and nurturance, not with punitive and rejecting fathering ... Fathers seem to be most effective if they are warm and affectionate towards their sons; characteristics that are often typically thought of as feminine ... The male teacher who disciplines by sarcasm and by verbal abuse will not be an effective model.' Secondly: 'The lives of both one- and two-parent children may be enriched by contact with male teachers whom they like and respect. Some recent New Zealand data [this was the late seventies] shows that middle class fathers spend less than seven hours per week caring for their children.'

From the interviews, Viviane thought that the parents consistently underestimated 'the capacities of children to perceive what is going on around them'. They therefore often would not talk about what was happening within the family. In her 1979 talk she said although children of separated parents can be at a disadvantage socially and cognitively, 'two recent New Zealand studies show that about 30 per cent of children show an immediate positive reaction to parental separation'. In practical applications from the research she suggested teachers encourage parents to talk openly about the separation with their children, and for the parents to give explanations that referred 'not only to the relationship between parents, but also to their hopes for the future relationship between parents and child'. In conclusion she said the most practical application was also an abstract one, not to give 'over-simplified answers' to complex situations.

Marie Clay, in a talk to the University of Auckland Education Department in 1986, referred to similarities between her and Viviane: 'Like Viviane I like to take my theory to the field to see whether it does in fact belong to real life or merely to the closed circuitry of minds and scholarly writing.' Practical application of theories was important to both of them, which is probably why Viviane's suggestion of a course for intervention for change brought a positive response. Reading Recovery is an example of this. Viviane said Marie did want to make things better.

Viviane concluded her tribute at the Maidment Theatre: 'Despite her busy international schedule and intermittent poor health, Marie always had time for her students. I still went to her home to seek her support and advice about book proposals, research funding or to celebrate something that one of us had achieved. On my last visit I was once again struck by her combination of sharp intellect, political astuteness and deep caring for the individual. Marie was a great mentor.'

Sources

'For Marie Clay, My Mentor', Viviane Robinson's talk at the Marie Clay Memorial Service held at the University of Auckland Maidment Theatre, April 2007.

Geraldine McDonald: Information re NZARE and Marie Clay.

'Children of Parents Who Separate' by Marie M. Clay and Viviane M.J. Robinson, University of Auckland, published by New Zealand Council of Educational Research, Wellington, 1978.

'The Children of Separated Parents: Testing Some Assumptions', Viviane Robinson, University of Auckland. Published with four papers from the 15th Extension Course Lectures (1979) of the Auckland Primary Principals Association

Interview with Viviane Robinson, January 2008.

Marie Round About 51

Andrew Sharp

Lecturer in Political Studies at the University of Auckland from 1971 to 2006, retired as an Emeritus Professor

I'm not sure when Marie conceived the idea of studying Form 2 (Year 8) children in New Zealand, or the division of labour between her and Ronald Oates in the production of their book *Round about Twelve* in 1984. But she was contracted to do the research by the Department of Education in 1977 or 1978. The terms of the contract meant that before they could begin, and at crucial points thereafter, they needed to get the approval of a weighty Advisory Committee: one member appointed by the Research Division of the Ministry, one by the Auckland Primary School Inspectorate, one by the New Zealand Federation of School Committees, one by the New Zealand Education Institute, and one by Catholic Education.

This did not deter her at all. The committee, she thought, would ensure that the proposals for research would be run past a wide range of people representative of educational interests; and, once satisfied, they would be a great help in eliciting the cooperation of (among others) the district senior inspectors, regional education boards, school boards and the heads of state schools, together with the education offices of the four Catholic Dioceses and the heads of independent schools. She was right; and she was, as always, quite undeterred by what others might regard as political or administrative challenges. Rather, she saw such challenges as opportunities to be energetically exploited. Her aim was to study every kind of child, from every kind of school, and to do it as usefully and strategically as she could, taking careful account of what was already known and avoiding those few areas already being studied, in particular the drinking habits and sexual knowledge and practices of her subjects. Everything else that research and common sense suggested to be relevant to understanding the children would be examined: what they did during the weekends, where and how they travelled, what impact the news media had on them, what they thought of their families (and their parents compared with their peers and their teachers), what they worried about, and what they thought about gender roles. In pursuing her aim she would cheerfully and relentlessly mobilise every resource she could.

I'm not sure either when I joined the project, though I can remember how it happened. It could have been the Wednesday morning of any Faculty of Arts meeting over the long summer of 1977–78. We were walking back together to our offices after a meeting. She was the first woman professor ever appointed at Auckland, with piercing light blue eyes, a commanding vocal tone, and a formidable reputation as a researcher and university politician. She was, I now realise, aged 51 then, and at the height of her powers. She was wearing a bright floral dress and was chatting freely; but that did not make me less respectful of her power and position. I was a senior lecturer, and thought myself not likely to go further. I was 37 with very little published research to my name. Most of my time and interest was taken up with domestic life, and I could see that a dilettante's interest in far too wide a range of subjects was going to blight my academic future. In fact, though, my dilettante's interest reawakened academic ambition in me by triggering in Marie an invitation to work with her.

As we walked that morning in the sun she told me of her idea: to find out in the simplest and most direct way possible — with a battery of questionnaires — just what 12-year-old children thought and felt. Only in the light of that knowledge could the planners of public policy decide what might best be done for the future; and if the study were made replicable for future cohorts of 12 year olds, then what a mine of data could be accumulated to be mined in the future. 'What a waste of time and money,' I cried (or something to that effect). 'I could tell you what they're like and what they'll be, simply by reading what they read, watching the TV they watch, and listening to the music they listen to.'

'You're on,' she said, to my astonishment — since I had meant to offer provocation, not help. But within a few weeks she had provided me with research funds to hire some research students to help me, and I could not back down.

The rest is history, contained in the fascinating if slightly forbiddingly utilitarian book she and Dr Oates produced: one of the last ever done in 10-point typewriter typeface. For my part, I did as much as I could of what I had rashly claimed could be done, applying the techniques of the history of ideas to what 12 year olds encountered in the media. I set out to discover the main kinds of human character and life themes that the children would have come across there, and set about inferring from that (give or take a good deal) how they would view the world in general. A rereading of the result certainly takes one back to 1978: to Rob Muldoon, to Telethons and TV news; and to the heroes and heroines of TV to be found in *Happy Days*, *Welcome Back Kotter*, *Starsky and Hutch* and *The Good Life*. The satirical show *A Week of It* was the only New Zealand-made show they watched, because it was all that there was. The reader may also discover, for instance, what was in the Trixie Belden stories for girls and in the Hardie Boys series. Yet I can remember uneasily thinking at the time that the essay showed far less than I had claimed on our morning walk, and was more flatulent and biased than was ideal.

My alarm at the essay's shortcomings increased when, after I had handed it to her, Marie told me that she now proposed to 'operationalise' it into a series of propositions which she proposed testing against the evidence abstracted from the questionnaires. So it was with great trepidation that one day in 1984 when *Round about Twelve* came into my hands, I scoured the new publication to discover in 10 pages or so an appallingly fair and accurate attempt to assess my 'excellent, courageous, and eminently sensible predictions'.

'Excellent' and 'sensible' I liked: and it was typical of Marie to be so generous to those she worked with. 'Courageous' seemed equally kind at first glance; but soon the description emerged as one not to be entirely happy with. As I read on I was gently led to see that it might also mean 'foolhardy' (that is, pathologically risk-taking) and even, slightly, 'unscientific': yet for all that, she wrote of me as a colleague, and took seriously what I said.

Of course she herself was courageous and a risk-taker: how else to explain her ambition and the wide range of collaborators she attracted worldwide? Nevertheless her research aims and methods were fully thought through and her execution was meticulous. She was a thorough professional who put finding out the truth about her subject above everything else. She put this even above her other driving passion: the wish to help those she studied. I was to find these things out at little cost, and to my great benefit. I will always be grateful to her for inviting me to work with her, and will not forget the lessons I learned in the process.

A Colleague

Based on an interview with Nicholas Tarling
Professor Emeritus, The University of Auckland

Professor Marie Clay and History Professor Nicholas Tarling served on many of the same committees at the University of Auckland, where they formed a friendship from working on mutual tasks.

Nicholas Tarling started at the university after Marie in 1965. Nicholas was Dean of the Arts Faculty, and he was also Chairman of the Dean's Committee from 1977 to 1992, and as such Assistant Vice-Chancellor for this time and Deputy Vice-Chancellor for six years to the Vice-Chancellor, Colin Maiden. Marie was Deputy Dean of the Arts Faculty from 1984 to 1986. When Marie chaired the Student Accommodation and Welfare Committee, she was an assistant to the Vice-Chancellor. She was Chair of the Discipline Committee in the late seventies and early eighties, a voice of reason and tolerance, and Nicholas was also on this committee.

Research, and the recognition of social science research in particular, was always important to Marie. From 1979 to 1981 she was on the Social Science Research Fund Committee of New Zealand. Marie was a member of the Research Committee at the university from 1983 to 1986, and at the same time she served on the National Research Advisory Council of New Zealand. During the late eighties when various university departments were reviewed, including the Education Department, she was the chair for the review of the Anthropology Department. Often Marie Clay was the only female representative on the university committees. In 1979 the New Zealand Vice-Chancellors Committee selected Marie as their representative for the National Advisory Committee on Women and Education.

Nicholas Tarling and Marie Clay also worked together on proposals for credits for the Auckland Teachers College. In the late seventies Nicholas was chair of the Liaison Committee between the Teachers College Council and the University of Auckland, and Marie was on this committee. The Liaison Committee could award students up to four papers towards a degree, based on the individual's performance, for completing the Primary Training College course. Duncan McGhie, the principal of the primary teachers college, wanted the students to receive two-thirds of the credits towards a Bachelor of Education for their course. Nicholas met with Marie several times to discuss the Bachelor of Education proposal. The preference at the university was to retain the existing framework of the Bachelor of Arts degree as a more general degree with a wider range of subjects, rather than adopting a Bachelor of Education. In the history of the Auckland College of Education, *Making a Difference*, it says in 1978 'Professor Nicholas Tarling (Dean of Arts) and Professor Marie Clay (Education Department)' put forward a compromise proposal that was 'partially adopted. Students who graduated from the three-year division A course were now entitled to seven unspecified papers towards a BA degree' (p. 182). This included some advanced papers, and as a third of a degree was 'considered a significant breakthrough'.

After nationwide education reforms, where Marie was one of four independent evaluators, and the subsequent New Zealand Qualifications Authority legislation of 1990, institutions other than universities had the ability to give degrees. The Auckland College of Education began teaching a conjoint Bachelor of Education degree with the University of Auckland. In 2004 the Auckland College of Education merged with the University of Auckland to become a joint Faculty of Education.

Nicholas remembered that Marie slowed a little after she was diagnosed with polymyalgia rheumatica in 1990. When he encountered her on the way to the university common room, on the pathway between the old buildings of the education and the history departments, she looked 'very buxom' from the drugs. She was prescribed a steroid called prednisone to alleviate her symptoms of the polymyalgia, the stiffness in her limbs and spine, which for her also caused weight gain in her body and face. She reduced the dosage when she thought she could, but continued to take the steroid for around 10 years.

On retirement from the University of Auckland in January 1991, when others might have chosen to take it easy, Marie Clay instead became president of the International Reading Association and taught Reading Recovery Tutors as a visiting professor at the University of London. In her speech on her retirement she talked about coming to the university with a particular speciality as a clinical child psychologist, and going away with a much 'wider range of skills: the intricacies of student welfare and accommodation, the ins and outs of disciplinary issues, the inside story of departmental reviews, the outside view of the university from … the tomorrow's schools evaluations, how to get Social Science research accepted and funded …, how to live and work in historic buildings, and how to start a world movement from a little lean-to in Wynyard Street'.

When after about 10 years her polymyalgia rheumatica seemed to be coming under control and the drugs were no longer needed, Marie was diagnosed with Type 2 diabetes. As it progressed she would test her sugar daily, taking pills when necessary. She had special travel insurance so that she would be covered despite various physical conditions, including long-term hypertension. She continued what others would have found a gruelling worldwide schedule. For her it was an enjoyable part of her life, meeting with colleagues in many countries.

In 1990 Nicholas Tarling began to take opera tours annually to Australia and some to Europe. At the University of Auckland he had been involved in the Theatre Workshop and had performed in outdoor Shakespeare productions; and he had been a member of the Mercury Theatre Board in Auckland. Although interested in attending shows, Marie seldom took much time out from her work, but after 2000 she began to regularly join the Australian opera tours organised through Continuing Education of the University of Auckland. Nicholas said he always knew where Marie was on the tour and where people were having a good time by her laughter.

In 2006 she decided to go on the Eastern European Opera tour, in the middle of the year, through Germany, Poland and the Czech Republic, as a rare treat. She had recently completed work with her editor on *Part Two* of *Literacy Lessons*. Being on the tour reminded Marie of times when she was growing up and of her mother, who taught singing and had wanted to be a professional opera singer.

One day in Prague, Nicholas had the morning off from being tour leader, and Marie and he decided to explore the city museums. Marie began to flag in the old city. 'I must have a coffee or something sweet,' she said. Strangely they were in a street that had no cafes, but they managed to make it to the end of the next street and sit in a cafe until she felt able to go back to the hotel.

Marie wrote at the end of her notes about the Eastern Europe opera tour that it had 'been a fantastic tour, interesting things to learn, good company and organisation … I would like to do this every year.'

In September, after returning from helping with a Reading Recovery Teacher Leader Development course in the United States, Marie attended Nicholas Tarling's talk on the opera *Faust*. He invited her to the opening of the opera. In late October she went on the brief Australian Opera tour, and visited with her grandson, Michael, and granddaughter, Manuka, while in Sydney. Back in Auckland she invited Nicholas to an Arts Laureate event.

In the first half of November she was due to travel to Hong Kong and Taipei when her left leg expanded with liquid and her doctor told her not to fly. For the first time in her life she was unable to travel to fulfil work commitments. The swelling in her leg went down, but her tiredness, aches and the heaviness in her lungs remained.

Nicholas Tarling made contact again in February 2007. Marie told him Auckland Hospital's diagnosis. 'I won't be going on any more opera tours,' she said. She talked with him about wanting to donate her papers to the University of Auckland. She had been approached by the Texas Woman's University several years earlier regarding her papers, but her preference was to leave her history in education to the university where she had become the first female professor and where she had taught for 30 years. Nicholas Tarling approached the Special Collections Librarian at the University of Auckland, and a meeting was arranged at Marie's townhouse. Some matters were discussed and although no final arrangement was made or signed until after Marie's death, she had been grateful that this had been broached by him with the University of Auckland Special Collections.

A Student's Tribute

Seok Moi Ng

*Language Education Consultant to Curriculum Planning Development Division,
Ministry of Education, Singapore*

When Marie had to cancel her presentations in November 2006 because of ill health, I was disappointed. But my own disappointment was nothing compared to that of the many literacy leaders and educators who were eagerly anticipating her talks at a series of Asian seminars. While her work did not lead her as much to Asia as it did to America, Europe, the United Kingdom and Australia, she was known and revered by many there. I was helping to organise the November presentations

Seok borrowed Marie's gown to be capped for her doctorate.

and there had been a scramble from many to get her to other parts of Asia at the same time. Marie was not able to do the long stints that she had done in the past and she accepted only two other invitations that were near the main venue in Taiwan.

It was never easy to get Marie to speak at the Asian venues that I proposed to her over the years. After her retirement, she still had an incredibly busy schedule and even if we could spot a spare slot, there was inevitably an intense discussion about why I wanted her to speak at those places. Since she could only speak English and worked mainly from a first-language perspective, what on earth would she have to say to Asian audiences who spoke languages that are so different from English? If I crossed that first hurdle and she liked my arguments, she would then ask numerous questions such as those in her email about the talks scheduled for November 2006:

> Tell me what you would talk to those audiences about, if you were filling in for me. And what titles would interest my audience? Given that I am mostly familiar with issues about young children and young learners of the English language, what would you want them to go away with in their heads? I need to know your thinking of what would be helpful to the conference attendees.

Over the years, I grew to admire Marie's tenacious commitment to 'read' her audience and to make every presentation count for those she was talking to. Unlike some sought-after speakers, she never merely recycled a previous talk. She had the traits of a great teacher and it is Marie as a teacher that I will always remember.

It was at the University of Auckland in 1970 when I first had Marie as my lecturer for a Year 3 education paper. Fresh from a couple of years of pre-service teaching in Singapore, I had grabbed at the chance offered by a Colombo Plan scholarship to study for an education degree in New Zealand. I thought it would be a great opportunity for me to learn how to solve all the problems I had as a novice teacher. I soon found out that there were no straight answers and most lectures ended with '... and more research needs to be done'. I used to nod off in some of the lectures after lunch but never during Marie's. It wasn't the fear of being found out — I had to be wide awake to take down as many notes as I could. Marie did not use very difficult language but the concepts and ideas presented in her lectures were complex. I always had the feeling that those concepts and ideas were within my reach and if I worked at them, I might begin to grasp some of her important messages. What also fascinated me was that she was not only talking about other people's work but also about her development of the Reading Recovery intervention to help struggling readers. Here was someone who had studied the very children she was lecturing about. While her lectures did not provide all the answers to my teaching problems, Marie stood out as someone attempting to address the real concerns of a practitioner.

When I enrolled in 1975 to do my doctoral work under Marie, Reading Recovery was still in its early stages. During and after my doctoral studies, we discussed on several occasions the possibility of my working in Reading Recovery. I had tested the early cohorts of Reading Recovery children in 1978 as a research assistant and later trained as a Reading Recovery teacher, experiencing first hand its power for supporting slow-progress readers. However, I opted for a career in a different area, but what I had learnt from Marie then, and continued to learn from her over the next 20 or so years, has been invaluable to me.

My years as a doctoral student were hugely satisfying under Marie's tutelage. She guided me in areas such as developmental, cognitive and educational psychology and applied linguistics, areas in which I learned to evaluate the integrity of academic work and grapple with the complex issues and controversies in each. However, her demand for excellence coupled with her deep understanding about cognition and children's literacy development often drove me to despair. During those four years, the drafts I had laboured over would be returned, always kindly but inevitably with suggestions for improvement. Often it would be at least a couple of weeks before I could work on them — only to be annoyed to find that Marie was right once again and I had to dig deeper and work harder to clarify my thinking and writing.

As part of my Chinese culture, we observe the tradition of holding our teachers in high esteem so although she suggested it, I was unable to call her Marie like the other students. While I was at the university, to me she was always Doctor or Professor Clay. Only much later, when we occasionally shared meals at reading conferences in venues such as Georgia, Texas, Louisiana or Hawaii, was I able to call her Marie. Because we were both small eaters, we would often share one meal between us and would divide the entree, the main course as well as the chocolate dessert that she used to love. Although I always enjoyed having a meal with Marie, it was our conversations that were the highlight of these occasions. Whenever I was near her home in New Zealand, I made a point of calling or visiting her and we would chat sometimes about family, but mainly about work, both hers and mine.

Whenever we met, Marie always took an interest in whatever project I was involved in. I would tell her about my current projects and often show her video clips of the project children in the classrooms, seeking her comments about them. Like no one else could, Marie would comment on my work just as she did during my university days. While she did not always have a solution, her responses would shed some new perspectives on the challenges I was facing. Despite a difference in focus — Marie worked predominantly with children who had difficulties and for most of my career I have worked with average-progress children — we shared the same practice of collaborating with teachers when working on classroom problems in search of ways to maximise literacy learning.

In an early version of Marie's diagnostic survey for observing young literacy learners, she drew an analogy between conversation and teaching:

> Sensitive and systematic observation of young children's reading and writing behaviours provides teachers with feedback which can shape their next teaching moves. Teaching then can be likened to a conversation in which you listen to the speaker carefully before you reply.

Like the best of teachers, she practised what she taught. As both a scientist and a teacher in her well-known Reading Recovery project, she observed faithfully what children were doing and attempted to understand their understandings before making recommendations for optimising learning and development. We often exchanged experiences of applying those same principles to different educational systems as our conversations turned to the diverse cultures and people we worked with in various countries: children and their teachers, school administrators, teacher mentors, tertiary educators and researchers, Education Ministry officials and government leaders. We debated how best to manage the processes of change to ensure survival of the innovation, given that there would always be tension between innovation and cultural systems.

Because I had learnt so much from our conversations, I wanted Marie to share her knowledge and wisdom with the people I worked with and cared about in Asia. I began to search for such opportunities. The first such occasion materialised in Singapore in 1985. At that time, my first major language project was about to go nationwide. We had used some of the tasks from Marie's *Observation Survey* and the project team members had read some of her work. Maureen Khoo, one of the team members, said: '... it was her gift to explain complex cognitive and linguistic behaviours of a young reader in the simplest of language. In my early days as a beginning teacher educator, I was inspired by her work and am indebted to her for a sound understanding of early reading behaviours.' My other colleagues were also keen to invite Marie to Singapore as the third distinguished educator in a lecture series held in honour of Dr Ruth Wong, a former director of the local teachers college and who, like Marie, was not only a household name with locals but also had international acclaim.

It was not coincidental that in that same year in Singapore, a voluntary Society for Reading and Literacy was born. Marie had been responsible for sparking my interest in professional voluntary work with the International Reading Association (IRA), an association of literacy professionals devoted to improving literacy worldwide. During her term as one of the few non-US IRA presidents, Marie pushed for more international involvement from IRA members. Since then, IRA has granted more recognition to the committees set up for various regions in the world, the International Development in Asia Committee (IDAC) being one. The IDAC has worked through many literacy leaders and local reading associations in Asia, including those in Thailand, Hong Kong, the Philippines, Singapore, Malaysia, Japan, India and China.

The next occasion arose in 1995, when the IDAC members endorsed my nomination of Marie to do the opening plenary for the 1995 Asian Reading Congress to be held in Singapore. To mark the significance of the event, the drums of a Chinese lion dance pounded out a welcome for the Singapore Minister of State for Education and the delegates from 11 countries of Asia as well as from far-flung countries like the United States, Canada, Australia and New Zealand. Asian delegates still recall the event as providing important opportunities to network with other literacy leaders. In all her presentations as in this one, Marie's meticulous preparation enabled her to communicate to and 'teach' the audience, an audience comprising mainly Asians who she professed to know little about. The then IDAC chair wrote this of Marie's speech:

As I reread her Keynote Address for the Asian Reading Congress in Singapore 1995 ... I marvelled once again that anyone could analyse and discuss with such clarity an impossibly complex subject like 'Literacy and Bi-literacy in Asia: Problems and Issues in the Next Decade'.

The IDAC which was meeting in Taiwan also helped organise the November 2006 talks. A series of talks (two in Taiwan and one in Hong Kong) were to be part of the literacy seminars that IDAC combines with its committee meetings each year. When Marie was unable to attend, one of the overseas speakers volunteered to do the opening plenary in place of Marie for the IDAC event in Taiwan, and her other talk scheduled at a nearby local university was cancelled. But it was done differently in Hong Kong.

There, the invitation came from the Chinese Department of the Hong Kong Institute of Education (HKIED). Rosalind Wu, who had met Marie at the National Institute of Education in Washington, DC, had done some work using Marie's *Concepts About Print* tasks. She recalled that it took her a while to convince members of the department that someone who did not speak, read or write Chinese could have relevant messages for reading in Chinese, but she was eventually successful and the invitation was issued.

Preparations in Hong Kong for such an honoured visitor had been extensive. Emails, flyers and posters had been sent out announcing the visit. Prior to the talks, the library had collected and held an exhibition of Marie's publications, and a couple of Marie's papers had been translated for handouts. When news came a few days before the event that her doctor advised against travelling, the possibilities of teleconferencing or videotaping her talk were discussed and rejected as there wasn't enough time. Cancellation would be difficult since there had been an overwhelming and unusual response from schools and kindergartens, unusual because it was to be a weekday event. The local organisers finally decided to go ahead with the event. They were aided by Marie's characteristic trait of always being prepared ahead of schedule — she had already produced nearly full versions of her two papers, along with the visuals.

I was in that HKIED lecture theatre on 8 November 2006, having flown in the night before from the Taiwan IDAC conference. Even before the scheduled opening time, it was jam-packed with people who had to hunt for seats. I remembered being a bit apprehensive about whether the organisers had made the right choice — how would the audience react when they heard that Marie was not going to be there and that the paper would be read by someone else in English alternating with the Chinese translation? I need not have worried. The audience stayed through the reading of her first paper and the Chinese translation in the morning and returned in full force after lunch for her second paper. They listened intently to Marie's papers about young children making the transition into dealing with a written code — how individuals, who are different, construct reading and writing processes that link a spoken code to a written code in interaction with knowledgeable teachers — whatever the language or the script. At the end of the reading, many of the questions and comments that were raised were redirected to me as her former doctoral student — a particularly harrowing experience as I was unprepared for this awesome task of responding to questions directed to my teacher.

Rosalind Wu copied to me an email she sent to Marie:

Although we did not see you in person, we did hear the sound of your voice in the reading of the papers ... Seok was a great help. She came and explained many of your concepts, and answered questions as you would have done.

I am glad I was there to be a small part of Marie's presentation as it was probably her last one.

For me, Marie's legacy to the world is not only Reading Recovery, although that alone is achievement enough. She also has opened our eyes to a wider vision — to what we can discover and learn if only we allow the children we teach to show us what they are capable of doing. If we listen very carefully, we may be able to find and show them the next link to new learning. Her voice will continue to be heard and her influence felt through her books and papers and by those of us who have been influenced by her academic integrity and wisdom and continue to work at enhancing the lives of future generations of children. There will be other innovations but they will be built on what she started. Many academics and researchers have worked on what would help improve education but they have neither been able to put the ideas into practice in schools nor been able to support them until they produce good outcomes. Marie has shown by example to her students worldwide how to persist in striving towards understanding the complexity of language learning and how to communicate this understanding to others in the hope of putting improved practices within the reach of teachers.

Thank you, Marie, for being my teacher.

Acknowledgement
I would like to acknowledge the contributions of several people to the development of this tribute, all admirers of Marie's work: notably Maureen Khoo (IDAC chair, 1994–96, lecturer, National Institute of Education, Singapore), Rosalind Wu (Hong Kong Institute of Education), Claudia Sullivan (former lecturer, National Institute of Education, Singapore), Linda Gan (Assistant Professor, National Institute of Education), Christina Ratnam (former head, Pre-School Education, Ministry of Education, Singapore) and Cheah Yin Mee (Learning Venture).

What I Learned from Marie

Stuart McNaughton
Professor, The University of Auckland; Director, Woolf Fisher Research Centre

My relationship with Marie encompassed a variety of roles. She was a teacher and mentor, she was a colleague and she was a dear friend. I learned a lot from her in each of those roles. I have written elsewhere about her as a scientist and researcher and will not repeat those things in this piece. I want to stress the influence these roles had on me personally.

I first met Marie during my second year at the University of Auckland, in 1969. I was in her laboratory class on individual differences in which she introduced us to assessment tools and testing. In essence she gave me my first sense of trying to make a difference through the science in her positive reactions to a case study I completed on a close friend of mine who I thought far brighter but who had dropped out of university. In the battery of personality and intelligence tests and informal interviews, I had tried to summarise for him how he might better cope at university while realising his was a rational response to a set of circumstances. The grade Marie gave me was great, but it was the query many months later after the course about how my friend was now coping that impressed on me the need to consider and keep considering outcomes.

Marie supervised parts of my MA and, on returning to the University of Auckland with an almost competed doctoral dissertation from the University of Kansas, she was on my doctoral committee for one of the remaining studies. When I joined the Department of Education in 1976 she helped me to find research paths and funding. I co-taught developmental courses and research seminars with her.

I agree with others' experiences of her as a committed and effective teacher and mentor. At her memorial a letter was read out from one of her students, a Chief Executive of the New Zealand Ministry of Education. Dr Maris O'Rourke called Marie's courses 'tough', 'uncompromising' and 'relevant' — and pointed out the rigour never stopped.

What I would add to this description is that I learned from her the role of the academic mentor including the mutual obligations in the relationship of student and mentor. She was instrumental in my being awarded by the International Reading Association in 1983 the prestigious Albert J. Harris award. She helped me get research funding and introduced me to research and publishing opportunities. I reflected on this when I read an account in Stephen J. Gould's book *Wonderful Life* in which he says that universities are one of the few survivors of the old apprenticeship system in their doctoral programmes and that he could not imagine a better system. I could not have experienced a better system.

My academic apprenticeship with Marie taught me that she was a scientist studying children's development. She was quite insistent, as only Marie could be, that it was her developmental science that was the basis of what she did. I remember her saying to me many times that she hated being introduced to conferences as the 'Reading Lady'. Her point was that this was the rigorous base upon which her thinking about literacy and language sprang, although I'm not sure being introduced as the 'Developmental Lady' would have had quite the same ring.

Marie and Stuart McNaughton.

There were several things I learned about that were quite important to being a developmental lady in the context of New Zealand. One was that she was passionately interested in children and their well-being. Shortly after I had been appointed to a tenured position in her department, my wife and I and our very small baby were invited to a dinner at her place with some senior academics. Just as Marie was about to put the soufflé on the table, my wife, who was breastfeeding, had to feed our son. Marie heartily endorsed this and was very accommodating, insisting the guests all wait. The soufflé was ruined but Marie was unfazed: this was what the baby needed.

At dinner parties and gatherings we would swap stories about children and their views of the world. She loved hearing these. She was an inveterate collector of anecdotes about children. She would have loved one about Reading Recovery. One might think that the negative effects of being labelled would occur with an intervention such as Reading Recovery. Not so … Sian, a close family friend, came home recently to announce at the dinner table some very happy news. 'Guess what?' she said with considerable pride. 'I got chosen for Reading Recovery.'

Marie's fascination with children permeated her work. In this sense she taught me about a tradition in our science that keeps the research close to children's worlds and tries to make sense of these worlds as much from the child's perspective as from the adult's. Marie had included a piece of emergent writing from one of my children in one of her books and gave me the confidence to do likewise. In a book I wrote on emergent literacy, there are photos of my children in their early literacy activities to illustrate theoretical ideas and one whole chapter devoted to my youngest son, Harry, and his emergent writing attempts.

A more personal reflection of this love of children was how Marie's focus in her science changed, seemingly in parallel with the ages of her much-loved children. In the earliest years at the university the focus in her teaching and research was early development. As her children got older she developed courses in middle childhood and when older still, in adolescent development. I think if she had continued at the university longer there would have been a course on grandparenting. The point I took from this was that family is a source of important insights and the important insights are a means for contributing to the well-being of families.

I learned a lot about writing as a developmentalist through Marie. She was a very clever writer and she enjoyed thinking about her writing. I remember sitting with her through an interminably boring conference presentation which was saved by engaging in something like passing notes between naughty schoolchildren: Marie and I were swapping ideas for good titles to books. One of the titles she passed to me was the title of her book on emergent writing: *What Did I Write?* That is a great title for a book, not the least because it was a direct quote from one of the children she had observed, again reflecting her love of children's worlds.

A very recent example of her search for titles occurred when a family friend, Rangi King, found out we were visiting Marie and were worried about her health. When told Marie was the designer of Reading Recovery, she was greatly moved to hear Marie was so unwell. Her granddaughter Tracey had gone to Reading Recovery and had benefited enormously. She exclaimed, 'Reading Recovery — that's the bomb!' The story doesn't stop there. My wife Trudie was telling Marie this in the hospice. Marie, as fond as ever of searching for labels, had asked Trudie what to call their visit together. The answer was clear: 'Reading Recovery, that's the bomb'.

She deliberately wrote for at least two audiences, and taught me the importance of doing this. One is an international audience, the audience of peers who provide quality assurance and with and through whom scientific advances are made. But she said we should try to publish and disseminate locally so that colleagues and communities who might not have access to the research literature or, indeed, not be interested in the technicalities of that writing nevertheless could learn from our work and perhaps provide feedback on the usefulness of that work.

Something that I thought at the time was standard to doing science but I later found out was unique for her time was her attitude to the policy applications of science. Her definition of our science included contributing to optimising development. This latter she took to be as much a part of what it meant to be a scientist as the usual theory building and fact finding. The significance of this was that she spent time with policy makers, with bureaucrats and executives and studied how to embed new and better systems in real everyday contexts. This meant deliberately informing those involved in policy making, and she was very good at that. In at least two elections in New Zealand and one in the United Kingdom she managed to get opposition political parties to adopt Reading Recovery as a plank in their party's educational manifesto. The almost unique relationship between researchers and the Ministry of Education in New Zealand over many years has something to do with there being only 0.5 degrees of separation between us all, it's true; but it also has a lot to do with a history of close cooperation at which Marie was a pioneer and a teacher of others including myself.

As I have said, being a developmental scientist in New Zealand meant that Marie was committed to contribute to the well-being of all of our communities. But she also modelled a particular research commitment to the educational well-being of Maori communities. Her contribution to Maori educational concerns started early on in her career. In the 1970s, funded by the Maori Education Foundation, she developed for research purposes a language tool that assessed Maori schoolchildren's comprehension of following directions or answering questions using a graduated sequence in Te Reo Maori. These days many of us would recognise some of the earliest questions and comments in the sequence such as E tu (Stand up) and E noho (Sit down), or Kei te pehea koe? (How are you?)

Marie saw the need from those earlier studies to put in place programmes which build the language and she contributed to the development of Reading Recovery assessments and procedures for Maori educational contexts. It is interesting to see how far New Zealand has changed since her time, at least in some areas. In the 1990s a number of us repeated that study using the original tools, but with younger preschool children in Te Kohanga Reo (early childhood education 'language nests' designed to regenerate language as well as cultural practices). Marie was intrigued and impressed by an interesting finding. When we gave the original assessment to the children, they were so confident they even queried and corrected some of the original language, considering it too simple for them.

I have written about one of the very few disagreements I had with Marie. The occasion was her farewell speech to the then Department of Education when she apparently retired. I say apparently because she then worked harder and travelled more than ever before. She used analogies to great effect in her work and she used an analogy at her farewell that typified her humility. She described her times during Christmas holidays playing on a family farm. She and the other children would make trails through the bush. When she returned the next holidays, the trails were overgrown. She said that her work had made trails. But they

Young Marie (standing) and a friend in the bush.

would disappear as others would find new trails. I think she got the analogy wrong. True, others will make new discoveries; they will add ways of researching with and optimising children's literacy development. But these accomplishments will be done standing on this work, and in reference to this extraordinary body of work.

Earlier I described Sian's enthusiasm for being in Reading Recovery. Her mother Heather was telling Sian about Marie's death and how Marie had helped her and millions of other children around the world to read, but that many of them wouldn't even recognise Marie's name. Sian immediately responded, 'She's like a secret agent doing amazing things, and no one knows her name!'

Those of us privileged to have worked with and been mentored by Marie know about the amazing things and we will miss Marie. She typified what is excellent in an academic. She was a tough but nurturing mentor, fiercely protective of and an advocate for her students. She was an exemplary researcher blurring naive distinctions between being 'basic' and 'applied'; she was both — we all have taken inspiration and knowledge from her work — and she was a caring and stimulating colleague and friend.

The Journey to Reading Recovery in New Zealand and Australia

Marie Clay's Contribution to ERIC

Shirley Nalder
Former Reading Adviser

During the early 1970s, the Early Reading In-service Course (ERIC) was developed in Auckland. At the time, John Penton was the district adviser on reading, Shirley Nalder an adviser on reading, John Slane a primary school inspector, and Don Holdaway a lecturer at Auckland Teachers College.

The Early Reading In-service Course (ERIC) was an extensive course of 12 units designed to train all junior class teachers in the teaching of reading. The units were of tape, slide and booklet format. Teachers took these units individually in a booth at a centre once a week. All staff members from a school were involved at the same time so that there could be follow-up staff discussion and in-school tasks carried out. Each booklet included a professional article, and other professional reading was suggested.

Marie Clay had completed her PhD thesis based on observations of the reading behaviour of five- to six-year-old children. This work developed new knowledge of the strategies children use in learning to read, particularly a self-improving system, explaining how they get better and better as they read. Don Holdaway had spent a number of years developing reading programmes for students who, for many reasons, had not usually found learning to read easy. Shared Book Experience was a procedure that he developed at this time. It embodied the notion of the bedtime story in a classroom context to develop a knowledge of book language for those children who had not had much experience with books; this included children for whom English was a second or other language. ERIC included material based on both Marie's work and Don's work.

ERIC essentially helped teachers develop better understandings of the reading process and the process of learning to read as well as sound teaching practice, including such well-accepted procedures as language experience and guided reading with the addition of Don's Shared Book Experience. Diagnostic teaching and early identification of children who were likely to have reading difficulty was an important part of the course.

There was a development team consisting of John Slane, John Penton and Don Holdaway. Many teachers were involved in different ways, such as working on particular aspects in their classrooms and doing model lessons from which teaching examples were drawn for the units. ERIC began in Auckland then spread New Zealandwide.

Don Holdaway and John Penton initiated a plan for ERIC that was to feature Marie's diagnostic work. At that stage she agreed to participate in the project. They needed to learn how to take running records, so Marie decided to teach them.

Marie wrote: 'I remember so clearly one afternoon in a South Auckland school. Don, John Penton and I sat around the table … They were constructing a slide and audiotape programme for training teachers and they were considering using one of my research techniques with the teachers. It was actually a way of recording what a child was doing, word by word, as he or she worked through the pages of a book.'

Marie found that they were difficult pupils! In order to record accurately there seemed to be so much to remember. John and Don wanted to do it their own way. However, they did succeed, and also saw the value of using standard procedures.

Unit 2 — Sensitive Observation of Reading Behaviour, Unit 3 — Observing and Interpreting Early Reading Behaviour, and Unit 10 — Diagnosing Early Reading Needs were based on Marie's work. Units 2 and 3 were about taking running records and were intended to help teachers understand the reading process and the process of learning to read.

As a result of the problems he himself had experienced, John decided to design Units 2 and 3 in a way that would make it easy for teachers to learn easily and proficiently how to observe, record and analyse young children's reading behaviour. In taking running records, teachers needed to do what Marie had done in her research: become a neutral observer, and so record what children did without any preconceived ideas of what they should do.

In the two units John designed, teachers had hands-on practice at recording reading behaviour from tapes using the very innovative booklets, with half pages where they could check their efforts. New reading behaviours and the conventions for recording these were introduced very slowly throughout the units, so that proficiency could be developed before moving on to something new. Marie was thrilled with these units and used them in her own work when training students to record reading behaviour accurately.

In Unit 2, Marie's article *Early Reading Behaviour: A Guide to Sensitive Observation* was included as the professional article, and in Unit 3, her article *The Early Detection of Reading Difficulties: Some Investigatory Techniques* served the same purpose. Both of these articles had previously been published in *Education*, a journal for teachers published by NZEI (New Zealand Educational Institute), numbers 1 and 5 (1970) respectively.

Traditionally, reading programmes have been provided for all children, and then remedial programmes at a later stage after children have failed. ERIC presents a different model, where it is envisaged that within the framework of a developmental reading programme there will always be diagnostic teaching based on the results of diagnostic work. All children's reading should be checked at the age of six years, and those who are thought to perhaps be at risk should be given a full Diagnostic Survey to reveal what they know and where to go from there.

Marie wrote: 'They devised a way of training teachers to use this tool [running records, and] put it in their ERIC programme. Starting with my research they devised and spread a reliable tool throughout this country, and it is used in most English-speaking countries today. They also trained these teachers in a series of tasks which evaluated children's reading progress after one year at school — still used, and referred to in New Zealand as the six-year-old safety net.'

The purpose of Unit 10 was to train teachers in the techniques of the full Diagnostic Survey (as opposed to running records only, as in Units 2 and 3) and so to analyse many more aspects of a child's reading. An analysis of one child's reading at the ages of 5.5, 6.0 and 6.5 years showing growth in all aspects of the survey over this year of development was presented in this unit, and a model of the integration of cue sources Marie had found to be important in early reading was included.

During the 1970s and early 1980s, Reading Recovery developed and new editions of *The Early Detection of Reading Difficulties* were published. After the third edition in 1985 became available, Unit 10 was updated to come in line with these developments. This new version presented one child at the age of 6.0 years, indicating this was the stage of a child's schooling when a careful survey of reading was necessary to determine whether satisfactory progress was being made or whether some special intervention, in the form of Reading Recovery, was necessary. By this stage procedures had become much more specific and standardised.

Unit 10 also included the first publication of Marie's article *Organising to Prevent Reading Failure* preceded by the following introduction: 'The professional article for this unit is the text of the inaugural address given by Dr Clay to launch the first Auckland term-long in-service course on Reading in the Junior School for a selected group of Resource Teachers. The talk was presented to a large invited audience drawn from the schools, the Department of Education, and the Teachers Colleges on the evening of 11 February 1975.'

The procedures for observing, recording and analysing reading behaviour developed by Marie Clay became an integral part of the ERIC programme and were thus introduced widely to many teachers throughout New Zealand. Since then they have been promoted by advisers (reading, junior class and rural) and literacy facilitators. They have become an integral part of New Zealand reading programmes at primary and secondary levels, of specialist reading services such as Resource Teachers of Literacy (RT Lit) and special programmes such as Rainbow Reading. They are now the procedures teachers look to for obtaining information on children's reading.

The author would like to thank John Slane for his assistance with ideas and final suggestions for this article.

The Beginnings of Reading Recovery

Barbara Watson

Former National Director of Reading Recovery, New Zealand

Everyone who has known Marie Clay as friend, mentor and teacher or colleague has stories to share of her influence upon their lives. I have many memories gathered in our 30 years of shared experience during the development and implementation of Reading Recovery. Marie was an amazing scholar, an astute researcher and an exceptional educator and individual. At the 5th International Reading Recovery Institute in Baltimore, Maryland shortly after Marie Clay's death in early 2007, I talked about this remarkable woman whom I felt privileged to call a friend. The following account is based on that tribute.

An idea conceived ...

When the Reading Recovery story starts in 1976, Marie Clay had just become the first woman professor and first woman head of department at the University of Auckland. Early literacy was only one of her many areas of interest, but that year class teachers challenged her to pay particular attention to early reading and writing. By developing a set of observation tasks, Marie had made it possible for experienced teachers to identify the children falling behind. But what, the teachers were asking, can we then do to help those children become effective readers and writers?

Explorations and surprises ...

Marie set out to seek an answer 'simply by sailing in a new direction', to use a favourite quotation she drew on in later years by poet Allen Curnow from 'Landfall in Unknown Seas'. From her early research it seemed that extra, one-on-one help for struggling readers and writers might open up possibilities for success. Sue (Sarah) Robinson, a Masters graduate and an experienced teacher, was available. Under Marie's direction she taught two children individually in reading and writing. Starting from their strengths and observing them closely, she noted every step of their progress for Marie's critical attention.

Pleasing developments led to a second year of exploration. Marie now needed to observe more good teachers. She gathered together a group of seven, of which I was asked to be one. We met with her often and took turns to teach a child. Can you imagine regularly teaching before Marie? She would ask us why we had done what we had done. Mostly, we couldn't even remember doing it, let alone knowing why! In this way the Teaching Procedures emerged. Many activities were tried; many were discarded. Already a central Reading Recovery principle of accelerative progress was taking hold. There was an emphasis on recovery of lost time for young learners with temporary difficulties: they must be enabled to catch up quickly with their peers. So Marie would allow only the most accelerative teaching activities to remain.

By 1977, other educators and administrators who were to be significant players in the novel literacy intervention had become interested in what was happening. In a key position as Auckland District Senior Inspector of Schools was Terry Walbran. He knew and admired Marie's work. He had already assisted her in a practical way by arranging a training venue and the essential one-way viewing window for observation of lessons. When Marie asked for support to carry out field trials in five Auckland schools using the recovery procedures developed, he was immediately receptive and made the necessary arrangements.

This 1978 field trial research was outstandingly successful — 'breathtaking', according to Marie, not one for overstatement. Terry Walbran ensured that the Director-General of Education was well informed of the research results and their implications for the country's education system. Both knew that funding would be crucial to any implementation of Reading Recovery. In the next five years, Terry was central to the administrative efforts to facilitate expansion of the fledgling intervention.

An unbelievable journey begun ...

'I believe it is going to be the evidence from the research that will convince principals to come aboard,' Marie stated. And so it was. Surprisingly, the very next year, 1979, with the assistance of Terry Walbran and other top administrators, 48 schools put forward one of their junior school teachers to undertake a year of Reading Recovery in-service training. This was indeed sailing in a new direction, into uncharted waters. How could so many teachers be trained to use the novel procedures?

At Marie's request I assumed the responsibility of working with her in designing the training course, and undertook the training of the teachers. Marie was thrilled with the exciting results. They showed that the early success could be replicated with many teachers and many children. A milestone had been reached. Marie published the data, to great interest throughout the country, in the first *Reading Recovery Guidebook* for teachers. Reading Recovery was born.

Then came a startling discovery. As time passed, trained Reading Recovery teachers were veering away from the procedures. We were concerned, seeing this deviation as a threat to the integrity and effectiveness of Reading Recovery. A battle with senior educators followed. 'These teachers have already had a full year of training,' they protested. 'You can't want more!'

But finally, arguments for quality assurance proved persuasive. Permission was granted for ongoing professional development support to be offered to teachers for as long as they continued teaching in Reading Recovery. The design features integral to Reading Recovery teacher training and support were established. And so, the first chapter ended.

Full implementation and international expansion ...

The last elements to be set in place came a few years later. In the early 1980s the high demand for teacher training across New Zealand indicated an urgent need to train more Tutors. My role now became that of Tutor-Trainer, later national director of Reading Recovery in New Zealand — eventually assisted by others trained in their turn as Trainers.

Marie continued to be involved in varied ways in aspects of the training of all these people. Her influence came not only through her writing but from the academic courses she offered and the frequent talks to Tutors and teachers. Her emphasis on meeting the needs of the children was always uppermost.

By the mid-1980s, overseas interest in Reading Recovery had steadily mounted. Marie was closely involved with each new implementation: Australia, USA, Canada and the United Kingdom.

All have honoured this brilliant, single-minded scientist and innovator who has made such a difference to the teaching of literacy in their countries. Those of us who worked alongside her in those early years have powerful and persistent memories. I remember ...

Her input —
in collegial interactions, facing challenges, exploring possibilities, puzzling over issues, problem solving, steering the ship but fostering independence.

Her belief —
in the power of teachers observing each other teach, learning from watching colleagues, not experts — articulating what was being seen and *heard*, as it was happening.

Her excitement —
after watching the first teacher groups near the end of the training year.
'They are helping each other, challenging

Marie and Barbara Watson.

each other, lifting each other to better understandings — and you are becoming redundant,' she said to me. 'That's good.'

Many of us do not achieve all that we aspire to. Not so Marie Clay. Her mind was constantly active, her focus unwavering, her zeal fierce, her research meticulous, her claims circumspect, her output prodigious.

Let us celebrate her: her work, her outstanding achievements, her supportiveness and especially what she offered to each of us, as individuals.

Eleanor Roosevelt wrote: 'The future belongs to those who believe in the beauty of the dream'. In honouring Marie Clay we could say: 'The future belongs to those who believe in the vision of her dream.'

Interview with Terry Walbran

District Senior Inspector of Primary Schools (retired 1983)

Terry Walbran was instrumental in the introduction of Reading Recovery into New Zealand primary schools in the late 1970s and facilitated the expansion nationwide in the early 1980s. Terry first encountered Marie Clay's work when he was District Senior Inspector of Primary Schools in Invercargill. His own Masters thesis had been on the teaching of reading. He read a precis of Marie's doctoral thesis in the *New Zealand Journal of Educational Studies* in 1967. His attention was drawn by a university academic being prepared to go into primary classrooms to find out about children beginning to read.

When Terry Walbran was directing a course of National In-service Training for Infant Teachers at Lopdell House, under the Department of Education, he wrote to Marie Clay at the University of Auckland to ask her to give an address. She agreed, and her ability to talk to the primary teachers made a big impression on him and the teachers.

In 1972, Terry transferred from Invercargill to Auckland as District Senior Inspector. Reading Recovery started in 1976 with Marie and Sue Robinson, the beginning of the development phase. After a while Marie realised that she needed other good teachers to observe with children. She wrote: 'I started [Reading Recovery] in a lean-to room in an old house in Wynyard Street with a teacher teaching behind a one-way screen and me watching, [and] in 1977 we enlarged the team.' Terry Walbran organised discretionary funds to fit up the old house with benches, loudspeakers and the large one-way screen to enable the observation of the teacher interaction with the child reading. The enlarged team included supervising teachers, reading advisers and senior university students. Sue Robinson was there for the second year, and Barbara Watson was invited to join them.

Terry met Barbara Watson when she was teaching at Favona, a new open-plan school at Mangere, where from 1973 she was the senior teacher of junior classes. He regarded Barbara as a fine administrator and he thought she knew exactly what she was aiming at in the classroom. He recommended her when there was someone to be seconded to assist with Reading Recovery. Barbara remembers Marie saying to her when she had finished her last papers for a Bachelor of Arts and they were standing outside the Wynyard Street house: 'You could do a Masters part-time and assist with Reading Recovery part-time and we could start off Reading Recovery.'

Marie Clay talked with Terry Walbran about a trial of Reading Recovery in five Auckland schools for 1978. 'We felt we had something that worked,' she said. Five half-time teachers were requested and five full-time teachers were offered. There was 'a surplus of trained teachers that year to be placed', Marie said at the opening of the Auckland Reading Recovery Centre in March 1998, and Terry

Walbran 'was persuasive'. The five teachers taught the children using Reading Recovery procedures during sessions with the one-way screen, under the guidance of Barbara Watson; and the rest of the time they used the Diagnostic Survey with all the other six year olds in the junior part of their schools.

The results of the well-documented Reading Recovery trial seemed remarkable. Marie wrote that 'the Chief Inspector of Primary Schools sent the report we sent him (in exchange for the five teachers) to the Director-General of Education [Bill Renwick]. He told the Chief Inspector to find what funds he could to support the expansion of the programme in Auckland.' In February New Zealand hosted a meeting of the Directors-General of Australia and New Zealand at Waitangi, where, at the request of the New Zealand Director-General, Terry Walbran spoke comprehensively about Reading Recovery and its development in New Zealand.

The expansion in Auckland began with letters to schools offering training and support in Reading Recovery in 1979, and 48 schools responded. Three people from the schools had to come to the initial meetings: the principal, the senior teacher of junior classes and the proposed Reading Recovery teacher. All three had to be there for it to go ahead. Terry remembers some hurried phone calls as teachers realised this. The teachers were enthusiastic about innovation in improving the quality of education and opportunities for children, and schools supported the intervention to help to make every child a reader. Marie said Terry ran 'the first meeting for participating schools in 1979 with a firmness and insight which set us on the road to sound implementation, here and overseas'.

In 1980 the first Tutors were trained. They did the practical work with Barbara and university papers with Marie. In 1981 there was a decision by Terry Walbran and Bill Renwick to expand Reading Recovery beyond Auckland. The first group started in Hamilton, again with 48 schools participating. During the year other people around the country became interested, and there was a meeting in Lopdell House with school inspectors responsible for reading from every district.

Over the school holidays the decision was made to train Tutors for the whole of New Zealand. Fifteen people from 10 districts were sent to Auckland to train as Reading Recovery Tutors, including two from each of the big cities. These 15 Tutors were trained to go back and start Reading Recovery all around the country at once. In 1983 there was national implementation of Reading Recovery in New Zealand from Whangarei to Invercargill.

In 1983 Barbara also trained three new Tutors, two more for New Zealand and one for Australia, Joan Smith. Joan went back to Bendigo and with the assistance of Peter Hunt, the regional Group Manager of Educational Programs, began the introduction of Reading Recovery into Australia.

Terry Walbran believed that Marie gained the teachers' acceptance by her personal involvement and understanding. Marie noted, 'Sound practice does not arise from the application of research and theory to the classroom without very careful transmission of clearly understood messages.' Teachers acknowledged that Marie Clay knew what she was talking about, and this led to the successful start of Reading Recovery. Terry said it can be difficult for politicians to acknowledge the economic benefits: 'Yet where are you, if your workforce can't read?'

The Complete Professor

Peter Hunt

Former Group Manager Educational Programs, Loddon Campaspe
Mallee Region, Australia

I became an inspector of schools in 1978, and I was lucky enough to be appointed to Bendigo, the major regional city in an educational region with about 400 primary, secondary, state, Catholic and independent schools, staffed by approximately 10,000 teachers. The five inspectors covering this area were a close team, determined to lift the quality of educational leadership and the teaching of literacy and numeracy in all schools. We were young, enthusiastic and ambitious, and determined to succeed. Fortunately, we also had the strong support of the Education Faculty of La Trobe University and the senior officers within the regional and central offices of the Victorian Education Department.

The major strategy adhered to over the first few years was to encourage small teams of teachers and principals from individual schools to attend ongoing professional development programmes in Educational Leadership in Schools, and the Teaching of Literacy. These programmes were developmental and were sustained over several years. Many of these programmes were provided by the then Riverina College of Advanced Education (now Stuart University) by teams of enthusiastic lecturers under the leadership of Dr Brian Cambourne. Strong ongoing support was also provided by many dedicated curriculum consultants from the central and regional offices of the Education Department, and a group of independent consultants who operated on a freelance basis at that time, for example Lorraine Wilson, Di Snowball, Garth Boomer, Keith Pigdon and Marilyn Woolley.

All this activity led to my attendance at the Australian Reading Association Conference in Darwin in 1981 along with a strong contingent of fellow travellers/educators. We were looking for something more powerful and rigorous from what we had done so far. It became clear that we needed teachers and leaders to acquire explicit operating modes rather than intuitive modes that were more common at that time. We were ready for Reading Recovery. The small team of teachers, principals and administrators who attended from our region included representatives from the Education Department, La Trobe University and Catholic Education.

I heard Marie Clay give a keynote address on Reading Recovery, and was blown away by the rigour, detail and data from her presentation. Immediately, I sought her out to commence a dialogue that would lead me to an understanding of literacy acquisition and that gave me a rationale for the later development of the Victorian Literacy Strategy. We met many times over the course of the conference to argue, discuss, and plot and plan for the introduction of Reading Recovery into Australia. We agreed on a plan for this to happen at the final social gathering of the conference — a barbecue picnic at Fanny Bay watching the sun set over the Arafura Sea. The yacht that sailed across the sun seemed to signal the change that was about to occur in my own life's course.

On our return to Bendigo, I approached the Federal Government to fund a trial programme of Reading Recovery. I was advised that they were seeking to fund a major initiative in literacy and I was invited to Canberra to attend a literacy conference they had convened to discuss this matter. Attending the same conference was Anne Darwin from the South Australian Education Department. She had visited New Zealand the previous year and returned with a copy of the Early Reading In-service Course (ERIC), which she then modified for Australia and reissued under the title of Early Literacy In-service Course (ELIC).

I found it difficult to sustain the argument at the national level that Reading Recovery should take precedence over ELIC on the grounds that what was needed initially was a major reassessment to improve classroom teaching before Reading Recovery could be effectively implemented, that is, ELIC was an attempt to introduce a common set of principles for approaches to the teaching of literacy in schools.

As a result of these discussions, ELIC was launched and steps were set in train to prepare for the introduction of Reading Recovery into Australia. As a first step, the Australian Schools Commission agreed to provide funding to Victoria for a Travel Award for an experienced infant teacher to visit New Zealand in 1982 to report on the effectiveness of Reading Recovery, and the steps that needed to be taken to implement it in Australia. Joan Smith was chosen to take up this Travel Award. Joan's report in late 1982 led to her selection to be trained as a Reading Recovery Tutor in New Zealand in 1983. To enable this to happen, a teacher exchange was agreed to by Dr Norman Curry, Director of Education in Victoria, and his New Zealand counterpart, no doubt encouraged by Marie. As a result, Joan spent the year in Auckland training as a Reading Recovery Tutor.

During 1982 and 1983, the implementation of ELIC and the dissemination of information about Reading Recovery to schools provided the background for them to make a decision to be part of the first trial of Reading Recovery outside New Zealand in 1984. Schools had to find staffing for Reading Recovery from their current schedule, as no extra staffing was available. During this period very strong links were formed between the Catholic Education Office through their Curriculum Officer, and La Trobe University (Bendigo), through the Dean of Education, Hugh Wheeler.

Joan Smith successfully completed the Reading Recovery Tutor course, and in February 1984, began the first training course for teachers in Bendigo. An experienced New Zealand Tutor (Jeanette Methven) was seconded to Bendigo for the year to support the implementation, and her expertise was invaluable.

A group of 16 teachers from 14 schools across a number of inspectorial districts were trained in two groups. Great support was provided by Barbara Watson, the then New Zealand director of Reading Recovery, with regular visits from her and phone calls to her, to assist with issues of implementation in a different education system. The year proved successful, and a group of teachers was trained in the region each year thereafter.

After extensive evaluation of Reading Recovery by La Trobe and Wollongong universities, the Minister of Education, Ian Cathie, launched the funding of a system implementation of Reading Recovery in Victoria in November 1987. The statewide launch of Reading Recovery was held in the main auditorium of my old teachers college, Stonnington, which I attended as a trainee teacher in 1959–60. The launch opened to a full house of approximately 1000 teachers.

Marie Clay flew from Oxford University to be the keynote speaker on this momentous occasion, another extremely generous gesture on her part made possible by Qantas airlines upgrading her outward fare to business class. The only sour note to the occasion seemed to be the continuance of the nonsensical debate between 'phonicators' and whole language experts, along with a general lack of acceptance by teachers at that time that *all* pupils could be taught to read and write once we had identified the appropriate teaching strategies. Bill Lomas, the Catholic schools coordinator from our region, thanked Marie and the Minister.

This allocation of funds assisted in the implementation of Reading Recovery across both the state and Catholic education systems. The lack of a common philosophical approach to teaching and learning was to slow the introduction of Reading Recovery into Victoria. In Marie Clay's analysis of the situation, 'the lack of a common reading programme across schools and a broadly agreed acceptance of a philosophical approach to the teaching and learning of literacy skills by teachers caused unnecessary delays and false trails to be dealt with'.

Schools and teachers were enthusiastic about Reading Recovery, and it forged ahead. The first Reading Recovery Tutor training course in Australia was conducted at La Trobe University (Bendigo) by Joan Smith and Gwynneth Phillips in 1987. There were 10 teachers from both the Education Department and the Catholic education system in the group. After completing the Tutor training, they went back to a range of locations and in 1988 commenced the training of Reading Recovery teachers across the state. By the end of 2007, around 87,000 children had been helped by Reading Recovery in Victoria, and 4627 teachers had completed the 12-month in-service course for teachers.

I attended the memorial service for Marie Clay at the Epsom campus of the University of Auckland in 2007. The immigration officer who oversaw my departure enquired as to the reason for my visit. When I told him, he thanked me, and this Maori gentleman told me with pride that 'he had also been a Reading Recovery boy'.

To me, this summarised what we are all about — thank you, Marie.

Marie Clay — Agent of Change

Joan Smith
Former Reading Recovery Tutor, Victoria, Australia

Marie Clay's work has had a powerful impact upon my life, both professionally and personally. I had been a teacher of children in Prep to Year Two for many years, and was always fascinated by the process of learning to read. Despite my best efforts, there were always some children in my class who did not respond as fully as I would have liked. I searched for ways to help them, and when I became a coordinator in schools I was often able to devote time to small groups of children who were perceived as needing extra help.

In the mid-1970s I became familiar with Marie Clay's *A Diagnostic Survey* (Heinemann, 1972), and while I was working with small groups, I utilised the tests in the book to try to inform my teaching. While this helped me to understand some of the difficulties that the children were having, I was a long way from an understanding of Marie's theories. I enrolled in further study, worked as a language consultant, and pursued many avenues to help me become more effective as a teacher. This was all helpful, but nothing provided the solutions I was searching for.

In 1978, I moved to Bendigo to work. Peter Hunt was inspector of schools for the district, and I became involved in the excitement of the time when there were many teachers like myself searching for solutions. I was a member of the District Language Committee, and attended a number of in-service programmes for teachers organised by the district which had the aim of improving teaching and learning in schools.

By this time, I had a copy of Marie Clay's *The Early Detection of Reading Difficulties* (Heinemann, 1976), and was trying to implement some of the suggested teaching procedures. This was more effective than anything I had used in the past, but without the support of the Reading Recovery training programme, I was still not achieving the results I believed were possible.

In 1982, I was awarded an Australian Schools Commission Travel Award to go to New Zealand to study Reading Recovery. The two weeks I spent in Auckland were an exciting revelation to me. Barbara Watson, the then coordinator of Reading Recovery, arranged for me to spend time with the 1982 Tutor training group, and I was stunned when it was arranged for me to sit in on the university lectures that Marie Clay was delivering to these students. This was my first real contact with Marie, and I took copious notes in the lectures, in order to reflect upon them at a later date.

In addition to attending lectures, I sat in on Barbara Watson's sessions with the Tutors in training, and visited schools to observe experienced Tutors such as Margreta Chance, Sue McLaughlan and Jeanette Methven. These were two concentrated weeks and it seemed to me that Reading Recovery was what was needed to help children who needed assistance with their literacy. It all made sense, and upon my return to Bendigo I wrote a report expressing my positive observations of the programme.

I applied for a teacher exchange to New Zealand, and in 1983, with the support of administrators in both education systems, was able to enrol in the Tutor training course in Auckland. This was an intense year, as I was enrolled in two Auckland University courses that were taken by Marie Clay, as well as sessions with Barbara Watson, daily Reading Recovery teaching at Grey Lynn School, and participation in the In-service Training Course for Teachers.

I can still remember handing in the first university assignment I had to complete for Marie. Upon its return to me I was so nervous about the outcome that I didn't read the comments until I had plucked up the courage the next day.

I soon found that I needn't have worried, as Marie had put into practice her theory of learning and was always positive in her comments, and yet would take my thinking to another level by opening up new avenues of thought. It was a privilege to have the opportunity to participate in her lectures.

I learnt a great deal in that year, including how to spell 'independent' correctly. Marie must have been frustrated with my constant misspelling of it, as she finally wrote at the bottom of one of my essays 'independent/independently/independence'. I have never spelt it incorrectly since that time!

I successfully completed the year with the support of many people, including my two fellow Tutors in training, Blair Koefoed and Ian Morrison.

On my return to Bendigo, I found a great deal of groundwork had been undertaken by the region in order for Reading Recovery to start in February 1984. Peter Hunt, by then the group manager in charge of educational programmes, was responsible for this, and had arranged for two groups of teachers from 14 schools to complete the year-long in-service course for teachers. I was fortunate that Jeanette Methven was seconded to Bendigo for the year to assist with the first implementation.

Reading Recovery went on to greater successes in the Victorian education system, with Marie Clay and Barbara Watson providing much-needed support and encouragement along the way.

Reading Recovery opened many doors of opportunity for me. In 1994, I was invited to participate in the New York University Reading Recovery Project, so I resigned from the Victorian Education Department and went to live in Manhattan. This was quite a change from Bendigo, and once again a wonderful experience, both personally and professionally.

I met Marie on many occasions during my time in the United States, both at Reading Recovery conferences and at professional development organised by New York University for both Reading Recovery teachers and Teacher Leaders (Tutors). I continued to be stimulated and to learn so much from each encounter with her. I don't know anyone who has influenced my understanding of how children learn as much as Marie.

I am constantly surprised and delighted with the opportunities my involvement with Reading Recovery has opened up for me, and when I look around at others who have participated in it in any way, I know it has opened doors for them as well. I have learned to be positive, to build on the evidence of what I observe children and teachers *can* do, and to act on those achievements in a precise and concrete way. Above all, I now *know* that all children can learn to read, given the opportunity and a well-trained Reading Recovery teacher!

From the
Eighties

During the Eighties

The eighties were a period of expansion and recognition for Marie Clay. Reading Recovery began to move into Australia and America; and in 1987 she was listed in the Queen's Honours and became Dame Marie Clay. She attended the investiture in Wellington with her friend and colleague Courtney Cazden and members of her extended family in May.

In the middle of 1987 she also took long service leave from the University of Auckland. This was mainly to work in the Department of Experimental Psychology at Oxford University, but also to complete two writing tasks, and to visit the Ohio State University for two months at the invitation of Ohio State Reading Recovery Programme.

In her application for leave to the University of Auckland, she described her two writing tasks: 'The first is to write a replacement for my text on reading acquisition. The second is to develop a series of papers, possibly involving research with small groups of children, related to the theory of complex action systems (for example in the analysis of meaning, language actions, or academic behaviours) and what this implies for interventions like teaching or remediation. I hope to use a well-researched intervention programme as a tool for exploring the theory of complex action systems (applied to reading and writing behaviours in the early acquisition stage).'

At Oxford University she planned to work in the research laboratory of Professor Peter Bryant, Watts Professor of Psychology, at the Department of Experimental Psychology. Marie said: 'Professor Bryant is a developmental psychologist with several longitudinal projects under way. I will join the research team to work on two of these.' The first was 'a longitudinal project [that] has followed children from three to six years and in the final six months staff will be carrying out experiments on the role of phonological awareness in reading acquisition' and the second was 'a project on spatial development in young children and early mathematical learning'.

Lynette Bradley was also working at the Department of Experimental Psychology. She had grown up and taught in Australia, before moving to England. During Marie's sabbatical year at Oxford, she and Marie formed a lasting friendship.

Remembering Marie's Year at Oxford

Lynette Bradley

A.C.E. (Special Education), Oxford

Clearing out the cupboard under the stairs recently, I found years of unsorted photographs. One is of Marie with my grandson, who must have been 20 months old at the time. The photographs had been taken on the towpath of the Thames in central Oxford, where we had been feeding the ducks and swans. As my grandson is now a university student, my friendship with Marie has spanned some 20 years.

Marie had arrived to spend a sabbatical year in Oxford in the University Department of Experimental Psychology, where we were investigating the acquisition of reading skills and children's learning difficulties. My early work on phonological awareness and learning to read, grounded in my teaching experience and my work with children at the Park Hospital for Children, Oxford, had already been published in *Nature* and other publications. In a longitudinal study that followed young children before they learned to read until the age of 13 years old, we showed that training children in phonological awareness had a significant effect on their progress in reading and spelling. Their preschool skills predicted success in reading and spelling.

Like Marie, I grew up in the Antipodes, and we quickly found that we were on the same wavelength. Though my early career was in Australia while Marie's was in New Zealand, our experiences were similar, perhaps the heritage of our early pioneers, like Schonell.

Marie during her sabbatical year in England was attached to my Oxford College, Wolfson, and my husband David and I helped her settle in there. She often came to our home, Mahana, and on one occasion I managed to get tickets for *Penguin Café* at Covent Garden. As it was a short ballet, featuring on the same programme was the world premiere of the ballet to Holst's *The Planets*. Marie had a meeting in Bristol that day, so David and I had arranged to meet her at Oxford Station and then drive to Covent Garden.

It was the hottest day on record. The train wheels could not hold the tracks.

The train came in very late, and we arrived just in time for the performance. Going inside the opera house, all velvet and plush, was like stepping into an oven. The start of *The Planets* was delayed as the stage machinery would not function in the heat. In both ballets, the dancers had to wear all-enveloping costumes. I don't know how they did it. The performance was punctuated by the sound of fainting bodies in the higher and hotter tiers of the theatre. In the interval we joined most of the audience in the foyer. All the fashionably dressed 'first night' audience were by now barefooted and stripped to the minimum, shirts and dresses undone as far as decency permitted. It was still 80°F (27°C) at midnight that evening in London.

We continued to correspond and meet up over the years. One year David and I flew to New Zealand, where Marie met us, gave us the keys to her house and car and then left for an engagement in America. On another occasion, we spent time at the annual Craft Fair in Abingdon, England, where we tossed up as to who would buy a wall-hanging which both of us admired. The last time I was in Auckland for the day, Marie collected me from my ship, took me to eat green-lipped mussels by the shore, then home to admire the wall-hanging 'in situ'. She was disappointed not to be able to make her last planned trip to London, but hoped she would be able to get across to Sydney to see me when I flew out there. She wrote to say that she was not well enough to manage it.

Marie and I bonded because we shared a passion: wanting the best in education for all children. I will miss this lovely, warm, dedicated, generous and fun-loving lady.

NEW ZEALAND PROVIDING LEAD IN
READING INSTRUCTION

When Professor Courtney Cazden was visiting Auckland, New Zealand in 1983, there was an extensive article in the New Zealand Herald *about her visit, her work, and Marie Clay. These are some extracts, reprinted with permission, from the article, Saturday 19 February 1983, p. 7.*

Harvard professor of Education Courtney Cazden had been one of the keynote speakers at the International Reading Association's first South Pacific conference in Auckland [in January, and would be working alongside] Professor Clay ... at the Auckland University until May ... Professor Cazden, a language development specialist, is particularly keen to get to grips with Professor Clay's Reading Recovery programme. It identifies six-year-olds who are in difficulties with the printed word and, using individual instruction, leads them to sound reading skills.

Courtney Cazden has a hunch that the programme and how it is being applied in New Zealand schools with Department of Education backing may be the most important thing happening in the world of reading instruction.

'I want to learn more about the ideas of this woman who would, by anybody's standards, be one of the top people in reading and education in the English-speaking world.'

At Harvard in Cambridge, Massachusetts, the former primary teacher lectures students at the graduate school of education on teaching, curriculum and learning environments.

Here her lectures will deal with how children learn language — identifying the universals in language development and the cultural differences — and the implications for education.

Outside the university she wants to see how teachers work with diverse groups of children and children who have different cultural backgrounds from their own.

Courtney Cazden had previously been involved in studies in the United States concerning issues in multiculturalism and classroom education, and wished to see how these would be addressed in New Zealand.

Marie Clay's Career-long Work for Maori Children's Literacy

Courtney B. Cazden

Professor of Education Emerita, Harvard University

Some chronology

I came to New Zealand the first time with an invitation to speak at the First South Pacific Conference on Reading and a follow-up invitation from Marie Clay to stay on and teach a course at the University of Auckland. We had met earlier at a set of conferences on research on early reading at the University of Pittsburg in the late seventies, but the 1983 term afforded more extended personal and professional time together. The photo reprinted from the *New Zealand Herald* story on the 1983 conference shows us holding *Language Programmes for Maori Children* (Department of Education, 1972) — an appropriate illustration for this little article, and for Marie's career-long contributions to Maori children's literacy.

Maori educator Cath Rau, in her chapter in this volume, recounts how in recent years she and her Maori colleagues worked with Marie over several years on the 'reconstruction' of Marie's *An Observation Survey* in the Maori language (Rau, 1998). That may stand now as Marie's last contribution to Maori children's literacy development, this time towards literacy in the Maori language rather than English, but it is far from her first.

When Marie received a Lifetime Achievement Award from the National Reading Conference (in the United States), she gave an autobiographical talk with a sailing metaphor: 'Simply by sailing in a new direction you could enlarge the world', and spoke of her publishing life: 'I am fond of my first book, a peer-reviewed monograph for the Society for Research in Child Development [SRCD] in 1971' (Clay, 2004/2007). The monograph reports her study of the English language development of four language groups of children, including Maori children monolingual in English, using a sentence imitation test (commonly used in the then burgeoning field of language acquisition research).

Another of Marie's studies involving Maori children had a very different focus. It was on teacher-child classroom interaction rather than individual children's competencies. During my 1983 visit, while I was teaching a course on 'Classroom discourse', Marie told me about this observational research in new entrants' classrooms that she was then finishing. In her always meticulous way, she had written down and coded interactions between the teachers all 'European' (as she then referred to Pakeha) and their European, Maori and Pacific Island children. Marie found the most interesting results in the individualised teacher-child interactions, often as many as five or six for each child each morning. 'Teachers started as many contacts with Maori children as with European or Pacific Island children but they asked less often for verbal elaboration' (Clay, 1985, p. 3). This pattern of differential experience was the same across two terms, although the children she observed — always being the new entrants — were different.

Marie concluded that the cumulative impact of such differential school experience could have a significant impact on Maori children's language development. She ended by calling for further research that tries to identity classroom situations that maximise opportunities for more extended conversations between the teachers and their Maori children. So before the end of my teaching term in Auckland, we started planning how I could apply for a Fulbright fellowship to return to New Zealand for such follow-up research.

Due again entirely to Marie's support, I received that fellowship in 1987. When I arrived back in Auckland, Marie's research had then been published (Clay, 1985). And one of her students, Adrienne Kerin, a primary teacher herself Maori, was finishing a smaller replication for her Masters thesis with Maori as well as European teachers (Kerin, 1987). The important aspect of this set of studies is that the problem being diagnosed had much less to do with what Maori children did or did not know, and much more with the support their teachers did or did not provide.

In contrast to Marie's and Kerin's research — with their careful sampling of children and situations and careful recording of the sampled talk — my 1987 Fulbright classroom observations and those of my Maori associate, Marie-Anne Selkirk, were more informal. Through our observations, and informal interviews with the teachers, we simply tried to identify those situations and topics that seemed to make it easier or harder for teachers and Maori children to extend their talk together.

After my Fulbright ended and I returned to Harvard in September 1987 for our new academic year, I wrote up this work for New Zealand teachers (Cazden, 1988, as well as a more academic version, 1990). On subsequent trips to New Zealand for other reasons, I found no evidence that these ideas had been picked up by local teachers, Pakeha or Maori. After all, the original problem came not from them but from researchers. Moreover, although the majority of Maori children continue even now to be in mainstream classrooms, beginning in the early eighties the priority for Maori educators became the continuing effort to revitalise Te Reo, the Maori language, through Maori immersion schools. 'Sailing again in new directions' when a shift in prevailing winds required a change in tack towards the constant goal of Maori children's literacy development, Marie worked with Cath Rau on reconstructing her Reading Recovery *Observation Survey* for those Maori-medium programmes.

When last in New Zealand in July 2007, after Marie's death, while tracking down the now-35-year-old booklet in the *Herald* photo, I found Marie's classroom interaction research positively cited by Maori researcher Russell Bishop and his co-author Ted Glynn in their book, *Culture Counts: Changing Power Relations in Education* in their final chapter on 'Power-sharing relationships within classrooms'

(1999, p. 201). I can only wonder whether Marie herself was aware of this appreciative Maori reference to her work so many years later.

Some reflections

In our 30-year friendship, for me three special moments stand out. For the first two, I just happened to be in New Zealand at the time of two special and very different occasions. One was being able to join in celebrating the launching of the *Maori Reconstruction* in Hamilton, as Cath Rau mentions, where there was appropriate Maori protocol and a delicious dinner.

The second was in British style. Marie invited me to accompany her family to the Wellington ceremony at which she was knighted as a Dame Commander of the British Empire at the hand of the representative of the Crown, Governor General Sir Paul Reeves. Formerly Archbishop Reeves, this Governor General was the first non-British person to be so appointed and a Maori. Of course I was thrilled to meet him, but my most vivid memory is Marie's *deep* curtsy. My knees ached as I watch her kneel almost to the floor and then stand up with seeming ease and enormous grace.

The third moment was the one time Marie and I co-authored an article (Clay and Cazden, 1990/2007). I had been invited to contribute to an edited volume on Vygotsky and education. I knew I wanted to analyse Reading Recovery as an intervention that was developed independently but in theory and practice exemplified many Vygotskian ideas, and realised I could only do it well with Marie's collaboration. Marie agreed, and serendipity favoured us with a time to talk and write together. I happened to be in London for a conference while Marie had a sabbatical at Oxford, and she arranged a guest room for me in a nearby Oxford college for a few intense talking and writing days.

Since Marie's death, I have been reading and rereading Marie's writings, and thinking hard about what made her such a beloved colleague. I have already mentioned her meticulousness as a researcher, and as a writer too, as both Cath Rau and I have known first-hand. Two other qualities stand out. One quality is her insistence that research has to become what some now call 'usable knowledge':

> However impressed the educator in the 1970s may be with concepts of rule-guided behaviour, information-processing, linguistic competence, and dialect or second-language problems, his prime concern must be with the 'match between these new linguistic and psychological insights *and his actions as a teacher*' (Clay, 1971, p. 1, emphasis added).

The second quality, paradoxically, is that the most effective instructional support will come not from teaching techniques alone but from theoretical understanding of how and why they help. Like the first, this idea was already clear in Marie's mind in the seventies:

> If teachers are to generate individual programmes to meet particular needs, and if the matter of strategies for processing information is critical for some learners, then this must be written down in a way that enables teachers to

go easily from behavioural signals, *through theoretical constructs*, to programme. By offering teachers the means to sensitive observation of children's reading behaviour, I hope I have not merely opened a Pandora's box of creative teaching gimmicks, unchecked by reference to theory (Clay, 1979, p. 170, emphasis added).

Sitting with her daughter, Jenny, on the 'Dame Marie Clay' bench looking down on the space in the lovely glen where her ashes had been placed three months before, I wished I had found a time to thank Marie for giving me so much of herself and also for giving me, in a very real sense, the opportunities to begin to understand the valiant efforts of so many, Pakeha as well as Maori, towards Aotearoa/New Zealand as a bicultural nation. In a public talk at the University of Auckland at the end of that first visit in May 1983, I explained why this meant so much to me:

When I came four months ago, I was … not aware of how much I would come to identify with Pakeha New Zealanders, as we try — in your country and mine — not only to change our schools but to change ourselves. After all, I have come to realise, I'm just a descendant of an earlier tide of British colonialism on another shore (Cazden, unpublished ms, 1983).

For all that and so much more, to Marie with love.

References

Bishop, R. and Glynn, T. 1999. *Culture Counts: Changing Power Relations in Education*. Palmerston North: Dunsmore.

Cazden, C.B. 1983. Meanings of Multicultural Education in the United States and New Zealand. Invited talk during the centennial celebration of the University of Auckland, 7 May.

———. 1988. Interactions between Maori Children and Pakeha Teachers: Observations of an American Visitor. Auckland: Auckland Reading Association.

———. 1990. Differential Treatment in New Zealand: Reflections on Research in Minority Education. *Teaching and Teacher Education*, 6 (4): 291–303.

Clay, M.M. 1971. Sentence Repetitions: Elicited Imitation of a Controlled Set of Syntactic Structures by Four Language Groups. *Monographs of the Society of Research in Child Development*, 36 (3, Serial No. 143).

———. 1979. Theoretical Research and Instructional Change: A Case Study. In L. Resnick and P. Weaver, Eds, *Theory and Practice of Early Reading* Vol 2: 149–71. Hillsdale, NJ: Erlbaum.

———. 1985. Engaging with the School System: A Study of Interactions in New Entrant classrooms. *New Zealand Journal of Educational Studies*, 20 (1): 20–38.

———. 2004/2007. Simply by Sailing in a New Direction You Could Enlarge the World. *The Journal of Reading Recovery*, 7 (1): 7–12.

Clay, M.M. and Cazden, C.B. 1990/2007. A Vygotskian Interpretation of Reading Recovery. In L.C. Moll, ed., *Vygotsky and Education: Instructional Implications and Applications of Sociohistorical Psychology*. New York: Cambridge University Press. Reprinted in *The Journal of Reading Recovery*, 7 (1): 40–50.

Department of Education. 1972. Language Programmes for Maori Children. Wellington.

Kerin, A. 1987. One-to-one Interactions in Junior Classes. Unpublished Masters thesis, University of Auckland.

Rau, Cath. 1998. *The Maori Reconstruction of An Observation Survey of Early Literacy Achievement*. Ngaruawahia: Kia Ata Mai Educational Trust, PO Box 166.

'THERE IS NOTHING LIKE A DAME'

When Professor Marie Clay was listed in the New Zealand Queen's Honours awards, she could not be found by the media as she had gone on a short holiday with her friend Eleanor England. They were staying at a motel at an unknown location. Her son, Alan, who was living next door to her home at the time, was unable to assist the print and television journalists who phoned him wanting a comment from the new 'Dame'. Was her absence a coincidence? Hardly! She did appreciate though the letters and cards that flowed in during the early part of 1987.

Eleanor England and Marie.

Graham Nuthall, Professor of Education at the University of Canterbury, wrote that her having been 'made a Dame Commander of the OBE ... is a tremendous honour and very thoroughly deserved. Over the years you have done so much for educational research. I remember in the early years when it was hard to get the cooperation you needed ... It is such a delight to know that you are the person to receive the first significant honour for educational research in this country.' He hoped 'the award not only feels like a reward for work well done — but that it may be of some use to you in the future — in getting the things you want to achieve accomplished.' Marie also hoped for this, that the honour would advance research and education.

Arthur Fieldhouse, a Professor of Education at the University of Victoria, wrote that he was pleased 'to learn of your inclusion in the New Year Honours list — and at such an exalted rank! It is a fitting recognition of your contribution in your professional field. Also, I regard it as an achievement on behalf of the standing and significance of Education as a university discipline.' Tony Taylor, also of Victoria, congratulated her as the 'first titled ... psychologist in New Zealand'.

The chairperson of the New Zealand Council for Educational Research, Jean Herbison, said: 'We were all very gratified to see such high recognition given to the very distinctive and enduring contribution you have given to educational research and more particularly to the better learning processes for young children. We know this work is recognised internationally and we are delighted that "the public" of our own country is now conferring this very appropriate honour. As a research institution we reflect in this honour and trust you will continue with your highly valued work in the future.'

Letters were exchanged between Clarence E. Beeby and Marie at this time. He had been the first director of the New Zealand Council for Educational Research, and the Director-General of Education in New Zealand from the 1940s until 1960. He became an ambassador to France and a delegate to UNESCO, he worked at Harvard and London Universities, and was an educational consultant in many countries. He was also Director Emeritus at NZCER.

Beeby wrote to Marie that 'it was gratifying that educational research should appear at the top of the Honours list after never having made it before even at the humblest level'. He emphasised 'whatever assistance you have had from colleagues, at the heart of your success lies your own originality, courage and tireless belief in your cause'.

In a draft of her reply, Marie said: 'My deepest appreciation for your letter, the thoughts it expressed are insightful as ever. It is a long way back for me to the time in Wellington when I worked for Jim Caughley [as a psychological assistant in 1950] and shared an office with Moira Gallagher. On some momentous occasion (the exact moment escapes me now) I was invited to Head Office to a social occasion when the Director-General (of Education) Dr Beeby was in attendance. Very impressive for a young educator.

'I will be particularly pleased if this award is seen as a tribute to educational research (and Graham Nuthall, like yourself, saw it that way), for recognition of good work carried out here in New Zealand is rewarded all too rarely. I hope that I can claim just a few of the personal attributes you suggest.

'Who better than you would know the resistance of institutions and tradition to original ideas. I once asked if it was possible to heave the elephant over, and get the programme going in the education system … We must have done it. I am greatly honoured by your tribute.' She also congratulated Clarence Beeby on receiving the Order of New Zealand in the same year, 1987. He was one of five foundation members.

In his reply Beeby admitted it was an exclusive award, but added, 'There's nothing like a Dame' (the title of a song in the musical *South Pacific*). He said he hoped to see Marie in Wellington that year. 'The only travel I have in view is a possible job in Dar-es-Salaam in July, as a consultant to the Aga Khan Foundation. Their invitation is firm, but the idea of an 85-year-old consultant seems a touch ridiculous …' Marie had mentioned two overseas professors would be visiting, and Beeby said he would be 'happy to meet your two visiting professors when they come to Wellington. Courtney Cazden I have met once already and shall be delighted to renew the acquaintance. They will be more likely to get in touch with me at home than at the NZCER, where I go less frequently now that I have a happy *maison a trois*, with my word processor and my Siamese cat, and no longer need secretarial help.'

At the memorial service at the Maidment Theatre of the University of Auckland for Marie in April 2007, Raewyn Dalziel led the welcome as the Deputy Vice-Chancellor (Academic). She had met Marie at Fulbright and University Alumni occasions. In 2004 Marie had been given a Distinguished Alumni Award by the University of Auckland. Back in 1987 Raewyn Dalziel had said, 'It is great to see such different and significant work being recognised.'

Ross Howie of the Department of Paediatrics, National Women's Hospital, was also delighted to see Marie's name so high on the list because 'it is so rare for education to feature in these awards. Is it possible that our national priorities may be changing?' His reservation that 'commonly such honours signal retirement', which he hoped wasn't true, was certainly not borne out by Marie Clay, who continued to work for the next 20 years.

The Institute of Education, University of London

Professor Dame Marie Clay

Barbara MacGilchrist

Deputy Director (until 2006)
Institute of Education, University of London

Learning to read is critically important. It opens the gateway to further learning, particularly in the context of the school curriculum. It enables young people to develop as independent thinkers. It provides a much better level playing field for young people to make the most of their schooling through the ability to access with confidence new knowledge in its many forms, be it from first-hand experience or vicariously.

Underachievement in reading is critically important. It is an issue that continues to be a systemic challenge in the English education system. The relationship between socio-economic disadvantage and achievement and, in particular, the relationship between disadvantage and underachievement in reading, has been the subject of substantial research evidence over many years. The relationship between effective schooling and pupils' progress and achievement and, in particular, the impact effective schooling can have on the reading progress of children from disadvantaged backgrounds in the primary years of schooling, has also been well documented in a number of longitudinal studies.

Programmes designed to combat the underachievement of disadvantaged children emanated from the United States from the mid-1960s beginning with the Headstart initiative and were followed by programmes targeted at disadvantaged children in the early years of schooling with the aim of providing teaching programmes specifically designed to combat underachievement in reading. However, it was Marie Clay's Reading Recovery intervention that particularly caught my attention, not least because of my personal experiences as a teacher and school inspector in London.

I trained as a primary school teacher back in the sixties, and spent most of my time as a teacher and primary head-teacher in a school serving a mainly disadvantaged community in the inner city area of Hackney in London. This experience brought home the realities of the research referred to earlier that was beginning to emerge. It became clear to me that through good teaching it was possible to break the relationship between disadvantage and underachievement. However, it also became clear to me that by the age of seven, despite good general class teaching, too many of the children in our care were still falling behind in their reading progress, and that this was having a serious impact on their confidence, self-esteem and their ability to make the most of the experiences we were trying to offer them. I knew then that for those children, the only answer was some form of early intervention in their literacy development that would require specialist teaching skills.

I subsequently became a primary inspector and then chief inspector in the Inner London Education Authority (ILEA), and the inherent challenge of combating underachievement in reading became even clearer to me. I gathered data on the relationship between the reading standards of all the children moving to secondary school across the inner London area every year and the catchment area of each of the primary schools. The relationship between children from disadvantaged communities and low standards in reading was self-evident. Having said that there were definite exceptions to the rule, the findings of the ILEA Junior School Study at that time led by Peter Mortimore were providing evidence that effective practice in schools can and does make a difference. The findings of the study by Peter Mortimore and colleagues coupled with my own experience told me, however, that general characteristics of effectiveness in a school needed to be combined with a specific early intervention teaching strategy to support those children who were falling behind their peers in learning to read. I also knew that this is much easier said than done, not least because of the ongoing debate in England about the teaching of reading.

How to teach children to read is probably the most controversial issue in English education. Debates have raged over the years with opposing positions often being taken exemplified by the 'look and say' versus 'phonics' devotees and the recent government-sponsored 'synthethic phonics' approach to teaching reading. Government concern with the need to address underachievement in literacy, in particular reading standards, gathered momentum in the late 1980s to early 1990s with reports by the national inspectorate being commissioned, such as the one into reading standards in 45 inner London primary schools in three local education authorities including Hackney. Unfortunately this and other earlier reports that were looking at primary practice led to a blame culture that implied that poor teachers needed to be rooted out and that there was a need to return to the 'basics' if standards were to improve. The National Literacy Strategy was born in the late 1990s and the testing regime was strengthened and coupled with national targets to be achieved in reading levels by all schools.

In 1990 I moved to the Institute of Education, University of London, and my first job there was to develop in-service training programmes for teachers in collaboration with local education authorities. Fuelled by my interest in early intervention in the teaching of reading, I became increasingly impressed with the work of Marie Clay. The starting point for the development of her Reading Recovery intervention in her home country of New Zealand was the observation over a long period of time of how teachers taught young children to read and what it was that proved to be successful practice.

Marie was very concerned about underachievement in reading and recognised that catching children early was essential. She knew from her observations that there will always be children, from both advantaged and disadvantaged backgrounds who, despite good classroom practice, will find learning to read difficult for various reasons. She knew too that these children are likely to be the hardest children to teach. She worked with practising teachers to draw out the key elements of learning to read that needed to be combined together to form a one-to-one personalised programme to give children experiencing the most difficulty in learning to read a second chance. Her vision was of a programme that enabled young children to catch up with their peers and so be able to access the general classroom setting in such a way that their progress would be sustained over time. Through her passion, commitment and sheer determination, she and other researchers were able to demonstrate the efficacy of the programme she developed with her team, integral to which is an intensive training and support programme at a local and national level. The outcome in New Zealand was the systemic adoption of Reading Recovery that incorporated all the key elements of the programme.

Convinced by the findings of her work, I decided to see if I could persuade Marie to come and work at the Institute to develop her training programme here in the UK. Much to my delight, she expressed an interest in working with us. In collaboration with Surrey LEA and with the full support of the then Director of the IOE, Sir Peter Newsam, I approached the Paul Hamlyn Foundation for the necessary funding, which they willingly provided. The rest is in part history and will be described in detail by others contributing to this book. For my part I want to express a sincere thank you to Marie and to her colleagues who came over from New Zealand, along with colleagues at the IOE and our partners in the schools and local authorities with whom we worked, for enabling us to get the programme under way, initially in the London area and then spreading to all corners of the UK.

It was a privilege to meet and work with Marie Clay. She was in the room next to me and I have fond memories of the many conversations we had about the programme itself and about the best ways of trying to get it integrated and embedded in, to begin with, the English education system. Marie was a very wise, astute academic with her feet firmly on the ground. She appreciated the political challenges of introducing her programme over here and I was full of admiration for her tenacity and ability to liaise with our politicians and the media in such a way as to get them on board as far as was possible. It is fair to say that the journey of trying to embed Reading Recovery in England by securing a long-term funding commitment from successive governments has been, as others will describe, a rollercoaster ride of uncertainty and still is. Like Marie, however, I am forever the optimist and know that there is compelling evidence developing year on year that Reading Recovery is making a difference for an increasing number of young children in this country and I remain hopeful that the long-term success for these children will, in the end, determine the need to embed the programme through appropriate funding into our education system. It is a credit to all those involved that the programme is still alive and symptomatic of the deep commitment to Reading Recovery inspired by the pioneering work of Marie Clay. Marie was genuinely inspirational. She is an example of someone not just expressing an interest in improving the life chances of individual children and their families but doing something about it.

Reading Recovery Comes to London

Peter Mortimore

Former Director of the Institute of Education, University of London

Marie came to London in the early 1990s at the invitation of Barbara MacGilchrist (then the Institute of Education's Head of In-service Training and, in later years, its Deputy Director). Colleagues at the Institute of Education welcomed her arrival as part of the continuation of the tradition of strong women like Susan Isaacs, Dorothy Gardner and Barbara Tizard, all of whom had helped shape the Institute's work with young children. She came with Barbara Watson and Susan Duncan, supported by a grant from the Paul Hamlyn Foundation, to launch Reading Recovery in the UK. The country which produced Chaucer, Shakespeare and Dickens was also generating more than its fair share of poor readers and needed some extra help. Surveys such as that undertaken for the (subsequent) 1999 Moser report (Department for Education and Skills, 1999) showed that even then 20 per cent of the adult population had less than functional literacy. Marie came to launch a rescue service.

With her unshakeable belief that many more young children could master literacy if they were helped by highly skilled — and appropriately trained — teachers, Marie threw herself into establishing Reading Recovery at the Institute. By 1993, supported by a three-year grant from the government, 32 Tutors had been prepared and were working with 26 local authorities, training 350 teachers and reaching about 2000 pupils.

By 2007, almost 4000 teachers have been trained and over 60,000 pupils have completed the Reading Recovery programme. Research shows that success rates are high with 85 per cent overcoming their literacy difficulties and gaining access to the mainstream curriculum alongside their classmates. What is more, Reading Recovery is still growing in the UK, with eight new centres opened in September 2008 to train a further 760 teachers as part of a government programme entitled Every Child a Reader.

For me, one of the most remarkable features about the establishment of Reading Recovery at the Institute was the reaction of the teachers. Those recruited to the Reading Recovery Course tended to be experienced, very competent practitioners, greatly valued by their local authorities. Yet when I met them after the course, they bubbled with enthusiasm for their new knowledge. Many claimed that they had really grasped how to listen to a child accurately for the first time in their lives. What Marie had taught them was how to observe the way a child approached the reading task, taking advantage of every possible cue, and how to interpret these actions so as to be able to understand the child's mistaken strategy and see how best to correct it.

Such highly sophisticated practical skill was built on sound theory. Marie had been developing this since publishing, in 1966, her first painstaking clinical exploration of children's weekly reading progress. Unlike so many who work in the social sciences, she was able, easily, to integrate theory and practice so that each was able to inform the other. She was an academic and she used academic tools but her purpose was always practical — helping children to read and thereby to learn.

As with the best teachers of young children, Marie could tell a good story. Her accounts of her travels could be hilarious as when she confessed that, despite her long experience of flying and her extensive knowledge of airport scams, she had became so absorbed by what she thought was a spontaneous fight in the departure hall that she failed to notice her baggage disappear. An infectious laughter about strange events, or at her own predicament, was a constant part of her teaching repertoire.

Marie's work has received national and international recognition. In 1975 she was the first woman to be appointed a professor at the University of Auckland. Among other honours, she was elected to the New Zealand Educational Institute, its Psychological Society and its Royal Society. She has been awarded the Mackie Medal by the Australian and New Zealand Association for the Advancement of Science and inducted into the international Reading Hall of Fame. In 1987, she was made a Dame of the British Empire. But pleasing though it is to be honoured, her true satisfaction stemmed from the knowledge that she had provided practical help to vulnerable children. As Paulo Freire — another distinguished visitor to the Institute of Education — has so passionately argued, without literacy there is oppression. Reading Recovery enables learning to occur and learning leads to emancipation.

In pioneering a way to teach reading to children who otherwise found it impossibly difficult, Marie has changed the course of the lives of countless children. The Institute of Education is proud that Reading Recovery found a home within its portals. In 2002, as part of the celebrations of its centenary, it awarded an honorary doctorate to its creator — Dame Marie Clay.

Listening to Marie

Angela Hobsbaum
Institute of Education, University of London

The first day of term

It is Monday, 7 September 1992, the first day of term of the new academic year at the Institute of Education in London. It is a warm day and the seminar room's south-facing windows let in all the late-summer sunshine. In the room is a group of teachers, 12 women and one man, who are beginning their course to train as Tutors in Reading Recovery. Although they are all experienced teachers, confident in their own professional roles, they are feeling slightly apprehensive.

Over the shuffles and rustles of papers, one woman's voice is heard. Marie Clay is introducing the course to them, adding details to the outline they have received in the course handbook. She is describing the course components, ensuring that they understand what lies ahead. Even if, this morning, they think they understand it, in a few weeks they will discover that this course is like no other professional development opportunity they have ever experienced. Today, her aim is to give them a flavour of how the elements of the course interconnect and what will be expected of them. She explains how each element will be examined, for this group of mature learners is, like any other group of students at the very start of their course, anxious about the assessment process.

Carefully, thoughtfully, and with never a hint that she might have done these explanations many times before, she describes the structure of the course. Her voice is lively and she isn't afraid to pause to give time for her listeners to contribute. She explains to them that, as well as working with children, they will have some challenging academic learning ahead of them; they will have to learn how to critique research papers, a task they have probably not undertaken before. But she reassures them that, through the supportive and helpful feedback they will receive, she is confident they will become proficient at this. She makes jokes, releasing the tension, and replies to their questions introducing some concepts, such as cumulative change, that will soon become familiar to them. 'Do you feel comfortable with that?' she asks, explaining how their work will be graded, and they laugh their assent nervously.

I am in the room too. I suppose I am making the tape-recording on which I have based that account. I am the course leader, and this is the first time that I've seen Marie Clay in this role, with a group of students. I'm also there to meet the group, to introduce them to the Institute of Education, and to make sure that all the administrative tasks of inducting the new cohort go smoothly. Although this is Marie's second year in London, I was almost unaware of the presence of the New Zealand team for most of the first year. They had been allocated rooms in the INSET department and they must have been so busy as they bustled in and out that they had not really registered on my radar. In her first year in London, Marie, together with Barbara Watson, Sue Duncan and Christine Boocock, had trained the first English group of Reading Recovery Tutors, a small group of seven, drawn mainly from London education authorities, together with a group of 42 teachers who were trained in Reading Recovery by the New Zealanders. My involvement with the first group of Tutor-trainees came late in their course, setting and marking their examination papers. I remember vividly their final end-of-term celebrations, when they fêted Marie with a musical offering, punning all the new terminology they had mastered, with the hilarity verging on hysteria that bonds those who have survived a baptism of fire. I realised then that this course was going to be unusual.

Preparing the ground

During that year, 1991–92, Reading Recovery had come under the media spotlight, and the fact that Professor Marie Clay herself was in England, training Reading Recovery personnel, attracted attention. Thus it was that, after some persuasive negotiations with the government on the part of the Institute of Education, the Department of Education earmarked a three-year grant to run from 1992 to 1995, to fund Reading Recovery Tutor and teacher training courses around the country. So, in September 1992, applicants from 25 local education authorities were accepted to train as Reading Recovery Tutors, 13 in London and 12 in Sheffield, and courses were set up to train teachers in London, Birmingham and Sheffield. Reading Recovery was expanding nationwide!

I was introduced to Marie early in 1992, when it became clear that, backed by the three-year government funds, Reading Recovery's future in England was secured for the next few years. With characteristic foresight, Marie set out to ensure that there were trained personnel in place to run the enterprise — not just to train teachers and Tutors, but to coordinate the implementation with the participating local education authorities. Because I worked at the Institute of Education, I had been identified as the new course leader and would eventually become one of the national coordinators. Like those students I met in September 1992, I too was ignorant of what lay ahead.

Lessons from the first year in London

Marie had done a lot of preparation already. At the end of the first year's training course, she had collated the experiences of the New Zealand team concerning conditions in England which could hinder a successful implementation of Reading Recovery. Some of the obstacles were part of our educational culture, like our tendency to allow children ample time to respond to school, which meant that we failed to identify struggling readers early enough and tended to be overly protective, 'cocooning the child in a bubble bath', as one New Zealander noted, rather than expecting them to be able to work independently. Other barriers were due to emphases in the current equal opportunities policy, such as a disapproval of any form of withdrawal from the classroom, which meant that the half-hour

Reading Recovery lesson was viewed as a form of negative discrimination rather than as a short-term measure to improve access to the curriculum.

Schools were not used to releasing teachers consistently to give their daily Reading Recovery lessons; Marie reports that 'Teacher absence was higher than we have worked with before.' Her non-judgemental tone belies the fact that, given her extensive international experience, this comparison is very unflattering. The first year's programmes were seriously undermined by 'lost lessons', when teachers in training had to cover for absent colleagues, or go on trips, or deal with the many unexpected events which crop up daily in busy primary schools. She concluded: 'Added together, teacher absence was a problem in achieving accelerative progress with children. The unfortunate effects of these absences on child outcomes must be discussed clearly in the first meeting with teachers.'

The other problems that the New Zealand team encountered, which Marie noted stoically under the heading of Troublesome Times, were the transition to local management of schools, the delegation of funding to schools, and the hiccups of a funding year which finished in April rather than at the end of the school year in August. Some schools found that the funding for their teachers ran out partway through the training course, leaving them with a half-trained teacher and children who had not gained full benefit from the programme. Marie's experience in many education systems in Australia and the USA enabled her to focus on what needed to be done to ensure that the programme was understood by administrators at national and local levels; and she was willing to explain it to them carefully and patiently to ensure that their commitment was backed by necessary support.

What strikes me now, as I look back, is her insight into how our overprotective culture (we called it child-centred) had led us to underestimate children and denied them opportunities to learn. To Marie this was obvious, because high expectations are set for every child in Reading Recovery, and their goals are continually reviewed. Today we have many governmental exhortations to aim high; 'high expectations, which are made explicit' have been shown to be an essential ingredient of effective teaching, and now every initiative has its targets and objectives.

Reporting the first year's encounter with English pupils in Reading Recovery, Marie and her team were shocked by the very low literacy skills of the children who came into Reading Recovery in London. As someone with considerable experience of working with the lowest-attaining cohort, she ponders whether their 'flat profiles, showing little literacy achievement in seven aspects of literacy-related performance' are the result of low expectations, the lack of any other intervention programme, or the lack of good first teaching since they came to school. Six years later, the introduction of the National Literacy Strategy in 1998 had as its goal to ensure good first teaching and, were she to return today, Marie would see some changes in the profiles of children entering Reading Recovery; no longer such flat profiles, but with some evidence of letter and sound knowledge, albeit still with significant difficulties in reading and writing text.

Embedding Reading Recovery

What was impressive, I see now in retrospect, though I wasn't aware of it at the time, was Marie's ability to combine two aims which might otherwise have been in conflict. She stressed those elements of Reading Recovery which could not be compromised, and which needed to be adhered to in every implementation. This was not blind faith, but an explicit recognition of the importance of researching and evaluating the programme; 'if the programme is varied in the training, or the teaching, or the implementation,' she wrote, 'then the research which supports this programme [that is, Reading Recovery] cannot be used to support the non-standard variant. New research would be required to see whether the effectiveness can be claimed under the variant treatment conditions.' She helped us to understand the importance of fidelity to the programme and the need to prevent 'drift'. But at the same time, she encouraged us to include in the training course materials drawn from the UK which fitted into our educational climate. Gradually we incorporated more English, rather than American, articles on our reading lists, and developed our courses to make them feel home-grown.

She was older then than I am now, and yet her stamina was amazing. She frequently caught the late train to Sheffield to teach the Tutor-trainees there, having taught the group in London in the morning, and would then pop off to speak at a conference, fly to America for an IRA or NRC committee, and fit in a meeting with some important government officials. It was a tough schedule, yet she made time to research her family tree, burrowing into the archives. She was the first person I met who pronounced the words *own* and *known* as two-syllable words, referring to the first sessions in a Reading Recovery programme as *roaming around the 'knowen'*. Not that it mattered; we soon got used to much stranger ideas which stretched our understanding still more.

A celebratory lunch on the terrace at the Institute of Education: Richard Boxall holds forth while Clifford Johnson listens.

After almost two years in England, she left behind 32 trained Tutors and two Trainers; over 160 teachers had learnt to become Reading Recovery teachers and 900 children had tasted the programme. She had planned the infrastructure for a national coordination network, written the job descriptions for coordinators, and prepared three of us for the tasks ahead. Sixteen years later, the legacy of her stay remains with us; Reading Recovery has survived some inclement conditions and is now acknowledged here as an effective early literacy intervention. Over 60,000 children in the UK have benefited from Reading Recovery. Clay's ideas have had an impact on our expectations of children's entitlement and our provision for the lowest achieving. The challenge of the hardest-to-teach children remains, but thanks to Marie's teaching, we are now better-equipped to meet it.

The Return of the Pioneer: Marie Clay in UK and Ireland

Julia Douëtil

Institute of Education, University of London; Trainer and National Coordinator, European Centre for Reading Recovery

Personal diary entry for 2007

Friday 13th April

It is 1.38 a.m. I was woken just after midnight by a phone call from Mary Anne Doyle. At eight this morning in New Zealand Marie Clay died.

After Philip and my parents, she was probably the person who had the biggest impact on my adult life. Since I heard the news, my mind has been racing with images of her, almost all a gentle, unassuming, almost grandmotherly figure. But with a perceptiveness and an intellect that was terrifying, challenging and awe inspiring. In all the obits and reminiscences in the next few weeks, that word 'inspiring' will dominate. That's what she did at every level, and through her inspiration millions of lives were changed for the better.

I remember my first sight of her, in September 1992, I assumed she was the course secretary, bustling through with a sheaf of papers. I thought 'she looks friendly, I'll try to get to know her, you can never underestimate the value of having the admin person on your side.' I had stumbled into the Reading Recovery course as a way of spending a year closer to home in Sussex, whilst being employed 200 miles away in Lincoln. If I had had any inkling of what that first year would involve, I would have been out of the room like a shot. If I had any notion of where it would lead me, I would not have believed it. Would I have stayed in the room, I wonder, if I had known?

So, we are in the Post Marie Era. Oddly, the thought that has been going through my sleepless mind is, the fact that Mary Anne knew who to ring, and I know who to ring, is one of Marie's last and most brilliant creations. She spent the past few years working for this moment, ensuring that there were systems in place that would bind Reading Recovery together across the world, and ensure we continued to function without her.

Within 24 hours of Marie's death, almost everyone in the UK, Ireland and Denmark who knew her, or had a close connection with Reading Recovery, had received the sad news through a personal call. The speed of that dissemination, and sense that this was news one should hear from a friend, not stumble across in the media, is

114

testament to the infrastructure she had created and to the regard in which she was held, not just as an inspirational leader and constant supporter through the highs and lows of Reading Recovery in the UK and Ireland, but as a person.

What made Marie so extraordinary was that she was, in so many ways, so very ordinary, so human. She was a towering figure in the academic world, a giant among her peers, yet when she visited she was one of the family. When called upon to introduce her formally we always found ourselves tripping over her many titles because, to us, she was simply 'Marie'.

She wrote and spoke with such depth and complexity that your head would spin, trying to take in a fraction of what she had to say; but she could demolish an argument in seven words. In 1991 Marie spoke at a conference at the Institute of Education, University of London, to present Reading Recovery to an unsuspecting nation. One school head teacher in the audience could barely contain her anger and rounded on Marie, accusing her of cruel and unreasonable expectations of children whose lives were already severely stressed. She described a child in her school, mistreated, malnourished, uncared for, unloved, and she challenged Marie to justify why this poor child should be expected to work so hard and so intensively every day. Marie listened quietly to the tirade and then asked, 'And you think being illiterate will help?'

Reading Recovery in the UK and Ireland

In 1987 Marie had been invited to visit Cambridge University. During her stay she spoke of the developing Reading Recovery intervention in New Zealand and, as a result, an experienced educator went to Auckland to train as the UK's first Reading Recovery Tutor. Britain's first Reading Recovery teachers were trained in Surrey in 1990, and in September 1991 the University of London Institute of Education invited Marie to return to the UK with a small group of New Zealand colleagues to set up a Tutor training course.

Meanwhile a controversial report, claiming that standards of literacy in England were in a dangerous decline, propelled debate about the teaching of reading out of schools and onto the front pages of the nation's most combative newspapers. Promising results emerging from the project at the Institute of Education were too good a lifeline for a beleaguered Education minister to ignore, and in 1992 a three-year, government-funded Reading Recovery project was launched. Once again Marie brought a team from New Zealand to England, this time to set up two parallel Tutor training courses, one based at the Institute of Education and a second in the Yorkshire city of Sheffield. New Zealand Trainer and Tutor teams were established in London and Sheffield, while Marie travelled weekly between them. Several years later a young and fit London-based Trainer team tried running a course in the north of England, and found it exhausting. Marie, already well over pensionable age, had not only nipped up and down the country every few days, but also regularly declared that she would 'just pop over to Ohio', or 'just drop into Texas', taking the gruelling transatlantic flights in her stride.

Educators in Northern Ireland recognised the potential in Reading Recovery to change the life chances of vulnerable children. The province was still, at that time, a community divided by civil strife, fuelled by poverty and low educational attainment. Many teachers had their first experience of coming to know, collaborate with and trust individuals from across the religious and social divide in Reading Recovery training groups. At that time London was on constant alert to the threat of attack by Irish nationalist groups, and bomb scares were frequent. Travelling with Marie on the London underground one day, we registered the alarmed faces of fellow travellers, and watched the carriage gradually empty as Marie talked animatedly about her recent meetings, until we gently asked her to stop referring to the International Reading Association as the IRA.

The implementation in Northern Ireland proved highly effective and impacted far beyond the children for whom it was designed. The expectation in Reading Recovery that children would independently compose and write their own stories was at odds with an assumption in Ireland that children were not capable of independent writing until the age of seven. When challenged about Reading Recovery's 'unrealistic' demands upon children 'who could not have developed sufficient manual dexterity for writing', Marie produced a drawing by a six-year-old girl, of a princess wearing an elaborately decorated gown. Teachers agreed that the frills and bows, the curly hair, the dainty shoes were typical of the fanciful fashion plates little girls love to draw. Marie responded with another of her famous argument-demolishing one-liners 'And you are telling me a child who could draw those frills could not form letter shapes?'

New challenges
By the mid-1990s Reading Recovery was available in schools in Jersey, Scotland and Wales and finally crept over the border into the Republic of Ireland. This brought new challenges, and Marie, who always took a great interest in the personal experience of those in Reading Recovery, was greatly amused by a Tutor's description of working between the north and south of Ireland, carrying two currencies, two mobile phones and an international driving licence.

As Reading Recovery began to take hold in the UK and Ireland, Marie challenged us to rethink our assumptions about children learning literacy. She taught us that the learner does not act in a vacuum — however puzzling and inaccurate a child's responses may be, he or she is guided by some internal logic. That logic may be shaped by confusion, misunderstanding or partial knowledge, but if the teacher could try to understand why this child should think as he or she did, and if the teaching could start from the child's view of the task, then it would be possible to help the child find more effective ways of thinking about reading and writing.

In 2002 the Institute of Education marked its centenary and chose, in that most prestigious of years, to honour Marie, as one of its most prestigious associates. She was presented with an Honorary Doctorate in Literature by Her Royal Highness, the Princess Royal, Princess Anne, for once someone with even more titles than Marie. We all felt for Marie at that ceremony, drowning in hot and heavy robes, dripping with gold braid, her feet dangling from the huge chair as her life story was orated in front of her. We knew that those events were torment for her, and she did not need the honour, but she submitted to it with grace because she knew how much it would mean to her colleagues and to the hundreds of Reading Recovery teachers across the UK and Ireland, as a way of recognising their efforts.

Her respect for and belief in ordinary teachers was yet one more example of Marie's willingness to challenge current orthodoxies. At a time when the political trend in England was towards 'teacher proofing' the literacy curriculum through a highly prescriptive national literacy strategy, Marie argued that the person best placed to make decisions about a child's learning needs was the teacher sitting next to that child. Her trust in the ability of ordinary teachers to achieve extraordinary things enabled them to change the life chances of the most vulnerable children. While the government provided teachers with manuals and scripts, Marie bade us focus on their professional learning. She was frustrated when writers 'wrote down' to teachers, and annoyed when administrators treated them as education machines, programmed to turn out lessons according to a generalised notion of what worked for most children.

As she prepared both Tutors and Trainers to work with teachers, she urged us constantly to refine our thinking and our language until the message was clear. As Trainers in training, our task had been an essay on the theorist Frank Smith. She passed the essays, but asked us to rethink *how* we had written them and be more succinct. We resubmitted, but she was still not satisfied. 'I want Frank Smith in a nutshell!' she declared. It happened to be the season for fresh walnuts. Carefully opening a nut and cleaning out the insides, we wrote a message in the tiniest of letters, on a narrow strip of paper: 'What the brain brings to the eye is as important as what the eye brings to the brain.' The message was scrolled into the nutshell which we tied with a pink ribbon. The next morning, we trooped into her study to deliver our latest version of the 'essay'. We presented the walnut. Marie looked puzzled. She untied the ribbon, opened the shell and unrolled the strip of paper. We waited: had we overstepped the mark? Do professors accept 18-word essays? Marie's delighted laugh relieved us all. 'Perfect,' she said. 'Now you know how to talk to teachers.'

In her many visits to the UK, and to Ireland, Marie always found time for teachers and Teacher Leaders (as our Tutors became known). Returning to support our national conference one year, she slipped while out walking in the Surrey Hills, and broke a wrist. At the conference the following weekend, she still had a generous smile for every teacher who, not noticing or choosing to overlook the plaster on Marie's arm, asked her to sign their copy of the *Guidebook*, and she did.

Marie was due to return to Europe in March 2007, to join our professional development meeting in Limerick, in the Republic of Ireland. We knew when she had to cancel that trip that all was not well, for she had always been such a stalwart supporter, and had been especially looking forward to returning to Ireland, where she felt a special bond. She had traced her family history to Ballygawley, a small village in Northern Ireland, and discovered links with Ireland's famous linen weavers. Another branch of her family in London may have been Huguenot silk weavers. Marie's fascination with her ancestors, and what led them to uproot their lives in Ireland and London to establish themselves in a new country on the other side of the world, reflected her own pioneering spirit. A keen collector of miniature books, she once explained the intrigue of these tiny gems of literature for her. The early pioneers had to carry everything they possessed; they could not afford to take anything that was not essential to survival. Yet even in the harshest of conditions, life without books was unthinkable. So books were miniaturised, to ensure that even the most remote of settlements could have their 'stores of civilisation'. At her home in Auckland, Marie showed me her collection, beautifully arranged with her artistic eye. And there among them was a walnut shell, tied with pink ribbon.

International Reading Association

Marie M. Clay: Educator and Friend, Fondly Remembered

Carl Braun

Professor Emeritus, Applied Psychology, University of Calgary

I begin with an intriguing image, metaphor if you wish, credit to Lorri Neilsen, Poet Laureate of Halifax, Nova Scotia. In a recent article she muses over the many writers, both met and unmet, who will for ever share the dinner parties of her imagination. It is with awe and the deepest respect that I acknowledge a guest who shall always occupy the chair of honour at my dinner party, the late Dame Marie Clay.

Early encounters of the IRA board type

Marie and I first met as members of the International Reading Association board of directors in 1984. Although she and I reserved a comfortable 'just met' distance for a short while, I was soon drawn by the passion in her voice whenever discussion got close to the hearts of children and teachers. Her contributions on the board were nothing short of stellar. First and foremost, she was a woman with a vision. It was clear from the start that the lens through which she viewed literacy issues transcended conventional ways of doing business in the 'how to teach reading' arena. Her insights derived from extensive language study, developmental psychology and decades of child observation, a multi-textured context that served her in depth examination of issues. In spite of her scholarly prowess and her vast knowledge of literacy and language, she never felt the need to flaunt her expertise. On the contrary, she approached debate with a sense of humility and always with a view to learning from discussion rather than to educate the 'unwashed'. Debates had a purpose — to clarify, to bring to light new issues, perhaps to resolve issues; they weren't there to expose winners or losers. She was businesslike, and exemplified wisdom. She quickly garnered the respect even of those who didn't necessarily share her views. While Marie didn't compromise her position easily, if at all, she was always respectful of the person with differing views.

Practised in the art of silence and diplomacy, Marie patiently endured long debates around the ebbs and flows of 'what's in/what's out' issues she regarded as peripheral, even anathema, to literacy learning. She would, however, break the silence, even compromise that vintage eloquence, but only when discussion teetered on the cusp of a motion at risk of unexamined, unintended consequences. Only twice do I recall her being pushed to the brink of a snarl, but only to the brink. When I risked one day to make reference to the hint of a snarl, she was ready with a quick retort: If I was going to resort to metaphors of the 'canine kind', she had one in reserve for me. Indeed, she had concluded one day during my chairing of a 'thorny session' that I shared some critical attributes with the New Zealand sheep dog. I think it was meant as a compliment. I simply accepted the remark as clear licence to engage in light banter.

People come and go. Some loom in memory as shadowy figures of the past. I think for all who met Marie as a member of the IRA board, the image and the voice will never fade.

First visit to New Zealand
In 1986 my wife, Evelyn, and I travelled to New Zealand. Marie met us at the airport and casually announced that she had cancelled our hotel booking, a surprise as we knew that she was assuming a new post as department chair the following day. However, recognising that voice Marie reserved for non-negotiables, I offered no argument. Cordial, yet business-like, she ordered (kind of ordered) us to unpack our bags and meet her for tea in her garden. Then she whisked us off in her little blue Honda for a beautiful panoramic view of Auckland, atop Mount Eden. Typically organised, Marie remarked, 'This gives you an overview of the parts that form our local geographic mosaic. Should you get lost in your wanderings, you'll soon get your bearings.' Aha! The teacher setting the stage for us to solve our own problems. But that wasn't all. We learned through the most captivating language so much of the history of this city she so proudly called home.

I was fascinated to observe Marie in her home. She apologised that she would be too busy to do a lot of cooking, but would we help ourselves to anything in her flat. No sooner said, she obviously was planning to cook dinner. Interesting! We offered to assist. No negotiating there. She directed Evelyn to some reading material, asked me to go to the back to pick a lemon, and then to entertain on the baby grand piano (which had belonged to her mother). Lemon picked, the kitchen door swung behind her, and we wouldn't see her till dinner was ready. What a meal! Marie was a solo cook, and in spite of her apologetic comments earlier, meal preparation appeared to be as natural for her as all that language, literacy and learning talk.

The remarkable discovery that night — a mutual passion for rich desserts. She had observed my 'weakness', and had decided to challenge the 'experienced palette.' Ice cream submerged in passionfruit sauce, second serving as good as the first. Later that week, the big surprise, brandy snaps, those wonderful crispy cylindrical creations oozing at each end with whipped cream. When Marie visited us in our home a few years later, she had, indeed, remembered to bring brandy snaps. (PS: Barbara Watson, Marie's neighbour/friend/student, it turned out, was not new to desserts either. Kindred spirits!)

Barbara graciously arranged classroom and Reading Recovery seminar visits for me. Among other things, Marie arranged for a visit to a school with a large Maori population (ties with Don Holdaway), a memorable experience, particularly as it revealed her deep appreciation of the Maori culture. There were other surprises. A devoted parent, she made frequent references to camping trips, trips to the

UK, family events with son, Alan, and daughter, Jenny; and there were nostalgic references to her two 'Swedish granddaughters'.

Times together on the IRA executive

When I was elected to the IRA executive a few years later, I invited Marie to consider a nomination for the presidency. Her refusal was vintage Clay: 'How could you wish that on me? I have nothing to offer!' However, I was surprised and elated when a month later, she decided to honour my invitation. I was proud, conflict of interest aside, to have blatantly hand-picked, ever so wisely, a colleague, a friend, a cherished mentor. Marie and I would be the first two (and to this day, the only two) non-US presidents. How fortunate for me, and how fortunate for the International Reading Association.

Carl Braun, IRA President (1990–91), with Marie at the IRA conference in Orlando.

Busy times, indeed. Among many endeavours, members of the IRA board endorsed with enthusiasm Marie's and my view that International Literacy Year should highlight special literacy thrusts, certainly to raise literacy awareness worldwide. With Marie's support I proposed four major committees and commissions: Literacy in the Cultural Context, Family Literacy Commission, Children's Literature in Literacy, Gender Issues in Literacy. The issues embodied in these commissions captured Marie's interest as she shared my concern that the association should extend its mission beyond reading to the broader literacy domain. I admired Marie's insights, her uncanny sense to imagine things as they might be. Her energy, her creativity, her optimism, and her faith in human potential to transcend obstacles sustained us all. I learned to appreciate her commitment and the air of excitement in discovering a new twist, a new insight, the surprise of epiphany. The contagion of that spirit was one of many gifts that Marie brought to the office, and to me personally.

During my presidential year, I accepted an invitation to speak at the South Pacific Conference in Rotorua, New Zealand, a wonderful opportunity to interact with educators with wide-ranging perspectives. I became even more aware of the diverse intellectual threads that nourished Marie's ongoing reflection and writing — among others, the voices of Cazden, Margaret Clark, Halliday, Lindfors, Paley (and proud references to 'our own Peter Johnston'). Marie introduced me to a number of New Zealand authors, and with obvious pride. I was honoured to share the podium with one of the country's literary giants, Margaret Mahy. These were people at the heart and centre of her literacy world. I began to understand her defensive declarations, 'I'm not a reading specialist; I'm a developmental psychologist.' Indeed, she brought to her framework of reading and writing processes that rich knowledge of culture, language and children. The more I learned about Marie, the more I learned to appreciate the subtle coherence of her philosophical world. Not surprisingly, she shared my belief that music has the potential to enhance all language learning. Aware of my ongoing involvement in music, she listened with great interest to applications of music rhythms and poetry which my students and I had experimented with in clinical settings, especially in cases of brain injury or misguided disability attributions. She would probe, and tried unsuccessfully to push me towards a metaphor that might move her closer to a rationale. That exhortation endured, even haunted me until recently when I read Oliver Sack's *Musicophilia: Tales of the Brain and Music*, which has left me with a compelling metaphor I would love to have put to the ultimate Clay test.

Marie's sense of beauty, even awe, was apparent on many occasions. I remember especially an instance at the World Congress in Stockholm. In part to celebrate the emerging solidarity among member states of the International Reading Association, at least common dreams, I commissioned a patchwork quilt consisting of squares submitted by member organisations, each square to symbolise an aspect of literacy in a particular region. A group of women from Winnipeg, Manitoba designed and put together a magnificent quilt for presentation to UNESCO during the final congress session. Closing words had barely been spoken when I noticed Marie and Katherine Paterson heading for the quilt. Both were in awe, and both viewed the quilt up close, and then from a distance, then turned it around and finger-tracked much of the stitching. Marie's comment: 'The ultimate test of the expert quilter is to inspect the stitching on the reverse side.' And then, 'Not only is this a touching symbol, it is also a remarkable work of art.' As always, Marie was much more than a casual observer.

Reflecting on a unique legacy

The many children whose door to the gift of literacy has been opened through Reading Recovery will always stand as a memorial to Marie's creative imagination and her unflinching optimism about child potential. I can't think of a tribute more fitting than a resolve to plumb the depths of the theoretical constructs underpinning Reading Recovery to explore the yet 'unmined' possibilities for all young children. Such a foray would surely lead us to yet unimagined places as we re-examined tired and disparate 'research says' claims, and entrenched ways of assessing, sorting and programming young children.

Marie stood firm on environments which 'open doors to literacy', including opportunities to talk, to listen, to dramatise, to construct in an atmosphere alive with anticipation. Woven into the rich web of 'becoming literate' were intricate threads of reciprocal processes among reading, writing, drama, and so on — a textured kind of literacy designed to draw children deep into the 'intellectual life around them'. To paraphrase Vygotsky, the crowning feature of these environments was the freedom for the child to 'put things together' for herself or himself — 'to conduct the orchestra'.

Marie was equally explicit about environments which 'begin to close doors to literacy.' Prescriptions, artificially contrived text and sequenced curricula were anathema to motivation and constructive literacy processes. She was adamant in her belief that 'muddled learners' are victims of conceptual bias resulting from histories of inappropriate prescriptions and the chill of skill drill. She took a strong stance against interventions derived from deficit-driven beliefs. Her own observations led to a firm conviction that children learn their way into confusions ('learning tangles'), to the extent even that they frequently manifest profiles typical of neurologically damaged children. Marie promoted interventions based on a fully fledged reading process model, the bottom line always, whether or not the 'reading engine was humming'. The teacher's place in the process, the sensitive observer who works at the 'cutting edge' of the child's competencies, is to scaffold and to support only as much or as long as necessary — the antithesis of programmes that begin with a diagnosis of what the child is unable to do (what Marie referred to as a 'spare parts' approach based on 'shopping lists of assessments').

Teacher support, and the expectation that the child would 'self-orchestrate', would serve as the grounding for 'I can' self-attributions of success, a radical shift in control from teacher to child. While the child's change in reading and writing processes was of interest, so also was the change in the child's identity, an identity even capable of withstanding environments not necessarily conducive to literacy development. This is radical; this is visionary! It points squarely towards an ecology of trust. The question is, are we willing to risk taking steps that Marie dared to take on her own, because of her abiding trust in children and teachers?

Marie believed that the 'big discovery' in the past few decades had been the 'language of children', that 'gateway to new concepts, that means to sorting out confusions'. And within that broad framework she continued to challenge herself, always reaching higher, the consummate model of lifelong learning. I believe that she offered her secret to us all in her opening remarks at the 1992 IRA convention: 'Ideas that challenge what we are not comfortable with can open up new possibilities. From small cracks in the massive land formations, much of the geographical beauty of today's world emerged: it is the challenge of what we hear and discuss, and often the disquiet we feel, that can open up new insights and opportunities.'

Back to the dinner party
As guests of the Munich tourist and convention bureau, Marie and I were invited to a reception preceding the performance of a Mahler symphony. The matter of appropriate attire struck us only as our host announced that we'd be ushered to seats normally reserved for the Herr Burgermeister and his Frau — second row from the front. Marie was visibly embarrassed; I was uncomfortable. Both of us standing motionless, ready to be escorted into the hall filled to capacity, I offered a lighthearted (likely inappropriate) comment. Marie snapped, 'No time for levity, Carl, make yourself invisible.'

It was a beautiful concert, my first and only occasion to hear the Berlin Symphony. And in spite of my faux pas and that slap on the wrist, I'll still have Marie at my dinner party, and indulge myself fully in my eidetic cinema replete with replays of the Mahler in Munich, walks in Stockholm, and the conversations, sights and tastes of New Zealand — as I remember fondly. And I shall continue to consult *By Different Paths to Common Outcomes,* or *Becoming Literate: The Construction of Inner Control,* or even that daredevil piece, 'Learning to be learning disabled'. When I survey the scribblings on some of those dog-eared pages, I know I will continue to experience the serendipitous, 'Oh, I hadn't noticed that before,' as I hear the telepathic voice of the writer long after her departure to that 'great concordance in the sky' (Neilsen).

References

Clay, M.M. 1987. Learning to be learning disabled. *New Zealand Journal of Educational Studies*, 22, 2: 150–72

———. 1991. *Becoming Literate: The Construction of Control.* Portsmouth, NH: Heinemann Education.

———. 1998. *By Different Paths to Common Outcomes.* York, Maine: Stenhouse Publishers.

Neilsen, L. 2001. Dinner Party: Consuming Words. *The Art of Writing Inquiry.* Halifax, NS: Backalong Books (pp. 200–10).

'TO PLAY THEM IN BUNCHES'
Glenn Coats

Reprinted from 'Trying to Move Mountains — Reflections of a Reading Teacher', 2004, with permission from Glenn Coats and the Reading Recovery Council of North America, Inc.

To Play Them in Bunches

Peter has learned
that
if he stops at a word
his parents
will have him spell it
out loud.
Peter has learned
that
if he stops reading,
shakes his head
and says,
*I don't know this
word,*
a friend will read it
for him.
Peter has learned
that
it is easier to say,
*I can never think
of a story,*
than it is to write
one of his ideas
down,
than it is to hear
and record
all those sounds.

Peter has learned
that
most of the words
on Friday's test
will be spelled
wrong.
He has learned
that
a book is a story
he must remember,
and a book is hard
if he can't recall
the whole tale.
Peter has learned
to write more words
than he can read
and if he sees
one of those words
from his writing
vocabulary
in the middle
of a line
of text,
he will not know it;
he will not know
what to do,
and his head will bob,
his eyes flash
in the mirror.

I see Peter
as a new musician.
The words he can write
are like the first notes
a child blows
on the saxophone —
each one stands alone
stark
in the room,
for he hasn't learned
to play notes
in bunches,
or to use them
to predict
the next note
in melody,
or to use them
to create a rhythm,
or to match
each note
quickly
with his eyes.

Peter hasn't learned
to turn
the lonely notes
he blows
into a song.

Marie Clay and the Saskatchewan Connection

Lori Jamison Rog

Saskatchewan Reading Council, Canada; former IRA board member

Long before I ever met Dr Marie Clay, her writing led me to some of the most powerful learning in my professional life. This knowledge came at a particularly significant time, as it helped me understand how my own daughter was learning to read.

My literacy training had taken place in the 'reading readiness' era, back when many educators thought that it was a mistake for children to read before the first grade. Some 'experts' even thought early teaching of reading would be damaging to a child's future reading achievement. So imagine my surprise (and concern) when my daughter began interacting with books, and then reading signs, letters and words, long before she started school. Would my preschool Jennifer be hobbled for life?

Thanks to Dr Clay, I learned that there wasn't a magic age at which a child moved from 'getting ready to read' to 'reading', but that literacy was an ongoing — emerging — process that begins when children first connect meaning to symbols. What seems so obvious today was a breakthrough back then, and gave this nervous mother considerable relief.

At a time when many of us still used a 'deficit model' of intervention, my colleagues and I were fascinated by the early intervention work going on in New Zealand. Our teacher teams pored over Dr Clay's research, studying her techniques, learning her wisdom, even quoting her as if she were our next door neighbour: 'Marie says ...' (trying, of course, to show our worldliness by pronouncing her name the New Zealand way, and often having it come out more like 'Morry'). Through her work with emergent literacy and Reading Recovery, Marie Clay gave us many tools for teaching, but, more importantly, she offered us new ways of thinking about literacy development and using assessment to guide instruction.

When I met Marie, live and in person, at an IRA convention in San Diego, it was like meeting a celebrity! Dr Clay graciously posed with us for pictures, commenting more than once, 'Haven't we done this already?' This was just the first of what was to be many meetings over the years.

In addition to Marie's profound influence on my thinking about how children learn and how best to teach them, she also offered important lessons in literacy leadership. As the only president of the International Reading Association from outside of North America in the 50-year history of the organisation, Dr Clay broadened the perspective of all of us as members.

During her tenure as IRA president, Dr Clay took a special interest in Canadian councils. She visited every provincial council. She honoured our work in Canada and Canadian schools and reminded us of our leadership role in the literacy development of our students and the professional growth of our colleagues. I was inspired to run for and serve on the board of directors of the IRA, becoming the only Canadian from a K-12 (kindergarten to Year 12) school system elected to that position. Later, when I explained how important a role model she had been to me, Dr Clay told me how proud she was of the position I had taken.

While past president of the IRA, Marie made a visit to our Saskatchewan Reading Council. Needless to say, her august presence did much to enhance the stature of our local and provincial councils. More importantly, we were able to bring our colleagues and administrators to hear the gospel of early intervention for at-risk learners.

In a well-intentioned gesture at this event, one of our council members brought Marie a gift of a local craft. It was a large metal sculpture of the stalks of wheat for which our province is known. She accepted it with grace, though I'm sure she must have been thinking, 'Couldn't they have just given me a book?' I often wondered if that oversized piece of art ever found its way across the ocean back to New Zealand.

The phrase 'small in stature but large in ...' — take your pick: intelligence, foresight, knowledge, wisdom — will continue to be used in reference to Dr Marie Clay. Without a doubt, this small woman has left a gigantic legacy for us all.

The New Zealand Reading Association and Marie Clay: Some Personal Reflections

Heather Bell
Former President, New Zealand Reading Association

The New Zealand Reading Association (NZRA) acknowledges the contributions and commitment of Marie Clay to the national association and the local councils throughout New Zealand. Her involvement over 40 years has helped NZRA to be in the strong position it is in today.

The New Zealand Reading Association began life as the Auckland Council of the International Reading Association (IRA), with Marie as one of the key initiators. As more councils began to form, in part through Marie and her networking with her academic colleagues around New Zealand, the relationship with the International Reading Association strengthened. Marie became the IRA Coordinator for New Zealand. In this role, she was able to liaise with councils and to support further growth.

Marie became more involved with IRA, yet maintained her links with the New Zealand IRA councils. A number of key people within New Zealand began to consider establishing the New Zealand Reading Association as an affiliate of IRA. Marie's input was incredibly influential, with her involvement with colleagues around New Zealand, her knowledge of and experience with IRA, and the politics of international reading issues, and her desire to see a New Zealand Reading Association 'come of age'. The New Zealand Reading Association as an independent, interdependent and autonomous association was finally formed.

Marie maintained her close association with the Auckland Reading Association from its beginning. When Marie was awarded Life Membership of the Auckland Reading Association (ARA), she was unable to collect her award in person. She asked me to collect it on her behalf — to do so graciously and to acknowledge and thank the ARA for the added bonus of not having to remember to pay the annual subscription!

Being a plenary or workshop speaker at meetings, seminars and conferences around New Zealand became a regular occurrence. Organisers were always extremely grateful as Marie's presence almost single-handedly guaranteed a large attendance, and in addition to members receiving exemplary professional learning, the meetings were a financial success. This helped the fledgling councils to become self-supporting.

As NZRA began to have an increased international profile, Marie's wit and wisdom was always evident. We established the South Pacific Conferences on Reading in 1983 at the University of Auckland and really valued Marie's knowledge of how the university 'worked', as we were able to use facilities and resources that would not otherwise have been available. At the third South Pacific Conference on Reading, held in Rotorua in 1991, Marie introduced NZRA to Carl Braun from Canada. Carl had been IRA President before Marie, and was influential in Marie standing for the IRA presidential nomination.

When Marie was IRA president she had the task of leading the 1992 World Congress on Reading, which had to be relocated to Maui, Hawaii from Thailand. At the opening general session, Marie had the honour of presenting Warwick Elley with his International Citation of Merit in the field of literacy, one of IRA's most prestigious awards, and of controlling the enthusiasm of almost one hundred Kiwis who erupted with delight. Our delight was enhanced by having two Kiwis receive this award, and for the second Kiwi recipient to be receiving his award from the first recipient! Marie later commented on the behaviour of the Kiwis and said that she too had been very proud. At this opening there was a problem with the serving of food. Marie proposed that the IRA should get the New Zealanders to organise a World Congress — a real David and Goliath idea.

The New Zealand Reading Association offered a bid to host the 2000 IRA World Congress on Reading. Marie continued with her advice, guidance and participation in preparations. An initial site visit by IRA conference staff was planned. The local city arrangements were exaggerated in their cost and complexity. Marie's advice was to let the tourist and government agencies provide all the trimmings in support of the NZRA's bid, although the decision whether to grant the World Congress to Auckland would not rest on the trappings. We enjoyed the limousine rides, the presidential suites at one of Auckland most luxurious hotels, the cocktail party, the sightseeing, the dinner in honour of IRA — with Marie's esteemed patronage adding that touch of class. These activities may not have influenced the decision, but we won the bid.

As part of the 2000 World Congress preparations, we took a large contingent of Kiwis to the 1999 IRA annual convention in San Diego and promoted New Zealand and NZRA through our designated booth. We gave away New Zealand school journals (and free 'lessons' on guided reading), tourist pamphlets, initial congress registration forms, and little gold kiwi lapel badges. We had a roster so that there was always someone at the booth doing the promotions. One morning, while Marie was on the booth, a young American woman came up to collect information. She saw Marie's name badge and had a conversation something like this:

YA	You're Marie Clay.
MC	(*somewhat caustically*) Yes.
YA	Why are you working here?
MC	Because I'm a New Zealander and part of this team.
YA	Oh, in that case, I'd better come to the New Zealand World Congress.

Another person said that her school district would allow her to come if she had a photograph with Marie Clay, and Marie obliged. Several other people also wanted photographs and Marie refused, graciously but firmly. One of our team members suggested that we simply get a life-size cut-out of Marie and charge for photographs — Marie vetoed this suggestion!

By this time Marie had established her Literacy Trust, which was kept almost secret in its early days. She asked me to get two 'young' (teaching for six years or less) teachers from each NZRA local council, and the Trust paid the registration for these people to attend the World Congress. This generous, encouraging gesture continued for subsequent NZRA national conferences and has helped to strengthen NZRA and promote membership.

Marie's wise counsel was always sane, practical, relevant and appropriate — yet never patronising. When she had something to share she would telephone, tell me to get a cup of coffee and then get down to business. She encouraged people in New Zealand to apply for IRA awards and committees, constantly affirmed NZRA's position, generously gave of her time and knowledge, and created a legend.

ABOUT A MAP OF THE WORLD
Alan E. Farstrup
Executive Director, International Reading Association

Marie Clay and Alan Farstrup shared a podium at a conference in Buenos Aires in 1991.

'Marie had put a "reverse" map of the world — with New Zealand and Australia at the top — on an overhead. A young Argentine student helper rushed to the projector and inverted the map, thinking that it had been inadvertently placed upside down. Marie, of course, handled the situation with grace and good humour, pointing out that our habits sometimes get in the way of understanding and our openness to new ideas.'

Marie Clay: A Legend in Her Own Time

Linda B. Gambrell

President, International Reading Association, 2007–08
Distinguished Professor of Education, Clemson University

I remember that it was in the late 1970s that I first I heard about Marie Clay and the work she was doing with Reading Recovery in New Zealand. In the early 1980s, it seemed like everyone in the field was reading her book, *Reading: The Patterning of Complex Behaviour* (Clay, 1972). Marie was an international scholar and Reading Recovery had enjoyed successful field trials in New Zealand. The Reading faculty at the University of Maryland were quite interested and excited about Marie Clay bringing the one-to-one early reading intervention strategy to the United States. In 1985 Marie brought Reading Recovery to the Ohio State University in Columbus, Ohio. This was an exciting time. Field trials by Gay Su Pinnell and her colleagues at the Ohio State University indicated that Reading Recovery was a promising intervention and it began to spread throughout the United States. Marie's work rang true. It was based on three important notions about children who find learning to read difficult: it is critical to intervene early, the intervention must be intensive (one on one), and teachers who have received specific training must deliver instruction. In the 1980s the reading field was all abuzz about Reading Recovery and the children who were being well served by this early intervention.

My memories of Marie as president of the International Reading Association
In 1992, I had the good fortune of being elected to serve on the Board of Directors of the International Reading Association and to serve my first year on the Board under the leadership of Marie Clay, who served as President of IRA from 1992 to 1993. I had only known Marie through her research and scholarly publications. Needless to say, at my first IRA board meeting I was a bit in awe of this woman who had made such significant contributions to our knowledge of literacy teaching and learning.

Marie was a remarkable leader with a strong vision of IRA as an organisation that could make significant differences in the literacy lives of children and the professional development of teachers. She was always thoughtful and respectful of the views and opinions of others. I don't think I exaggerate when I say that each and every member of the IRA board adored this woman of strong conviction and boundless energy, and the board meetings were far from boring during her term. Marie's sense of humour would often come to the rescue as board members tackled difficult issues.

My strongest memory of Marie as President was her commitment to the 'International' in International Reading Association. Throughout her year as President, she travelled the world on behalf of IRA and the goal of literacy for all. She made a special effort to connect with IRA affiliates around the globe. At the conclusion of her year as President, she presented each member of the IRA board with a gift of appreciation. It was, very appropriately, an early map of the world (see page 136). She had purchased the maps at Harrod's in England on one of her IRA trips. I have treasured this beautiful gift and I think of Marie every time I use it — and it reminds me of her very effective work during her presidency to make IRA a truly international organisation.

A scholar and literacy leader

Marie Clay was not only an exemplary teacher and scholar, she was a wonderful, witty woman who lived life to the fullest. What a legacy she has left to those of us in the field of literacy. Marie Clay's research made a difference, leading to revolutions in literacy instruction for struggling readers. Her theory-driven research addressed important literacy issues and was elegantly designed and executed. Her findings were not limited to Reading Recovery, but rather she boldly speculated about broad issues related to literacy learning.

Clay is among the most frequently cited researchers in the field of literacy. In 1999, I conducted a survey with members of the National Reading Conference, considered by many to be the most prestigious literacy research organisation in the US, in order to identify scholars who most influenced literacy practices across three decades: 1970, 1980 and 1990. While many individuals in the field of literacy were identified for the significance of their work, Marie Clay was the only scholar who was identified as a major influence across all three decades. Clearly, her work has contributed in important ways to the heritage and history of literacy research and practice. Marie's colleagues spoke eloquently about her impact on the field of literacy and many of these comments reveal why she became a legend in the field of reading in her own time.

Reading: The Patterning of Complex Behavior opened our eyes to how children learn to read and write. It was a new view of how to do research in real classrooms. A seminal work.

— Margaret Griffin

The work of Marie Clay ... has had a strong influence on the instructional practices of early childhood educators in preschools and the primary grades.

— Patricia Koskinen

She changed the way we assess and teach beginning readers. Her influence is seen in the acceptance of observation as an assessment tool. Also, she influenced the shift from the medical model to continuous, naturalistic assessment.

— Anonymous

Reading Recovery has had a direct effect on instruction in the many schools where it has been implemented. It has also had an indirect effect on our perspective about remedial struggling readers. It is also consistent with the tenor of the times politically ... and remarkable in the sense that it has remained, for the most part above the fray — inside and outside the field. An instructional practice that has components to which a diverse range of researchers, policy makers and teachers can relate.

— David Reinking

Clay's work changed our paradigm concerning early literacy. She showed us that "waiting was not enough — that teaching concepts of print could enhance, rather than hinder, literacy development."

— Cathy Collins Block

Marie's work on early literacy development was very influential during the 1970s and a number of her publications made significant contributions to the field, including *Reading: The Patterning of Complex Behavior* (Clay, 1972) and *The Early Detection of Reading Difficulties* (Clay, 1972, 1979). These publications challenged current notions about the development of young children's reading and writing abilities. Her work during the 1980s built on and expanded her earlier work. The 1980s was a prolific time for Marie, and she published a wide array of books, chapters and articles that furthered our understanding of emergent literacy and the reading process. In the 1990s, Marie's work with Reading Recovery resulted in a number of publications. This work contributed significantly to a deeper understanding of how to effectively provide instruction for struggling readers.

Each decade of Clay's work gave us new ideas and understandings about literacy learning. In particular, she will be remembered for using observations of literacy behaviour to capture change over time, the notion of accelerated progress to bring children back to a normal trajectory of progress, and 'following the child' so that reading work and problem solving is within the child's capabilities.

Marie was, indeed, a legend in her own time. She will be remembered by all who knew her as a splendid international scholar and literacy leader. In addition, Marie was a wonderful person whose commitment to children inspired all who had the great pleasure of knowing her. She was a strong leader for IRA, had deep convictions and high ethical standards, and always kept children's literacy learning at the centre of her thinking. Literacy historians will undoubtedly remember Marie Clay as the founder of Reading Recovery, but we must all remember that her writings and research changed literacy and education's trajectory in significant ways.

References

Clay, M.M. 1972. *Reading: the Patterning of Complex Behaviour,* 2nd ed., Heinemann, Auckland, 1979.

———. 1972, 1979. *The Early Detection of Reading Difficulties,* 3rd ed. Heinemann, Auckland, 1985.

MARIE'S GIFT TO THE IRA BOARD

To the International Reading Association Board

This small memento carries with it my gratitude to each board colleague for the support and encouragement they have given me, for making my job easier, and for allowing us together to extend the activities of the association.

A little something to put on your desk for your coffee mug to prompt a thought about where in the world the first non-North American president of the International Reading Association came from (and don't mention the A — word). If you see any map of the current world without New Zealand, please complain on my behalf!

These maps clearly symbolise 'Emerging global issues'. New Zealand existed before the cartographers put it on the map, and into print. What IRA doesn't yet know about world literacies exists to be discovered. A comparison of these maps reveals the uncertainties, speculations and geographical controversies that only time and continuing exploration resolved into what is now familiar and certain. And that's very like our knowledge of literacy, isn't it? IRA is in the business of putting the unmapped on the map, and moving from uncertainty to more certainty.

This is one of a set of maps from the Henry Edwards Huntingdon Library in San Marino, California. The library contains a collection of 17th-century atlases and maps by great cartographers that have been selected for mounting: Gerard Mercator and Henricus Honius, Joan Blaeu, Frederick de Wit, Nicolaas Visscher, Petrus Plancius and Pieter Goos. Their maps documented the major geographical discoveries of European 16th- and 17th-century exploration and commercial expansion, delineating for their age a new configuration of the world.

Marie Clay
May 1993

The USA and Canada

Marie Clay at Texas Woman's University

Margaret M. Griffin and Billie J. Askew
Professors Emerita, Texas Woman's University

> Each of us has cause to think with deep gratitude
> of those who have lighted the flame within us.
> — Albert Schweitzer

Marie Clay's 30-year association with Texas Woman's University did indeed light a flame within so many of us. We pay tribute to her with gratitude for all that she meant to us personally and to the university community.

The early days — a historical perspective

In 1972, Margaret Griffin, then a faculty member at Indiana University in Bloomington, discovered a remarkable new book about early literacy learning. Marie Clay's *Reading: The Patterning of Complex Behaviour* so impressed Margaret that she urged others to read it. When she joined the Texas Woman's University (TWU) faculty in the fall of 1974, she gave the book to faculty member Rose Spicola for Christmas; the excitement about the groundbreaking work of this extraordinary New Zealander initiated a 30-year relationship between TWU and Marie Clay.

In May 1976, Rose Spicola attended Marie's session at the International Reading Association in Anaheim and invited her to speak at the Fall Forum in Reading at TWU. In the fall of 1977, Marie Clay was introduced to educators across North Texas as she gave the keynote address. Attendees, including Billie Askew, found her research on literacy learning of young children revolutionary. In the late 1970s Marie's work influenced a number of TWU doctoral students. She corresponded with Kaaren Perkins Day about her dissertation related to *Concepts About Print*, and all doctoral students at TWU began their studies by studying Marie's *Reading: The Patterning of Complex Behaviour*, causing them to think about literacy learning in new ways.

To learn more about Marie Clay's work and about literacy practices in New Zealand, Margaret and Rose took 18 graduate students to New Zealand

Billie Askew, Margaret Griffin, Rose Spicola and Marie.

in July/August 1982. They were warmly greeted by Marie and Barbara Watson who met with the visitors in Auckland. The thrill of this experience was enhanced by the opportunity to observe the early days of Reading Recovery in a New Zealand school.

Several other experiences built on Marie's developing ties with TWU. Marie and Barbara joined Rose and Margaret for a tour of Santa Fe following the 1984 Regional IRA in Albuquerque, New Mexico. Marie returned to Denton that same year as the keynote speaker for the North Texas Federation Reading Symposium. Friendships were now firmly established, and excitement about implementing Marie's forward-thinking ideas at TWU was a dream becoming a reality.

The introduction of Reading Recovery at TWU
In the fall of 1986, Billie Askew and several other district-level language arts administrators in the Dallas area approached Margaret about the possibility of bringing Reading Recovery to North Texas. Interest was mushrooming in Texas. Margaret excitedly began to investigate possibilities with Marie who responded, '... my plea is don't get involved in Reading Recovery unless there is an intention to establish it on a sound basis, and that takes time and preparation.'

The following excerpt from a 30 April 1987 letter written by Marie to Margaret reflects her early advice:

Now, some VERY STRONG cautions about Reading Recovery in Texas.
I am very anxious that any attempts to mount the programme, whether small or large scale, learn from the lessons of the past. These are:
1. We no longer have to prove the programme works. It does in three countries. I am currently putting a paper on this together.
2. We know what the organisational and institutional backing has to be and this is thoroughly analysed in a paper to be published in May 1987.
3. We know what mistakes have been made in the new implementations ... and what the faults in those programmes are. We do not need to repeat them.

If what I have to say sounds critical, it is the voice of hard experience and I have to say it. The American way is to start tomorrow, and see how the programme goes. The New Zealand way is to get the training of teachers and the understanding of administrators in place before the programme begins. Then the programme starts with at least half its problem-solving done.

Margaret and Texas educators took Marie's advice seriously. The first step was the training of Reading Recovery leaders and building the groundwork with school administrators. In 1987, Darla Shannon trained in New Zealand and Billie Askew was sent by the Richardson school district in the Dallas area to train at the Ohio State University. During this time, Margaret was busily laying the groundwork for Texas implementation with Marie Clay. Richardson employed Dianne Frasier, who was also training at Ohio State, to join Billie Askew as a Teacher Leader for the district. A visit from Marie in March 1988 was timely for her to mentor Margaret, Billie, Dianne and Darla as they planned the introduction of Reading Recovery in Texas.

Beginning in September 1988, the first Reading Recovery teacher classes in Texas became a long-awaited reality. Billie and Dianne trained teachers in Richardson and Darla introduced Northside in San Antonio to Reading Recovery. Margaret arranged for key TWU administrators to visit the class in Richardson. Dean Michael Wiebe's clinical background ensured his excited support, and visionary Provost Patricia Sullivan saw Reading Recovery as an important university function — including high quality academic courses, research and service to the educational community.

Because of the growing demand for Reading Recovery in Texas and the administrative interest at the university, Margaret initiated a proposal for the training of Reading Recovery Teacher Leaders at TWU. In 1989–90, Billie trained the first Teacher Leader training class in Texas for six school districts; the venture was co-sponsored by TWU and the Richardson Independent School District.

In 1990, Billie and Dianne became faculty members at TWU and established the Reading Recovery Center at the university. After visiting Reading Recovery teaching sessions, university president Shirley Chater and provost Patricia Sullivan requested funding from the Texas legislature. This biannual funding commitment was renewed six times.

The late Wilkes Berry, associate provost, worked closely to support Reading Recovery funding and became a champion for Marie and her university contributions. Across the years, university chancellors, provosts and deans have continued to recognise the importance of Marie Clay's work and have strived to institutionalise Reading Recovery within the university framework.

Marie Clay became our mentor and colleague as we expanded Reading Recovery in Texas and the region. TWU became a centre for the training of Reading Recovery Trainers, joining the Auckland centre and Ohio State University. Since 1989, TWU has trained 220 Reading Recovery Teacher Leaders and 16 Reading Recovery Trainers of Teacher Leaders. The university also became the centre for training in Descubriendo la Lectura, or Reading Recovery in Spanish — an important project to Marie.

Marie Clay's work in Texas
After TWU became an established university training centre for Reading Recovery, Marie became a regular visitor to Denton. The Center thrived with support from the Texas legislature and applications from numerous districts in Texas and beyond, and Marie was always available to offer counsel as we were growing so rapidly.

Marie was the TWU President's Scholar-in-Residence from February through December 1994. During that year she mentored Trainers at the Reading Recovery Center, supported members of the reading faculty, and held seminars for Reading Recovery and early literacy educators. Her two-semester research seminar for 14 TWU doctoral students resulted in a symposium, *The Current Status of Change Research*, at the International Reading Association Conference in New Orleans in 1996. TWU officials brought Marie back to campus for an extended stay in 1996 as a Visiting Scholar.

On all visits to TWU, Marie supported faculty research related to Reading Recovery and early literacy learning. She advised Reading Recovery Trainers on follow-up and longitudinal studies as well as studies that explored teacher–child behaviours. In addition to Billie and Dianne, Marie mentored a number of new TWU Trainers across the years: Connie Compton, Nancy Anderson, Yvonne Rodriguez, Betsy Kaye and Cynthia Rodriguez. Marie made significant contributions to two TWU dissertations: Yvonne Rodriguez, *The Translation of Marie Clay's* An Observation Survey of Early Literacy Achievement *from English to Spanish* (2000); and Elizabeth (Betsy) Kaye, *Variety, Complexity, and Change in Reading Behaviors of Second Grade Students* (2002). Both studies were important to the advancement of literacy learning and both doctoral students ultimately became Trainers of Teacher Leaders at the university. In 2003, Marie supported the transition of the centre to new leadership under director Anne Simpson.

The redevelopment of Reading Recovery in Spanish, Descubriendo la Lectura (DLL), was important to Marie. She was involved in the early work in Tucson, Arizona and worked closely with a national bilingual collaborative to move the effort forward. The publication of the bilingual version of the *Observation Survey* (*Instrumento de observación de los logros de la lecto-escritura inicial*) changed literacy learning opportunities for Spanish-speaking children in the United States. Marie worked closely with DLL Trainers and Teacher Leaders over the years in the reconstruction of Reading Recovery teaching procedures and supported Yvonne Rodriguez in the all-Spanish version of the *Observation Survey*. Her interest in the ongoing development and implementation of Descubriendo la Lectura continued throughout her relationship with TWU.

Marie Clay's own quest for cutting-edge research and theoretical arguments enriched all who knew her at the university. She became a regular (almost daily) visitor to the TWU library where she was immediately adopted by the reference librarians. She returned to her office daily with stacks of books to see what would be helpful in her forward-thinking work. The next day she exchanged those books for others. Often she brought books to our offices with an 'indirect' invitation to read and learn from them. While in-residence or visiting TWU, Marie shared her understandings and current thinking with the Reading Recovery network and the early literacy community. She graciously offered numerous sessions for Teacher Leader professional development across the years. She taught us all to become more flexible and tentative in our theory and practice, always pushing the boundaries of new knowledge.

Marie gave many keynote presentations at TWU across the years including *Research in Reading Recovery* and *Implementation of Reading Recovery* in 1988 and *Accommodating Diversity in Early Literacy Acquisition* at the TWU Reading Recovery Conference in 1993. During 1994 she ran several seminars, such as *Power in the Writing Component* and *Oral Language/The Low Language Child* and in September she gave the Distinguished Lecture in Education on *Constructing Independent Control Over Literacy*. At the GTE Eminent Scholar Series in April 1999 she delivered *The Challenge of Literacy Improvement*, and at the TWU Reading Recovery Conference in Dallas in November 2001 Marie spoke on *The Magic of Language*.

Marie's life in Denton

When Marie arrived for her year as the President's Scholar-in-Residence on 2 February 1994, she moved into the Board of Regents suite in one of the campus dormitories. In anticipation of her visit, TWU faculty members 'decorated' the suite and stocked the refrigerator with a few food items. The temperature on the day of her arrival was 80°F (20°C) — a bit warm for a North Texas winter day. We left Marie to settle in with arrangements for a late start the next day. In true Texas fashion, a 'norther' blew in during the night, dropping the temperature to 20°F (–7°C) and blanketing all of North Texas with a heavy coating of ice. When Billie called her the next morning to warn her not to step outside the dorm on the layer of ice, Marie responded that she was confident she could walk to the Student Union. After much persuasion, Marie acquiesced and said she would be fine with her refrigerator supplies.

Marie said in a letter:

On the television, from CNN and NBC or anywhere else for that matter, the forecast was unbelievable. Snowstorms from the north, looping down into north Texas ... during the night would bring the temperatures to below zero and there would be freezing rain. I left out my short-sleeved cotton clothes. It couldn't change that fast!

Today as I look out my third floor window with enough height to get a fairly long view, everything is white and grey ... In the parking lot cars are frosted over because there does seem to be more ice than snow ... My friend Margaret Griffin phoned. Schools were closing, some university classes were cancelled. Best to stay at home ...

Welcome to Texas weather! Three days later, Marie acknowledged that she may never eat spaghetti again.

After many unique experiences with dorm life, Marie lived in apartments on subsequent extended visits. Carolyn Roblyer, Reading Recovery office manager, enjoyed the role of taking care of Marie's living arrangements. Marie always wanted to live close to campus so she could walk to the Reading Recovery Center, the library and nearby shops, and be part of the university community. In addition to the two extended stays in Denton, Marie visited many times for shorter periods. We are fortunate to be near the Dallas-Fort Worth airport, which often served as a first and/or last stop to or from Auckland via Los Angeles.

Marie stayed at Billie's home when visiting Denton. Their breakfast talks often threatened timely arrivals to scheduled events. Weekends were special because there was time to visit and talk about so many things. They discovered a connection to the renowned Ruth Strang, Billie's major professor at the University of Arizona in the sixties, who introduced Marie and her groundbreaking research to the world at the World Congress in Copenhagen in 1968. During these breakfast conversations, Marie could make you forget that she was a Dame of the British Empire and winner of every major literacy achievement award. She could make you think about things that make a difference in this world, to look at issues through new and unusual lenses, and she could challenge you to enjoy and cherish the human experience. She was a warm and caring human being who was generous with her time and her knowledge — a person with the physical and mental acumen that we all envied — and most of all a person who was an extraordinary friend.

Although she worked tirelessly to support the TWU network, she also enjoyed some 'extracurricular' activities. Marie's varied interests were evident in her ventures in Texas. She became an honorary Rotarian in Denton, shopped with Margaret in Dallas, and enjoyed performances and theatre at the Dallas and Fort Worth symphony halls and opera houses. In 1994, after recovering from the initial wintery blast, Marie wrote in another letter: 'On Sunday afternoon Margaret took me to the theatre in Dallas, a kind of large-scale experimental theatre like the upstairs theatre at the old Mercury in Auckland. We saw *Das Barbecu*, a comedy musical with a Texas theme which was a take-off of Wagner's *The Ring*. I had big reservations … but it was excellent — great lyrics, good music, a cast of five who played 20 parts in fantastic costumes, staging and lighting, and very funny even though I missed 50 per cent of the Texan jokes. Next Friday night we have been given tickets for the Symphony Orchestra Hall … for a jazz concert with Dave Brubeck.'

In 1996, Billie and Dianne arranged for Marie to go to Galveston, Texas to visit with Helen Kirk-Lauve, whom Marie wanted to meet. They shared an interest in multiple births. 'We watched in awe as the two of them went through archived boxes and delighted in recalling accounts of these children around the world, and catching up with their lives today.'

Helen Kirk-Lauve, a specialist on multiple births, shares information from her files with Marie.

Marie liked travelling with her TWU colleagues. Margaret and Rose explored the historic town of Williamsburg, Virginia with Marie. Billie, Margaret and Rose took Marie to Little Rock, Arkansas, to visit the Clinton Presidential Center after a visit to Billie's first 'retirement' home in Hope, Arkansas. Margaret and Rose and Marie all enjoyed a cruise together around the coast of Norway. Wherever they went with Marie, she studied the history and enjoyed exploring the culture. Her sense of enquiry permeated all that she did.

Honouring Marie Clay's contributions to Texas Woman's University

Although TWU could never adequately acknowledge Marie's many contributions, efforts were made to honour her. In 1999, Marie was officially named an Honorary Reading Professor at the University. In May 2003, Marie Clay received an Honorary Doctoral Degree in Humane Letters from Texas Woman's University. The value placed on her influence is evident in that it was the first honorary doctorate conferred in 20 years at the university! Part of the Citation for the honorary degree, signed by Ann Stuart, the chancellor and president of TWU read: 'Dr Clay is dedicated to finding out what is possible and translating the possible into practice. Because of her search for the possible, millions of children have learned to read through Reading Recovery in English, Spanish and French; many thousands of

teachers have learned that all children can succeed; and scholars the world over have learned that a clear vision can change individuals and schools ... her influence transcends the boundaries of language, disciplines and nations. And we know the waters she has stirred will continue to expand our ideas of what is possible.'

The reading faculty presented Marie with a piece of art to celebrate the honour, a field of Texas bluebonnets (native wildflowers), so that she could take a bit of Texas with her back to New Zealand. In 2004, Margaret and Rose visited Marie's home in Auckland and saw the bluebonnets displayed. That year Marie organised their trip around New Zealand, and she travelled with them around the top of the North Island.

Marie's legacy

The gifts that our friend Marie Clay left to us personally, to our university and to our greater community cannot be measured. We are the beneficiaries of a very rare legacy — a legacy of knowledge, commitment, humanity and lasting friendship.

Our challenge is to ensure that her legacy lives on in the many lives that she influenced. She changed our conversations about what is possible for children and stretched our thinking in ways that we could not previously imagine. She shaped our personal and professional lives in ways that have influenced our future actions and conversations as we continue her legacy of searching for what is possible.

A quote from Norman Cousins exemplifies Marie's life and legacy — and her approach to immortality:

> If something comes to life in others because of you,
> then you have made an approach to immortality.

Marie Clay left an indelible mark on all of us in the Texas Woman's University community. Her legacy lives on and continues to rekindle the flame she lighted within us.

TWO NEWS LETTERS FROM MARIE IN OHIO, 1984

In September 1984 Marie Clay and Barbara Watson went to Ohio State University to begin the implementation of Reading Recovery in the United States, and stayed until early 1985. These are two general news letters from Marie during December:

Columbus, Ohio
3 December 1984

It seems as if I will never get my Christmas mail written if I do not resort to a duplicated news sheet so here goes. It is the last week of the Fall Quarter at the Ohio State University.

Barbara Watson, Beth (a graduate student) and I are living very comfortably in a little three-storey house (basement, ground and attic levels) in suburban Columbus. Our landlady is a British warbride, and her husband, a mechanical engineer now retired. They are on vacation in New Zealand and England for the duration of our stay. There are front and back lawns, many tall trees which have taken months to lose all their leaves and there has been much activity bagging up the dead ones ... We care for a neurotic cat who scoots for cover at the smallest sound, pleads to go outside, dashes away while we open the door, then dives out into the cold, only to make an equally quick return in a very short time. There are only three bird feeders outside the lounge window and many varieties of tiny birds, sometimes a blue jay or a cardinal, and almost always stealing from them half a dozen grey squirrels who are growing really fat on birdseed.

We have a Volkswagen Rabbit diesel car which goes very well and we are told will be trouble-free in the worst weather ... We finally got around to getting it steam-cleaned yesterday and discovered the Rabbit is a lot better looking than we had thought.

We try to fit in a little culture now and again. We went to the Gewundhaus Orchestra of Leipzig, to Marya Martin's solo recital to inaugurate the Young Concert Artists Series at OSU, to the Henry Moore Reclining Figure Exhibition at Columbus Fine Arts Gallery, the Ohio Artists and Craftspeoples Show, and we began our Christmas celebration with the Christmas Madrigal feast at the historic Ohio Village — holly and ivy, the processions of the Greens, the Wassail, the Boar's Head and the flaming plum pudding all accompanied by beautifully sung madrigals and carols, and the appreciative noises of a hundred guests eating an 1850s style repast in an English tradition as the early settlers remembered it.

It sounds as if we have not had much time for work. This is not true. We have 14 teachers working quite well with Reading Recovery procedures on a practice group of children and ready to begin the project in earnest in January. They are really quite excited by the procedures although they don't like the amount of work they have been subjected to. We have seven Tutors training, and they are just pulling ahead of the teachers and are beginning to look at the teacher training as well as doing their own teaching. Then I have just completed a course for MA and PhD students on the background theories that led to why we teach the way we do in Reading Recovery and have just graded 30 papers and 120 observation exercises for them. I have given my DIS VIS PRF (computer title) public lecture, and about 10 others to conferences or public groups. I have dined with the Provost and the other three Distinguished Visiting Professors (from Monash, Australia, Buenos Aires, and Lund, Sweden) and talked to the Faculty of Education. Most interesting perhaps (aside from attending NCTE in Detroit and staying 54 storeys up in the Renaissance Center and watching maritime activity up and down the lake, morning, noon and night) was flying off to Edmonton to the University of Alberta to examine a PhD. There they had snow! It was piled high at the sides of the river, and the roads. We celebrated with the successful candidate in the circular moving restaurant overlooking the river which was almost frozen over, and that was my scenic tour of Edmonton, a two-hour revolution over lunch.

Tomorrow it's the teachers' class. Wednesday we go by Greyhound bus to Shaker Heights out of Cleveland to do a four-hour workshop — Barbara and I will share it and then the next day by bus to take the last Tutors' session of the quarter and the last lecture. On Friday we head east to Boston where I have an IRA committee meeting and we hope to visit Courtney Cazden. Two days to enjoy Boston and then to SUNY at Albany where I will give a lecture for Peter Johnston and visit with some of the reading people. Then by Amtrak to Rochester where an ex-New Zealander is working a quiet revolution in teaching practices and where we will do a workshop on Observing Your Readers. This is to help the teachers document what is occurring in their classrooms. From there it's down to New York for about five days of vacation and home to Columbus by 20 December. We plan to spend three weeks working on our own writing projects and professional reading before the next mad rush of the Winter Quarter begins on 7 January.

Somewhere in there I managed to check the galley proofs of the next edition of *Early Detection* and mark University of Auckland exam papers. I don't seem to have done much else, but then I did write a whole new series of lectures.

There are a few trips planned for January and February. I have to do a two-day workshop at Tucson at the University of Arizona, and the IRA board meeting is in Albuquerque, and I will be at the Colorado State conference of IRA and, just prior to leaving, at the Far West Conference in Portland, Oregon. The calendar is full; and I am now saying, 'No more.' Except for the possibility that I might return home to New Zealand via Singapore and do some work for the Institute of Education there. We are still negotiating that one.

Columbus, Ohio
23 December 1984

While I was away so many people wrote to me and sent little packages that I feel totally justified in delaying the work for a further afternoon and sending off a news report.

Barbara and I set off on the last day of term, having finished the courses and marked all the assignments. We flew to Boston where I had two days of meetings for a subcommittee of the International Reading Association. On the Saturday night we had dinner with that committee at the top of the Prudential building in Boston, overlooking the whole city on a clear cold night. (We had had 8 inches of snow in Cleveland and Columbus in our last week over there and Barbara had driven the VW Rabbit in the snow and very well. However she couldn't make it up the drive so at 10.30 at night we had our first experience of shovelling the drive to get the car into the garage.) The snow has almost disappeared in Boston and we haven't seen any since. The weather is almost like a New Zealand spring at present but with very cold nights and frosty mornings.

Then we started to see Boston. Sunday morning — we went to the Free-for-All at the Museum of Fine Arts. We followed a mime artist around as he acted up to various exhibits — a Pharaoh waking up and going off to work, taking a Roman horse and later hitching this imaginary being to a statue's outstretched hand ... That made us late for the conducted tour so a lady that was extremely well-informed took us on a private tour of the museum and explained all kinds of things to us — including the fine silversmith's work that turned out to have been done by Paul Revere. We heard music on the strangest instruments ... Then it was time to take a taxi to *A Child's Christmas in Wales* at a little theatre like the Theatre Corporate in Auckland ... We walked home having had a cup of hot spiced cider at the theatre and turned on the TV just in time to catch an hour and a half of Baryshnikov in the *Nutcracker* suite, which is traditionally performed for children across USA at this of year. We missed the end of that because our day was not yet over. We had seats for the film of *Amadeus* ... What a variety of cultural activities in one day!

The rest of Boston involved a tourist tram ride on a vintage trolley, shopping, and last-minute seats to the Boston Symphony Orchestra presenting a dramatic oratorio by Arthur Honegger, *Jeanne d'Arc au bucher*, with three choruses or choir and actress Marthe Keller for the spoken part of Joan ... We visited Boston University and had lunch with Courtney Cazden in Harvard Faculty club.

Then we set off for Albany driven by Peter Johnston, a New Zealander on the Reading Faculty of SUNY. I spoke to the psychologists in training for school Psychology (at Frank Vellutino's invitation) and to about 50 people on Reading Recovery and fielded some good questions. Talked with Rose-Marie Weber, and Dick Allington, Sean Walmsley and Jim Fleming ... That evening was spent with some old friends of mine, Gwen and Willy Graham, who I first met in the Lake District on my first visit to England. Jenny will remember visiting their house (in 1968), which they plan to sell when they have built a winter house in Florida.

The schedule would not wait for further visits in Albany and we were, after a long wait, on the train to Rochester ... Barbara talked to a school district in-service group on shared book experience in the morning with a few asides from me, and then we began what had been called workshops. We had worked out who would do what — how to do reading and writing observations and some general introductory remarks, and the final session on Reading Recovery — until we found out they had enrolled 170 people! Hastily we backed up, changed gear, divided them into two groups and each taught everything. By noon on Saturday from a 4 pm start on Friday we had earned our keep and were rushed off to the airport and on to the plane for New York. This was to be our vacation.

We found the key to the Dean's suite (by arrangement) at New York University and rated it very comfortable for the next two nights. There were three lighted Christmas trees on the skyscraper horizon of New York — the Empire State building and two others and we had an unobstructed view. For our first theatre trip we aimed high, and secured seats at *The Real Thing* with Jeremy Irons for the Sunday matinee. We had, however, paid our due respects with sincere pride to the Te Maori exhibition at the Metropolitan Museum of Art first.

Monday morning brought an accommodation shift to the Barbizon Plaza on Central Park South ... Then came the obligation bit and we returned to NYU this time for me to give a talk — again Reading Recovery but this time in Columbus. I picked up some interesting ideas for a current policy paper I am writing from the questions asked. We couldn't stay too late because we were going to the opera at the Met. It was *The Barber of Seville* in ... magnificent surroundings ... Kathleen Battle, the soprano, was new to me, and wonderful in the part. The men had all been imported from Italy and could act superbly as well as sing. All in all, a good evening in New York.

Our last night in the city. The Royal Shakespearean Company was playing *Much Ado About Nothing* and *Cyrano de Bergerac* in a new translation of Anthony Burgess (of *Clockwork Orange* fame). I had studied the play in the sixth form and was very interested to see it again. In the romantic genre of *Romeo and Juliet*, it was nevertheless very funny and I have never seen such breathtaking sets. Many of you will know of my interest in stage costumes and sets. So that was our New York and Boston diet — historical French drama, a modern English play, a modern American play (Glengarry Glen Ross about salesmen in USA), *The Barber* at the Met and *Joan of Arc* by the Boston Symphony Orchestra. On our last day in New York we listened to a free lunchtime concert by a male quartet from the Julliard School of Music — Christmas music — and walked in the sun in Central Park. The New York shops had wonderful window displays and there were examples of every kind of Christmas tree you could imagine with every variation possible on the type of decoration — from only origami ornament to only storybook characters, to cookie and bread ornaments, or only glass or only gold ornaments.

[Charlotte Huck left them such a tree, fully decorated, for their Christmas in Ohio when she left on vacation, delivered, Barbara said, 'on the back of Gay Su Pinnell's husband's truck'.]

Christmas Eve. We were taken by one of our graduate students to a family celebration at Springfield, Ohio. The family farmhouse and farm go back three or four generations. The parents are dead but the extended family have kept the old home with all its traditional furnishings intact. Across the road is the share-farmer who runs the old farm and the farmhouse becomes the country home for any and all of the extended family. It was like a museum

of 19th century treasures, built in 1860 and full of handmade craft and needlework as well as magnificent antique beds, chests and tables. Yet it was a lived-in house. We sat around huge fires burning enormous logs while the cooks in the kitchen put together a turkey and ham dinner followed by a Christmas pudding.

Barbara has just heard the news. The outside temperature is below freezing and we may yet get snow for Christmas. We expect to have a quiet day tomorrow and then to begin some hard work writing and putting some thoughts together on our programme and other academic things.

Lectures will begin again on 7 January and there will be the teachers' course, the Teacher Leaders' course, and the graduate course to get under way and teach. Barbara will return to Auckland at the end of January and I will be home by mid-March. Time is passing very quickly ... I find the teaching leaves me little time to do other things I would like to do in academic areas because I have to write new material to suit the local scene, and because I have undertaken to give too many outside talks. I think we have learned a great deal more than we already knew about American education, at least in the junior school years which helps ... to understand what researchers and commentators are talking about.

With 1985 just around the corner, I want to wish you all a very Happy New Year.

What Would Marie Say?

Peter Johnston

Professor, University at Albany, SUNY

Marie Clay had a large impact on me, as a person, and on my thinking as a researcher. She was an unaffected, fiercely persistent, thoroughly curious, and deeply ethical pragmatist. For example, when asked by a basal reader company whether she would like a lot of money for helping them develop better literacy instruction materials, she could have simply said no (a simple yes was clearly not possible). Instead she said, 'Okay, but you can't use my name', which she hypothesised (but lacked proof) would be a deal-breaker, and an object lesson. Like most of her hypotheses, it was confirmed. She remains a role model for me as a New Zealand academic.

I first encountered Marie's work as a student teacher at Dunedin Teachers College. It would be another 10 years before I would meet her in person. I heard from Don Holdaway that she would be in Boston and invited her to come to Albany to give a talk to the faculty. I drove to Boston and brought Marie and Barbara Watson back to Albany in our little old Honda Civic. I remember being struck by how calmly and clearly she responded to critical questions. She simply loved an intellectual discussion, particularly when it involved productive disagreements. She deliberately sought out alternative views to explore the limits of her own theories. In the course of her visit, two colleagues, Frank Vellutino and Donna Scanlon, who viewed literacy teaching and learning from a different perspective, were persuaded by the importance of Marie's work on early intervention. Their subsequent work has led to changes in the US federal laws relating to early intervention and the classification of children as learning disabled.

When I first came to the University at Albany in 1981, I found myself teaching teachers. The views of literacy instruction here were on a very different page from the view Marie and Don had led me to (I recall taking shared reading for granted until a teacher asked me to explain what 'shed' reading was). I set about preparing materials for my teaching, one part of which became a book on assessment based on Marie's idea of the 'sensitive observer'. I saw her running records as central to assessment, so I constructed a set of audio examples, mostly of my children, to go with my book, which included a description of running records. In my youthful ignorance, at the last minute I contacted Marie to see if there was a problem with what would have turned out to be a violation of copyright. Marie generously worked with her editor Graham McEwan to make it possible to still publish the book and recordings. Though the book sold relatively few copies, the recordings have been duplicated and used many thousands of times so that a good proportion of the teachers learning to use running records in the United States have been introduced to them through those recordings, which would not have been possible without Marie's generosity. Indeed, my youngest daughter entering a teacher education programme recently called to say that her instructor was teaching them running records from those recordings. She was taking running records of her five-year-old self.

Since I began teaching teachers I have used Marie's books in classes on literacy. I have aspired to her writing style, which is elegantly clear and deceptively simple to read. Her books are densely packed with ideas and information so that I routinely notice things I had not noticed before in her work. From early on, the following related aspects of her work heavily influenced the development of my own thinking: the importance of the child being in control of learning and processing (following the child's lead); the idea of a self-extending system and the prompts for cross-checking; teaching *for* strategies; and the centrality of a teacher's dual attention to observing and analysing the child's behaviour and to her own instructional practices as mutually dependent (a sensitive observer and contingent instruction). The prompts were doubtless one stimulus for my thinking about the significance of teachers' language as a core teaching tool. Teaching for strategies, too, led to my thinking about the significance of teachers' decisions about when to be explicit and when not to be — how inviting strategic thinking is very different from teaching strategies. This led to my exploration of the sources of agency in teachers' language choices with children. In fact, Marie left me with a virus, a WWMS (What Would Marie Say?) voice in my head, and it is a virus that I pass on to my students.

I don't know why, but it never occurred to me to talk with Marie about her personal life, or mine, and it rarely came up. Yet, I felt a kindred spirit with her. I imagine I was not alone in this, perhaps because conversations with her about theory and research seemed so thoroughly personal, and she was such an intense and engaged conversation partner. Indeed, when she was engaged with ideas she could be impatient with distractions and a little blunt. Once at an International Reading Association meeting we split up into round tables and Marie came to mine. I had made an initial pitch inviting questions and comments. One of the participants took the opportunity to address the group and move the conversation a bit off topic. Marie succinctly explained that we weren't there for that and returned the floor to me.

In 2006, a year before her death, I was fortunate to spend some time visiting with Marie at Texas Woman's University where I had been invited to give a talk. I confess to some real trepidation in presenting my work with Marie in the audience. I know I am not alone in experiencing this, though Marie would be the last to make personal judgements. Nonetheless, her intellect was somehow intimidating. She was, after all, one of the great developmental psychologists, educational researchers and teacher educators of the twentieth and twenty-first centuries. I repeated this experience twice shortly afterwards at the National Reading Recovery Conference in Columbus, Ohio. That was the last time I saw Marie. We had breakfast together, and talked theory, a gift I shall always treasure. If I make any impact on teachers and children's lives, the lion's share will be traceable to Marie and her work.

Contacts with Marie

Celia Genishi

Professor of Education and Chair, Department of Curriculum and Teaching, Teachers College, Columbia University

Being a member of the faculty at the Ohio State University from 1986 until 1990 put me in touch with good fortune, for this was a time when, among other good happenings, Marie Clay made periodic visits to Columbus. What good fortune it was that my colleagues in the renowned programme in language, literature and reading introduced me to Reading Recovery and to Marie. From the Reading Recovery intervention and its many parts, I began to understand the depth and scope of Marie's contributions to the study of language and literacy. Teaching courses about language acquisition and language arts, I saw that there was little that Marie had not investigated about young children, reading and writing, and little that she had not communicated about her studies to teachers.

My thoughts here focus first on children and teachers as learners and Marie's ways of learning about both and, second, on the delights of knowing Marie. Throughout her work there is a persistent and insistent principle that *in order to teach children, we must first learn from them.* In these days of accountability and No Child Left Behind in the United States, when standardised tests drive the curriculum even in the earliest years, we can hear Marie reminding us that tests can never replace observant teachers. Thus in *By Different Paths to Common Outcomes* (Clays, 1998, p. 95), she wrote:

> So when I am in the United States and a question from the audience is 'What do children have to know when they come to school?', I have to say that is not a valid question. Individual differences, contexts, learning opportunities and culture all create the inevitability of different knowings, known in different ways, with different highs and different lows. Valid questions for the teacher who recognises the need to work with, and build on, what the child already knows are 'What does this child already control?', 'What can this child do?', 'How does he or she understand the task?'

Through the countless pages of her articles, books and assessments, there are always traces of what children can do, evidence that the major challenge for adults is not how to tell children what to learn but how to see tasks through the child's eyes and then offer tasks that are complex enough to show both what the child does control and what she or he needs to learn. Those tasks might be within a lesson or in an assessment that built on her observations of children and on previous research. Unlike many literacy researchers, Marie kept oral language in the foreground.

For example, in her book *Record of Oral Language and Biks and Gutches* (Clay, 1983), she drew on her knowledge of first language acquisition research (the Berko test of English morphology) and developed child-friendly test items for second-language learners, including children who spoke Maori or Samoan. It is noteworthy that Marie focused on English learners, what they knew, and what they needed to learn, at the same time that she published her and her collaborators' research findings and the assessment tools they developed for use by classroom teachers.

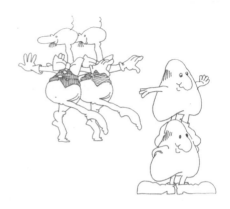

An illustration from Record of Oral Language and Biks and Gutches.

The same beliefs about research-to-practice underlay Reading Recovery, which was grounded in teachers' careful observation of children as they learned about print. I remember that Reading Recovery apprentices, observing each other behind the one-way glass at Ohio State, recounted how anxious they felt. I remember as well that they said this training process changed inalterably their view of children and learning/teaching, once they gained some experience and confidence. Marie viewed these teachers as colleagues who could learn to do the careful observation that she did and could then act on the results of their observations. She used the research tools of the educational psychologist and then informed teachers of what was relevant about her research for the classroom. The researcher was not an outsider to educational practice, but rather an insider-colleague. She viewed teachers as researchers well before teacher research was fashionable.

So those are key memories for me about Marie Clay, the brilliant scholar and pioneer in literacy research, which I'm sure overlap with the memories of many, many colleagues. My memories of Marie, the person, are hard to separate from Marie, the professional: we became acquainted because she invited me to teach a course on language acquisition at Auckland University while she was on sabbatical in 1988. Of course I said yes and began to learn about the delights of knowing Marie, not well, but enough to see what an unpretentious, generous and modest person she was.

One of my most vivid memories of Marie's enjoyment of life was of a field trip we took with friends, including Diane DeFord and Marge Cambre, then at Ohio State, to Chillicothe, Ohio, home of an historical drama called *Tecumseh!* It was performed in an outdoor amphitheatre and advertised thus: 'The epic life story of the legendary Shawnee leader as he struggles to defend his sacred homelands' in the late 1700s. And what a drama it was, complete with elaborately costumed actors and horses riding into the sunset of southern Ohio! Marie seemed to be thoroughly taken by the performance and curious about Tecumseh and his place in history. We all commented on the uniqueness of the venue and chuckled over whether any of us had ever experienced anything like it. I know that I had not and have not since.

Another memory that will always stay with me is of my second visit to Auckland, New Zealand, in 1998, when there was a power brown-out and drought, an odd and unique set of circumstances for an area of the world that is typically lush and never far from a breathtaking view of water. Marie invited my husband and me to her home and played chauffeur and tour guide to close-in suburbs that were still as inviting as they had been 10 years earlier. She chose a charming lunch spot and shared stories of her travels to remote pockets of the world. She showed us part of her collection of miniature books, all the while being as hospitable as she was interesting — and interested in our lives. This true interest in others, young and not so young, must be a shared remembrance with countless friends and colleagues of hers around the globe. What good fortune I had to be able to experience Marie Clay as a colleague, mentor and friend. How we will all miss her.

References

Clay, M.M. 1998. *By Different Paths to Common Outcomes.* York, ME: Stenhouse.

Clay, M.M., Gill, M., Glynn, T., McNaughton, T., and Salmon, K. 1983. *Record of Oral Language and Biks and Gutches.* Auckland: Heinemann.

The Pioneering Achievements of Marie Clay

Gay Su Pinnell

Trainer Emeritus, Ohio State University

In the spring of 1992, I received a phone call advising me that Reading Recovery was being considered for an award. Would I be able to answer some questions? During this busy day, I knew I had to stop and answer these questions, but I had no idea of their significance. My quick understanding was that Marie Clay and Reading Recovery might receive recognition. Of course, recognition of Marie was not a new or unique phenomenon, but positive attention would help Reading Recovery grow. So, I spent about an hour on the phone with the representative of the Charles A. Dana Foundation. The Dana Foundation is a private philanthropy with principal interests in brain science, immunology, and arts education. Charles A. Dana, a New York State legislator, industrialist and philanthropist, was president of the Dana Foundation from 1950 to 1966 and actively shaped its programmes and principles until his death in 1975. Perusal of its awards, most of which are in the area of medical research and the arts, reveals that Reading Recovery was a somewhat unusual choice. Other awardees in education are Robert Slavin, the creator of Success for All, and Uri Treisman, well known for mathematics education.

A few months later, I received another call informing me that Marie Clay and I would jointly receive the Dana Foundation's award for 'pioneering achievement in health and education'. A ceremony would be held in November 1993, at the Plaza Hotel in New York City. I informed them that Clay, not I, was the creator of Reading Recovery. The foundation board members were well aware of this circumstance. Their response was clear: this award was for the Clay's creative design and for United States implementation. Uri Treisman of the Dana Foundation had visited several hundred Reading Recovery teachers and had read just about everything that had been written about Reading Recovery and its history. I further learned that the original nomination had come in consultation with Angela Jaggar and Trika Smith-Burke of New York University. They had themselves been nominated for the implementation of Reading Recovery in New York City, and had referred the nomination to the national and international milieu.

I provide these details because they are evidence of the local impact of Reading Recovery everywhere it has come to exist. Marie Clay is a true pioneer in all of the ways detailed in the many articles in this book. But even more import — she has made it possible for thousands of people to be pioneers in their countries, states or provinces, and in their home towns. The award is given to people who have made a difference. Clay's 'making a difference' has been magnified by all of the pioneers she has empowered.

Marie, Gay Su Pinnell, and Charlotte Huck, with Evelyn Lucky, Associate Superintendent, and Jim Hyre, Superintendent of the Columbus Public Schools, during the mid-eighties.

Let's explore the roots of this award. Of course, its history goes back to Clay's landmark research in the 1960s when she studied 100 children in such detail and made groundbreaking observations. But my own history goes back not quite so far. In 1973, Moira McKenzie, my fellow graduate student, was browsing in a London book store and came across a little book called *Sand*. At the time, she was looking for a way of assessing young children's understandings about literacy. *The Early Detection of Reading Difficulties: A Diagnostic Survey* (later *An Observation Survey of Early Literacy Achievement*) was exactly what she was looking for. McKenzie was an unusual graduate student. In her fifties, she had had a long and very distinguished career as a teacher and headmistress in schools in England. The school she developed was the focus of investigations by professors Martha L. King and Charlotte Huck of Ohio State University. They were interested in the curriculum that was prominent in England at the time, and headmistress McKenzie's school was a prime example. McKenzie soon became interested in research and came to Ohio State as a graduate student. Her interest was in young children's literacy learning and Clay's work offered new and brilliant insights. Faculty and graduate students at Ohio State found Clay's research exciting, and soon everyone was reading and rereading *The Patterning of Complex Behaviour*, which figured prominently in my own essays for my doctoral candidacy examination.

Professors Martha King and Charlotte Huck brought Clay to Ohio State several times and they became fascinated with Reading Recovery, particularly the professional development for teachers. Together, they began to seek the funds needed to implement the early intervention effort in the United States. They enlisted my services as a former graduate student. None of us could have predicted the ultimate outcomes of our efforts.

In 1981, we all went to Auckland for the South Pacific Reading Conference. Charlotte and Martha were keynote speakers. They had arranged for me to do a session on the data from my dissertation. The conference was excellent, of course, and I attended many sessions, including one delivered by Marie Clay. The session was absolutely packed, with many people turned away. I was lucky to get in! It was puzzling to me that so many participants were from New Zealand. In Ohio, participants would avoid 'local' professors in favour of those 'outside experts' that they seldom got to hear. I asked the person next to me why she thought so many New Zealanders were struggling to get into this session. She replied that, 'We do not get to hear her often enough.' That communicated to me the value that Clay's countrymen place on her work — and that is ratified by the bevy of awards and the profound respect that have come her way.

The serious purpose of my first trip to New Zealand was to find out about Reading Recovery. We had already produced the draft of a proposal to the US federal government (with excellent prospects) for the implementation of Reading Recovery in combination with some classroom initiatives. The proposal was not complete, but our plan was to use Clay's writing as a basis and go from there. Charlotte, Martha and I interviewed many of the members of the first national Tutor training class in New Zealand. We looked at data. We heard detailed reports of the year of training. We looked at the rigorous design for implementing Reading Recovery within the national system of New Zealand.

Close to the end of this experience, our department chair called me and I took the call around 9 p.m. New Zealand time. I told him to throw the proposal in the waste bin. We were starting over. We had learned something about the complexity of intervention that would serve us well over the next 20 plus years. This event holds a lesson today for policy makers, who are seeking approaches that have been 'proved by' or are 'based on' research. We were learning this: *If you want to achieve the results of innovations, then you must implement them with integrity.* We examined as many aspects of Reading Recovery as we could; it was more than a way of teaching children. It was an intervention in the *system* and a powerful professional development programme for teachers. We talked at length with Clay, Watson, and the first Tutor group. Determined to implement Reading Recovery with integrity and to test the results, we went back to OSU to raise the funds for an implementation. It took until September 1984, when we brought Marie Clay and Barbara Watson to Columbus, Ohio, to train the first group of leaders who would set in motion Reading Recovery.

Let's move to a decade later. By the time the Dana Foundation selected its awardees, Reading Recovery was operating in 42 states, the District of Columbia, and four Canadian provinces. More than 5000 teachers at 300 sites had taken the training, and Reading Recovery reached more than 30,000 children in North America that year. The Charles A. Dana Foundation presented the award to Marie for 'helping tens of thousands of previously "low-achieving" first grade students in the United States master the skill of reading'. Of course, Marie Clay did not call reading '*a* skill'. Her theory encompassed the vast complexity of the act of reading. Further, Clay's work signalled a shift in philosophy from a 'deficit' view of learning

Marie, Gay Su Pinnell and the other awardees at the presentation of the 1993 Dana Foundation Awards, with David Mahoney (centre), the President of the Board of the Charles Dana Foundation.

common to remedial programs then and even now. The Reading Recovery system recognises and uses the knowledge that the child already has as a launching point for learning more.

Today, close to 100,000 children per year are served in Reading Recovery in the United States, and that is in addition to all of the children served in Canada, Australia, Bermuda, England, Ireland and New Zealand. This early intervention effort has been reconstructed in Spanish, French and Danish. The results tell a success story for many thousands of children. But the road has not been easy.

In the United States, Reading Recovery has been soundly attacked over the last 20 years (Schmitt, Askew, Fountas, Lyons and Pinnell, 2005). Why would something so cost effective and so beneficial to children come under attack? The answer lies in the competition that is foundational to education in the United States and perhaps in other countries. Publishing companies compete for sales; professors compete for grants and appointments. Let's be clear about the position of Reading Recovery. It is not a commercial venture. Reading Recovery has received a service mark '®' from the United States government and a similar service mark exists in all other countries, but it is not a business. It is rooted in schools and teacher preparation institutions. Clay has granted royalty-free permission for all sites that meet the standards of Reading Recovery (specified for each country).

Reading Recovery is an intervention with integrity; and protecting and assuring that integrity has been the pioneering work of educational leaders in local places across the world. When school districts implement it, they know that there are standards to meet but that if they do, they will have a high quality intervention with results. Of course, with thousands of implementations there are some alterations across the world; but, in general, Reading Recovery has been implemented with remarkable fidelity. In this case, fidelity means much more than the superficial aspects. It means that teachers participate in a full year of training during which they teach children behind a one-way glass, observed by their peers. They engage over the year in deep discussions of their detailed observations of children's reading and writing behaviours and, even after the end of the initial year, they participate in ongoing professional development as long as they are associated with Reading Recovery.

In the United States, this depth was and still is unique and unprecedented. Ten or 15 years ago, professional development typically consisted of a session or a few sessions given by an 'expert' who was selected by school district central office personnel. Teachers sometimes had a choice, but often were required to attend. There might be one day a year of released time, but often sessions were held after school on an 'early release' day. The prospect of a year of training plus ongoing professional development was astounding. While professional development is not at the level it should be in the US, many more long-term efforts are being attempted today. In addition, professional development for teachers often focuses on observation of children's reading and writing behaviours. Reading Recovery has contributed substantially to this change over time.

In 2007, Reading Recovery was recognised as meeting the 'gold standard' by the federal government (see *whatworksclearinghouse.org*). Reading Recovery works. We hope that it will expand in the US as it is in many other countries. But in a way, it is not so important how widespread Reading Recovery becomes or how it is regarded. The Charles A. Dana Award was an early recognition that Clay's achievements were changing the educational landscape in the United States. Her research, along with the example of Reading Recovery, has informed the thinking of a generation of teachers and researchers. Most profoundly, her work has enabled struggling young readers to make accelerated progress, illustrating that every child has the potential to become literate, with all that implies for the future. As a result:

- Teachers have powerful tools to help them observe and analyse the reading and writing behaviours of children.
- Early intervention and prevention efforts are valued and implemented.
- Children's strengths are noticed and recognised as the avenue for helping them learn more.
- Teachers engage in collegial dialogue that helps them solve problems relative to the children they teach.
- Professional communities of learning are created so that teachers become lifelong learners.
- Even the lowest achievers in reading are seen as learners with great potential.

Two words stand out in the Dana Award ceremony: *achievement* and *pioneering*. Achievement is certainly documented by all of the chapters in this book, but I like *pioneering* better. A pioneer is a person who goes before, preparing the way for others. In the United States, children study pioneers as individuals who went to the frontier in the Westward Movement, but a large number of teachers now see this New Zealander as a pioneer in literacy research and teaching.

Reference

Schmitt, Maribeth C., Askew, Billie J., Fountas, Irene C., Lyons, Carol A. and Pinnell, Gay Su. 2005. *Changing Futures: The Influence of Reading Recovery in the United States*. Columbus, Ohio: Reading Recovery Council of North America.

Marie, Maribeth, Metacognition, Margaritas, and Memories

Maribeth C. Schmitt

*Center Director, Jean Adamson Stanley Professor of Literacy,
Purdue University Center for Literacy Education and Research*

This is a story about my journey in developing an endearing friendship with Marie Clay. The first time I met Dame Marie Clay was when I was in my field year as a Trainer. She attended a Trainers meeting in Arizona to work with us on her new book, *Reading Recovery: A Guidebook for Teachers in Training* (1993). I was in awe of her for the entire day, just listening to her answer questions and discussing the content. She was being considerably more tentative in her responses than I had expected. During my training and even in my first year in the field, I was still operating on the conception of the rigidity I believed characterised the teaching of Reading Recovery. When I tried to at least look like a Reading Recovery teacher when working with a child, I continually heard (in my training year) or said (in my field year), 'Where is *that* in the *Guidebook?*'

So in that Trainers meeting in fall 1993, I was sitting and listening and trying to control my utter amazement: 'I cannot believe I'm in the same room as Marie Clay', and gradually, 'She seems like a really nice, friendly lady.'

I had the opportunity to sit next to her at dinner that evening and had hoped to get to know her. I didn't know which subject to broach; should it be personal or professional? Should I ask her to sign my *Guidebook* at the dinner table? Finally, near the end of the dinner, I spoke, but all I could muster was 'Are you enjoying your food?'

A few years later I arranged for her to come to Indiana to conduct an implementation visit with the Reading Recovery stakeholders in the state. Such a visit is intended to promote awareness of and the solving of implementation issues. We began communicating via faxes and email to orchestrate all of the logistics of the visit. It was very straightforward question-and-answer communication, but I was so excited to be corresponding with her. At one point, it became obvious there was a communication problem. She politely suggested that I should already know the answers to the questions I was repeatedly asking. Apparently one of her faxed responses to my long list of questions had gone astray (months later found to be attached to a fax to someone else in the college). I wasn't making a very good impression at this point.

To get her to Purdue for this meeting, I had to pick her up in Chicago, where she had worked with Illinois teachers before her trip to Indiana. Marie and I, and

Marie Clay and Maribeth Schmitt holding the resolution from the Indiana General Assembly to honour Marie's contributions to children's literacy programmes around the world.

two of my Illinois Teacher Leader friends, Bobbie Severing and Carolyn Sorsen, stopped at a Mexican restaurant for dinner. The waiter was very entertaining, really funny, and convinced us we should have margaritas with our dinners. We were laughing and joking around when right in the middle of a conversation about some informal topic, Marie turned to me and said, 'I have wanted to ask you if you consider "metacognition" to include that the learner needs to be able to know about and talk aloud about the strategy or whether that type of knowledge wasn't necessary.'

This theory-related question came out of nowhere! So we proceeded to have this great theoretical discussion regarding our opinions on the various aspects of metacognition in a Mexican restaurant, drinking margaritas. I remember feeling honoured that she wanted to discuss this construct with me, but I knew from her writings that she was sceptical about the topic and also that we didn't necessarily agree about it. It was also apparent that she had been wondering about my take on the construct. It goes without saying that we continued to discuss metacognition in a variety of ways over the next 14 years, but it was this first instance that broke the communication barrier and made me realise that she not only was fun to be around but also respected me as a professional too and that I didn't have to be so scared of her. Perhaps it was the margaritas?

During the implementation visit we rushed her down to the Indiana State House in Indianapolis 60 miles (about 100 km) away late one afternoon, so the Indiana General Assembly's House of Representatives could honour her with a resolution for her considerable contribution to children's literacy around the world. This was all the work of our state representative Sheila Klinker, who is an adamant supporter of Reading Recovery. She really wanted this to happen, so in a flurry of activity she was able to arrange for it to happen right before a late afternoon break in their session. Gay Su Pinnell from Ohio State was with us as an observer at the implementation visit, along with Purdue Teacher Leader Tammy Younts and site coordinator Deborah Dillon among others. We'll never forget the sight: there was state representative Klinker standing in front of the House of Representatives, ceremoniously reading the proclamation aloud with Dame Marie Clay standing by her side while our legislators were carrying on side conversations, and flipping rubber bands, like children who had just been told to sit quietly while their teacher spoke to someone who had come to the door! We were so, so embarrassed. Didn't they know who she was? But we all went to dinner at a nice restaurant afterwards and laughed about the scene.

At the end of the implementation visit, I drove Marie to the spring Trainers meeting in Dearborn, Michigan in my little black sports car. For five hours we talked, laughed, giggled, and really got to know each other well — no business or theoretical discussions; it was all personal information. This is when I learned that Marie lived at the Chi Omega house during her postdoctoral fellowship at the University of Minnesota. She had her wedding reception on the front lawn. Well, what do you know: I was a Chi Omega at Purdue back in the 1960s! I heard about her children, grandchildren, great-nieces and -nephews. We had a wonderful trip and our friendship was growing steadily. I was learning that although Marie was a world-renowned scholar, she was very much a delightful woman with a great sense of humour and a genuine interest in others.

Later, I proposed that the College of Education consider Marie for an honorary degree. In December of 2002 Purdue University bestowed an Honorary Doctor of Education on Dame Marie M. Clay of Auckland, New Zealand. Many things fell into place to make this more than just the bestowing of a prestigious academic degree, which is, of course, a remarkable scholarly award by itself, but because of Marie's unselfishness and genuine understanding that she is supposed to be 'shared', many stakeholders had the opportunity to interact with her and, as always, everyone benefited.

President Martin Jischke with Marie Clay, Tammy Younts, a Teacher Leader, Sarah Mahurt, director of Literacy Collaborative, and Maribeth Schmitt, director of the Center for Literacy Education and Research, at the awarding of Marie's honorary doctorate at Purdue.

At Purdue University, honorary degrees are awarded at only the spring graduation, where there are four different ceremonies during the weekend and approximately four honorary degrees are awarded at each ceremony. However, Marie's doctor advised against travel at that time and Marie had to decline the invitation from Purdue's president Martin Jischke. In an unusual move, the president said that if Dame Marie could come to Purdue in December for the winter commencement, he would make an exception and award the degree at that time. That decision set into motion many things that ultimately afforded many others to meet and interact with Marie. Many were acting like I did in my first interactions with her.

On Friday afternoon, the College of Education held a lovely reception in honour of its recipient of an honorary doctoral degree. That evening, we held a dinner at then Teacher Leader Tammy Younts' home for all of the Reading Recovery Teacher Leaders and Literacy Collaborative literacy coordinators who attended the reception.

As an example of her understanding that she must be 'shared' with others, she suggested that she could work with nearby Reading Recovery teachers and Teacher Leaders, as well as our project's literacy coordinators while she was here. So, on Saturday morning, we held a professional development workshop on campus, followed by an informal luncheon served at my home. It was a very informal opportunity for teachers, Teacher Leaders and literacy coordinators to interact with her. I noticed many of them were shy about speaking with her. I could relate. She loved my dog Alexandra, a shih-tzu who was not at all impressed by her scholarly accomplishments. She just thought she was a nice, friendly lady, who was happy to let her sit on her lap.

On Saturday evening, we attended a dinner at a literacy faculty member's home with the faculty and administrators from the college. It was another good chance for people to get to know her. Purdue President Martin Jischke and his wife invited her to the holiday party they hold for the upper level administration and Board of Trustees every year. I attended as her escort. The very formal dinner had a seating chart and Dame Marie Clay was seated next to the president. President Martin Jischke is a man who requires data, data and more data to be impressed with anything! He had often pressed us for details concerning how cost effective it was to work with one child at a time. Marie and Martin had a spirited conversation throughout dinner and I knew that she had straightened him out on the issue and he never mentioned it to us again during his visits to the college. I'm quite sure she changed his perceptions on several important matters that evening. It was very fortuitous because if she had come to the spring commencement, she would not have had the opportunity to interact with the Purdue president so extensively.

One of the most fascinating things that I learned about Marie from this experience is that these honours don't mean anything to her, but she knows they mean something to Reading Recovery in the university's eyes and she accepts them mostly for the Trainer — almost as a favour. Can you imagine reaching a level in your scholarly life, near the pinnacle of your academic career, being awarded such a high honour and accepting the honour in part as just a favour to the leadership of Reading Recovery in that state?

That's what it's like to be Marie Clay. God bless her. I miss her very much. I lost my beloved mother in winter that year and Marie in spring. It was difficult to lose two of the most influential women in my life in such a short time span.

Thank you, Marie, for being a nice, friendly lady. You were an amazing woman and I feel very fortunate to have been your friend.

Reference

Clay, M.M. 1993. *Reading Recovery: A Guidebook for Teachers in Training.* Auckland: Heinemann.

Adventures Above the Arctic Circle: Marie Clay Visits Reading Recovery in Alaska

Margaret Ann (Peg) Gwyther
Retired Reading Recovery Teacher Leader

It was spring of 1997 in Barrow, Alaska. The temperature had warmed to a balmy –15°F (–26°C) degrees and we'd already had a couple weeks of days exceeding 20-plus hours of light. The ocean ice-pack was still firmly attached to the shore and preparations for spring whaling were under way. Family ice cellars (dug into the frozen ground somewhere close to a door into the house) had been cleaned out of winter meat to make space for the fresh catches of summer. Kayaks, wooden freight sleds and snowmobiles were cleaned, packed, fuelled and stood ready in the front yards of numerous houses. Everyone was anxiously waiting for the first sighting of returning whales.

While students and teachers were still in school, it wouldn't be for many more weeks. With the return of the sun and eminent whaling season, spirits were high and villagers waited with much anticipation. However, for those of us in Reading Recovery, all the local excitement meant little when we compared it to the fact Marie Clay would soon arrive to participate in a week-long visit to the Reading Recovery Distance Delivery Pilot Project. The broadcast was from the North Slope Borough School District (NSBSD) technology classroom to the seven other village school sites all located above the Arctic Circle and distributed across 88,000 square miles (over 2 million hectares) of frozen tundra.

The project was conceptualised and designed as a pilot in cooperation with the Ohio State University as an opportunity to determine the feasibility of training Reading Recovery teachers in semi-isolated areas using interactive audio and video technology. Marie herself was coming to observe the process first hand. She was especially interested in the quality we were able to provide related to course instruction, behind-the-glass lessons, reflective discussions and the discontinuation assessment of students.

Two days after her arrival, we gathered in the distance delivery classroom in preparation for the one and only class Marie would have the opportunity to observe. The classroom was filled with five times the number of people usually in attendance. In addition to the six Reading Recovery teachers registered in the class, there were 14 local Ilisagvik College education students and their professor who joined us specifically to meet Marie Clay and learn more about Reading Recovery.

As each village signed onto the network, we had a brief round of introductions and greetings. Within 20 minutes we began the first behind-the-glass lesson. Fifteen minutes into the lesson the entire system was hit with sunspots, causing it to 'go down' thus ending our connection and any ability to communicate. This was not the first time during the year lessons came to an abrupt and complete halt due to natural or mechanical disruptions. However, it was probably the most inopportune time imaginable. In response to requests, and with Marie's encouragement, I led an information and discussion session about Reading Recovery in our local classroom while technicians frantically worked to regain connection. With an hour remaining in our course session, the connections did return. As it happened, during the down time, the children being taught in the distant Inupiat villages had to leave school and go home.

Marie had several opportunities to observe my coaching of lessons taught locally at Barrow Elementary, yet one of her most enjoyable interactions with an Inupiat child came just prior to her surprise dogsled ride. After attiring herself in full Inupiat outdoor clothing of atigi (coat) and mukluks (boots), she was assured by the young daughter of the musher the ride was nothing to cause fear and gave her a few tips on how to behave on the ride (photograph on page 244). The child's tips failed to include that in order to reach the trail, the sled would drop off a foot-high (30 cm) ledge of ice within seconds of her father releasing the dogs to run. This drop caught Marie by surprise and jolted her back, making the entire ride a painful attempt to shift position on the sled cushions in order to protect her back from the numerous bumps caused by travelling over uneven snow and ocean ice.

Marie's 'mush' around the perimeter of the village and out onto the ice pack of the Chukchi Sea in the Arctic Ocean was to be very memorable. Each of her remaining days in Barrow ended with a long soak in a hot bath. Sled dogs live to pull sleds, but never once did we think to ask Marie if she wanted to take a ride. One minute she was getting instructions from a six year old and the next she was flying across the ice with nowhere near enough cushions in her sled.

Expanding Perception, Sharpening Focus: Reflections on the Influence of Marie Clay

Noel K. Jones

Reading Recovery Trainer Emeritus, Associate Professor of Language and Literacy Emeritus, University of North Carolina, Wilmington

My first meeting with Marie Clay occurred in a hotel kitchen following a Reading Recovery conference. I was an outsider to Reading Recovery, a guest seeking to find a way to bring my university into Reading Recovery and to receive training as a Trainer. I had written to Marie two years previously when I began enquiring about her work, so I didn't expect her to remember me, but when I was introduced by name, she remembered my letter to her when she was in England, and she wished me well in my efforts to bring Reading Recovery to North Carolina.

Clarity of memory and an interest in other people were hallmarks of Marie Clay's personality, as I was to learn when I met her again during my year of training and then several more times over the years of my work in Reading Recovery. Recollections of personal interactions with Marie brought home to me many other aspects of her personality and her genius.

When we were in training, we were convinced that there were right answers to many of the issues and questions that arose during our teaching and training experiences. I remember a heated discussion after I had taught a lesson behind the glass for my colleagues. My book introduction was criticised because I had done something that was not listed among the procedures in *Early Detection of Reading Difficulties* (a previous Reading Recovery text). Marie was visiting our training class at the time, so I audaciously put the question to Marie whether my procedure was inappropriate. My memory of the experience is that Marie resolved the issue so that neither I nor my critics felt either vindicated or in the wrong.

Marie resisted requests for right answers about teaching procedures and many other issues. I recall another Trainer meeting at which we asked her to resolve an issue of coding running records. There was disagreement about the interpretation of self-corrections one group insisting that they must result from the child's notice of visual information (letters and words) causing the child to revise his or her response. Marie did not give us an absolute answer. Instead, she helped us understand more of the theory of children's early reading processing so that we could work out possibilities and be flexible in our thinking about what the child might be doing that brought about a self-correction. Marie's example, as a researcher and as an analyst, helped me establish a pattern of resolving teaching issues through close observation of the child's functioning, reconsideration of relevant theory, and hypothesis formation followed by further observation of teaching interactions.

Marie was always helpful to others in their thinking, writing, and implementation decisions. I remember submitting a draft article to Marie for her suggestions during her visit to my state to consult with administrators about Reading Recovery implementation. She took time to read and make notes on my draft even during the busy schedule of this implementation visit.

Marie's help was always given in the spirit of working alongside others in solving issues and concerns within Reading Recovery. She never acted as the person who had all the answers. She would consider what others proposed, think about the issue from many perspectives, and if she saw something that might have been overlooked, she made a suggestion or asked a question that led others to expand their awareness. She was always very humble in the way she dealt with such situations.

I remember working on the development of a Code of Ethics for Reading Recovery Trainers and trying to gain consensus on a much-revised draft from all the Trainers working as a committee of the whole. Marie, as a visitor, sat beside me and helped record revisions as I tried to guide discussion and contribute to the discussion. She participated as a working member of the group, but somehow I believe that the process of receiving suggestions, considering their import and limitations, and accepting or rejecting them proceeded in a more orderly manner just through her presence and the way in which she contributed to the task herself.

The opportunity for repeated interactions with a theorist and thinker of Marie's calibre was a rare and valuable experience for me, as for all of us in Reading Recovery. It was not the same as taking a class from a professor recognised as a leader in his or her field. My contacts with Marie were less frequent and much more limited than a class experience, but they extended over several years rather than one or two semesters. Meanwhile, my colleagues and I were avidly reading Marie's writing, and we were absorbed in our work with early literacy issues over this span of time — issues of teaching children; teaching issues shared with teachers and administrators; and implementation issues involving schools, school systems, regions, and universities.

These contacts with Marie, though infrequent, shaped my thinking in ways that a classroom or course experience usually cannot do. Sometimes these interactions resulted in the introduction of new ideas — things never before considered. More often, however, the effect was more subtle. A brief comment or a few words from Marie would lead to a new perspective on an unresolved issue or a revision in the way I might approach a problem or subject in terms of either thinking or decision-making. Over time, the effect was more profound than a course experience, or possibly even the experience of an entire degree programme.

Changes in my teaching as I worked in Reading Recovery parallel the changes in my thinking over the period of time that I had opportunities to interact with Marie Clay personally as well as with her writings. Learning to teach effectively requires a combination of theoretical understanding and practice — along with the communication skills, organisational skills and attitudes one would expect of an experienced teacher. I had studied theory quite extensively before I entered Reading Recovery training, and Marie's work extended the depth and specificity of my knowledge of reading and writing processes and about how literacy develops during childhood. In addition, I was introduced to new ideas that resonate with Marie's theoretical stance, including the writings of writers such as Bruner, Cazden, Stanovich, Tharp and Gallimore, Vygotsky, Vellatino, Wood and many others.

However, extensive experiences with teaching in Reading Recovery played at least an equal if not a more significant role in changing me as a teacher, and perhaps as a thinker, than the study of theory or the classroom study of teaching procedures. Everyone entering Reading Recovery — as a teacher, as a Tutor or Teacher Leader (one who trains teachers), or as a Trainer (one who trains Tutors or Teacher Leaders) — must teach children, not only during the initial training year but throughout their tenure in Reading Recovery. In addition to direct teaching of children, I observed and participated in hundreds of demonstration lessons during Reading Recovery training classes (lessons in which a teacher and child have a lesson behind a one-way screen while class members on the other side observe and engage in discussion while the lesson is in progress), and I observed hundreds of lessons as I visited teachers and Teacher Leaders at their schools. On more than 35 occasions I was the teacher behind the glass and my lessons were the subject of discussion both during and after the teaching experience.

Changes occurred gradually, over time, as intense involvement with teaching and the study of Marie's ideas caused me to confront and address subconscious ideas and attitudes that affected my teaching. I believe I understood intellectually the model of teaching inherent in Reading Recovery procedures. However, for some time, my teaching was not always consistent with this model.

At times, my focus during lessons was too narrow. On one occasion during our year of study at Ohio State, a colleague observed my teaching and recorded my teaching prompts. I was asking the child to attend primarily to visual information (letters, words and sounds) which was inappropriate, especially for a child early in his series of lessons. I understood the idea of balanced prompting and the idea of developing the child's strategic activity of searching for information, but my teaching was not consistent with what I understood intellectually.

Another revealing but embarrassing incident during my training year occurred when a little boy was reading the book *The Merry-Go-Round*. After several pages telling who got on the merry-go-round ending with 'The crocodile got on', the plot now shifts and the other animals take leave. When he came to the page that says, 'The tiger got off', the child stopped and said disgustedly, 'Ain't no tiger 'fraid of no crocodile!' and I was jolted to think, 'Oh, so that's what that story's about!' I was paying so much attention to how the boy was reading the words that

I didn't attend to the meaning. He was a better reader than I was because my focus was far too narrow.

The teaching procedures in Reading Recovery are based upon a model of teaching as assisted performance — the child's processing and problem-solving are assisted by the teacher in areas that he or she does not yet control, with the aim of developing as quickly as possible an inner control that enables independent reading. If a teacher is working from a different model of teaching, for example, word learning through drill and practice, or word learning through corrected performance (teacher correction of every error), struggling learners will not develop this independent inner control. Using myself as an example, it seemed to take considerable time, experience, feedback and interaction to allow me to see that I was still influenced by more teacher-controlling models of teaching. Clarifying one's vision of oneself — expanding one's focus to wider considerations — takes time, intensive engagement and observation, reflective analysis, and discussion with others.

My personal contacts with Marie Clay worked in much the same way as my experiences with teaching in Reading Recovery — they allowed an accumulation of small insights over time, leading to an expanded focus on many issues related to early literacy and the prevention of reading failure. In retrospect, one thing that amazes me is the manner in which Marie interacted with others. We considered her a guru; and others outside of Reading Recovery accuse Reading Recovery personnel of being a cult, but Marie never acted like a cult leader — quite the opposite. Her ideas were based firmly on reliable and valid research, but she was tentative in her adherence to theoretical positions (new research and evidence may be coming along suggesting new directions); she made suggestions rather than giving pointed advice; she was gentle and kindly in her manner rather than forceful or dogmatic; and she was always ready to expand her own focus by engaging with and listening to the ideas of other people, even those who at times had publicly disagreed with her.

In essence, then, Marie Clay's greatest influence upon me has been through the way that she went about her work. Her values, her integrity, her curiosity, her intelligence, her depth of understanding, her concern for others, and her unwavering commitment to the goal of helping all children learn to read and write successfully are just a few of her characteristics that begin to explain her influence and importance. Marie has broadened and extended my focus in many ways. She has made me a better educator, a better teacher and perhaps, in some small ways, a better person.

An Audience of One

Robert M. Schwartz

Oakland University, Rochester, Michigan, USA

RRCNA President, 2007–08

My mind was numb. I had stayed up most of the night before, mentally rehearsing the talk I'd just presented to Teacher Leaders at the 2001 Reading Recovery Institute in San Diego. Fatigue was setting in. Could I regain the energy to present this new research review to another group in just five minutes? Then Marie walked in and sat in the front row! A surge of energy carried me through as I re-envisioned my presentation for this new audience of one.

It is amazing how a small change in context can produce such a large change in motivation. Marie's writings have motivated me for over half of my professional life. Those of us who knew Marie remember her as a friend, a mentor and the epitome of a scholar. I can't claim to be her close friend ... but she was my mentor. We shared more than a few meals across the years and met in the strange and varied contexts that bring Reading Recovery professionals together around the world. But these social occasions pale in comparison to the hundreds of hours spent pondering her professional voice, the voice I brought to life as I read and reread her writings over almost 20 years.

Unlike her social voice, Marie's professional voice was never easy to understand. My understanding was limited by my experience, but each child that I taught, each teacher or Teacher Leader that I worked with, helped me to better understand Marie. She presented a new perspective in each book, along with her new knowledge from observation and theory. She never promised a simple view of literacy learning and instruction. She knew this was complex learning and she challenged us to learn.

I learned best by speaking and writing about Marie's theory. I based one of my first and favourite Reading Recovery presentations on one sentence from *Becoming Literate: The Construction of Inner Control.* It happened to be the last sentence in the book: 'Literacy activities can become self-managed, self-monitored, self-corrected and self-extending for most children, even those who initially find transitions into literacy hard and confusing.' Now there's a sentence! I've happily spent the last 10 years exploring its implications. In 1997 I published my perspective on self-monitoring in *The Reading Teacher.* This exploration of Marie's theory of strategic activity related to monitoring, searching and self-correction continues to help early literacy teachers develop their understanding of these complex processes. I shared an early draft of this article with Marie and felt fortunate to benefit from her feedback.

As I explored the implications of these ideas, my next set of talks focused on teaching decisions. Marie consistently maintained that accelerated progress for the most at-risk children depended on knowledgeable teachers making complex decisions based on the individual strengths of the child. Marie wrote lots of powerful sentences that express this idea. My favourite might be this one from *Literacy Lessons Designed for Individuals: Part One* (see page 23, but it also appears in earlier versions of the Reading Recovery guidebooks): 'Acceleration depends upon how well the teacher selects the clearest, easiest, most memorable examples with which to establish a new response, skill, principle or procedure.'

Of course, making these decisions for a particular child is complex and not easily explained. I presented my understanding of this complexity in my 2005 *Reading Teacher* article, 'Decisions, decisions: Responding to primary students during guided reading'. When Marie included a table in her latest revision of Reading Recovery procedures, *Literacy Lessons Designed for Individuals: Part Two* based on my article, I felt honoured. I took this as a very personal confirmation from Marie that I've helped describe at least part of the complexity teachers face in making these critical teaching decisions.

My last meeting with Marie was at a Reading Recovery Trainers meeting in Columbus, Ohio in September of 2006. She gave Mary Anne Doyle and me an article by a developmental psychologist, Robert Siegler. The article came along with the suggestion that we read his work and write about the similarities between the 'microgenetic method' he describes and Marie's 30-year exploration of strategic processes in early literacy. If I could, I'd thank Marie for this gift, the gift of a new perspective to again engage with her voice.

It is hard to express the mixture of emotions those of us who knew Marie feel. The joy in having had her as a mentor and a friend, the loss in knowing she is no longer with us. I want to share an introduction I gave on one of Marie's visits to Michigan, which was originally published in *The Journal of Reading Recovery*, Marie Clay tribute issue (Fall, 2007). I think it pleased Marie and it provides a small reminder of all she has done for us.

Michigan Reading Recovery Conference
Lansing, Michigan, 13 November 2001

It is my pleasure this morning to introduce Dr Marie Clay.

To introduce you to the remarkable individual, I would like to follow Saint Exupery's advice in *The Little Prince*. He warns that when you tell grown-ups 'that you have made a new friend, they never ask you any questions about essential matters. They never say to you, "What does his voice sound like? What games does he love best? Does he collect butterflies?" Instead they demand: "How old is he? How many brothers has he? How much does he weigh? How much money does his father make?" Only from these figures do they think they have learned anything about him.'

I know you would want me to focus on essential matters. So, I won't tell you how old Marie is! And I won't bore you by reading a long list of the books and articles she has written, though I'm sure you know many of them very well. And I won't even talk about the data on the remarkable success of Reading Recovery in America and around the world. Though I don't think it is boring at all that in the last 15 years Marie's work has touched the lives of over a million children in this country.

Instead, let me focus on essential matters. You might like to know that Marie does indeed collect butterflies. Her butterflies are ideas, ideas related to literacy learning and teaching. She has come across these ideas in the strangest way — by actually observing children over time as they learn to read and write, and by observing teachers as they work with children over time to support the learning of the most at-risk children. She has recorded these observations in great detail and shared them with us in books like, *What Did I Write?*, *Observing Young Readers*, *Reading: The Patterning of Complex Behaviour*, and *The Early Detection of Reading Difficulties*. She continues to reflect, refine and interpret these ideas in light of current theory and practice in literacy education and her ongoing observations. She shares this analysis with us in recent titles such as *Becoming Literate: The Construction of Inner Control*, *By Different Paths to Common Outcomes* and, most recently, *Change over Time in Children's Literacy Development*.

The butterflies she has collected form the basis for Reading Recovery, the foundation of our work with children. But Marie would be the first to admit the collection is not complete and the organisation only tentative. She provides the model and the challenge to remain tentative in our work with children; to always test the effect of our teaching by observing how children respond; to confirm our tentative theories by looking for signs of increased independence and acceleration in our students' reading and writing.

Now I think you'd want to know what games does Marie love best. Surely one of her favourite games is politics — the politics of literacy and the politics of education. There have been lots of great researchers and theoreticians in education, but few who have had the impact of Dr Clay. Some researchers would transform literacy education by freeing teachers from the constraints of basal programmes to pursue more authentic literacy activities. Other theorists would promote literacy for all children by tightly controlling the phonetic structures in early reading materials and carefully scripting teachers' interactions with their class. Marie has taken a different path. She has strived to ensure that the most at-risk children have access to individual instruction by the most highly qualified literacy professionals.

None of us would be here today if Marie just collected butterflies and, like so many educators, ignored the political game. She has played the game at the local, regional, national and international level. She has developed her game strategies and adjusted them for different situations and contexts. In doing so, she has modelled for us how to advocate for what is essential.

Finally, I know you would want to ask, 'What does her voice sound like?' The tones I hear are those of concern, compassion and commitment. She is dedicated to making a difference in the lives of teachers and children. Her voice is making possible the equity of educational opportunity that has often been promised but seldom delivered to many of our most promising but at-risk children.

It is my great pleasure to introduce a new friend to some and old friend to many, Dr Marie Clay.

Marie Clay: A Brilliant and Visionary Mentor

Carol Lyons
Trainer Emeritus, The Ohio State University

Reprinted from the Fall 2007 *Journal of Reading Recovery* with permission of the Reading Recovery Council of North America

From her revolutionary dissertation 'Emergent Reading Behaviours' in 1966 to nationally and internationally acclaimed 2005 books *Literacy Lessons Designed for Individuals: Part One* and *Part Two*, throughout her years as a cognitive psychologist, university professor, teacher, Marie M. Clay has conducted research to better understand how children think and learn and how to effectively teach struggling students to read and write. Throughout her life, Marie read widely, listened carefully, and closely observed children and teachers at work. Because of her acquaintance with so many fields of study, she enabled us to enter the worlds of literacy, language, psychology, neuroscience, and education.

Marie Clay always seemed to be just ahead of the curve, writing about the systematic observation of young children's responses in classroom reading and writing in the first years of schooling, before such scrutiny became commonplace, and making emergent literacy and early intervention metaphors for quality educational practice before everyone else did. Marie's scholarship is extensive, and her influence on both the science of learning and literacy learning and the development of application for this science through Reading Recovery is immense.

Marie Clay impacted my life as a university professor, teacher and researcher in three fundamental ways. When I met Marie Clay in 1985, she asked me why I wanted to become a Reading Recovery university Trainer. I told her because I wanted to better understand how researchers such as Bruner and Luria influenced her thinking and development of Reading Recovery. She looked startled and asked why Luria? I explained that I read Luria's 1972 book *The Working Brain: An Introduction to Neuropsychology* while a doctoral student in neuroscience. During class one day, my professor commented that Marie Clay had applied Luria's theories of the working brain to discuss the reading processes in *Reading: The Patterning of Complex Behaviour* (1972) and writing process in *What Did I Write?* (1975). Marie said my professor was right, but she wanted to hear an insider's perspective about the contribution of Luria's theories of learning to Reading Recovery. I agreed to come up with some potential answers.

During my training year, I wrote many references to Luria's theories of the brain's working system that seemed to support the teaching procedures in *The Early Detection of Reading Difficulties* (1985). I also decided that in order to better understand and describe emergent working systems for reading and writing text, it would be best to teach first grade Reading Recovery children who were struggling the most. The first grade classroom teachers in my neighbourhood school agreed that the very hardest to teach Reading Recovery children were also classified learning disabled (LD), however, federal and district policy prohibited the placement of these children into an LD resource room until third grade. I started teaching Reading Recovery students classified at LD that year and continued to teach this population of students until I retired.

The following year, Marie and I met for several hours to examine and analyse the Reading Recovery 'LD' children's lesson records and audiotaped teacher–student conversations and behaviours that I had collected in 1985–86. It was a memorable experience. Using specific examples of children's processing and my responses, we discussed how and why Luria's model of the functional organisation of the brain supports Reading Recovery procedures. The data revealed that once the Reading Recovery children learned to integrate and coordinate the parietal (motor), occipital (eye) and temporal (ear) lobes of the brain, their processing and problem-solving while reading and writing improved greatly.

In those few hours of conversation with Marie, I saw an astute, analytic, flexible problem-solver at work, a very personable mentor who never made me feel uncomfortable or inadequate. Marie encouraged me to incorporate the ideas discussed and illustrated in Luria's functional organisation of the brain into the Ohio State University Reading Recovery theoretical and clinical coursework if I thought it would be helpful to Teacher Leaders as they worked with the most difficult to teach Reading Recovery students. I did.

The second way Marie influenced my life is related to the first. During our memorable meeting previously discussed, Marie gave me a draft copy of her 1987 article 'Learning to be Learning Disabled'. I immediately identified with Marie's position on learning disability so thoroughly argued in this article.

As a first through fourth grade classroom teacher and primary learning disability teacher for eight years in the 1960s and 1970s, I was part of the emergence and growth of the LD field. In my opinion, the history of the LD field was a series of different renditions of the same tune that says the problems of children with LD can be attributed to a defect within the children themselves. The policy to remove children who were struggling to learn to read from the classroom and place them in an LD resource room to receive extra help was becoming institutionalised. Moreover, there was an extensive body of research that documented the ineffectiveness of these programmes. Once labelled, children remained 'learning disabled' for a lifetime.

Marie's influential article gave voice and validity to support the idea that many children who are labelled 'learning disabled' are, in truth instructionally disabled. That is, they are children who have no neurological disorder at all, but who had a series of unfortunate experiences, usually inadvertent, before formal schooling or during their first years of schooling that interfered with their developing the neural networks to learn how to read and write.

Marie Clay's classic article made a huge impact on my thinking, research, and reason for wanting to teach this special population of Reading Recovery students. As I worked with the Reading Recovery 'LD' children during the next 20 years, I accumulated substantial evidence to document that Reading Recovery intervention prevents learning disability placement. The 1987 pilot study and follow-up study from a population of 110 children independently classified as learning disabled prior to Reading Recovery intervention was published in 1989 in the *Educational Research Service Spectrum*. I continued this line of research interest and writing for many years.

Finally, Marie's collective body of books and articles and my own research investigating struggling readers' learning and teacher learning has helped me to better understand how and why learning involves active individuals reorganising and constructing knowledge *and* that thinking and decision-making is always tentative. From her early days working and writing in New Zealand, Marie found ways to encourage and engage teachers in processes that further their thinking, adapt their beliefs, and foster a desire to teach struggling children differently.

Marie also taught us that in order for struggling readers to be successful, teachers must bring to bear their own intelligence, experience, knowledge and feelings in their teaching. They must develop into self-directing, enquiring, reasoning and attuned decision-makers. Marie gave teachers their professionalism and asked them to assume a decision-making role in regard to curriculum, instruction and the assessment of student progress. I hope we never lose that professionalism.

Marie Clay's pivotal role in my life culminated in the writing of *Teaching Struggling Readers: How to Use Brain-based Research to Maximize Learning* (2003), which I started writing after our day-long meeting in 1987. After reading a draft copy of this book, Marie said she was happy that I had finally pulled all these ideas together. I felt very honoured that she agreed to write the foreword to my book.

Marie Clay was the most curious and enquiring person I have ever met. She spent her life incorporating recent research and theories of learning from multiple disciplines to help us better understand literacy learning and how best to teach struggling students. At a time when she could have lived a life of leisure, Marie continued to revise and update her influential books. When I last talked to Marie on the phone, which was three weeks before she died, she said she had worked hard during the last several months to get her 'ducks in a row'. Marie was happy to have completed the revision of *The Record of Oral Language* and thrilled that the political struggles Reading Recovery had been facing in the US the last few years seemed to have ended with the release of the What Works Clearinghouse report that establishes Reading Recovery as an effective intervention based on scientific research.

Marie Clay was driven by the belief that people who thought they knew it all and had done enough research, reading and writing were fooling themselves. She was one of the great minds of the century and her thoughts will continue to be my greatest source of intellectual stimulation, inspiration and motivation to continue her work.

The Legacy of Marie Clay: Influencing Education in Manitoba

Irene Huggins

Western Canadian Institute of Reading Recovery

Marie Clay has been described in many ways, as an outstanding scholar, eminent researcher, and even a genius. She won numerous awards for her research, published work and for the influence of both on literacy instruction. Her colleagues and friends recognised her contributions to literacy education internationally in two books, *Stirring the Waters: The Influence of Marie Clay* (Gaffney and Askew, 1999) and *Changing Futures: The Influence of Reading Recovery in the United States* (Schmitt, Askew, Fountas, Lyons and Pinnell, 2005). A modest Marie Clay (2004) also acknowledged her contributions to educational thinking in her National Reading Conference address, *Simply by sailing in a new direction you could enlarge the world.* However, her comments were focused on what is possible for the lowest achieving students. This tribute will concentrate on how she enlarged the world for both Reading Recovery and classroom teachers and, as a result, influenced education in a broader context.

The influence of Marie Clay's theories on the attitudes and beliefs of teachers is evident in Manitoba schools. Classroom teachers were introduced to her ideas when schools began the implementation of Reading Recovery in 1994 and Reading Recovery teachers began exploring her theoretical constructs as they taught children in individual lessons and in classroom programmes. The teachers in the first Reading Recovery In-service Course offered in Manitoba were challenged to consider alternative positions on key ideas that changed their thinking and planning for classroom instruction. In this tribute, I want to highlight three of Marie Clay's ideas that I believe contributed to these changes, altered the classroom programmes in fundamental ways, and contributed to better learning opportunities for all children. These ideas include the importance of early writing in literacy development; the importance of systematic observations of children's reading progress by taking records of continuous texts; and the consideration of what is possible for children when we raise our expectations. In this tribute I want to show how the changes in teachers' beliefs in these areas transformed classroom instruction in Manitoba schools.

Importance of early writing

One of the theoretical challenges for the first group of Reading Recovery teachers as they began the in-service course for teachers was to understand the contributions

176

of early writing in literacy development. As these teachers began teaching children in Reading Recovery, they included writing in the earliest lessons. This was a significant change in practice. Why was writing included as part of an intervention designed to teach young children to read? How would writing contribute to the students' learning of reading?

Marie Clay (2001) wrote that 'occasionally, even today in some education systems, writing is delayed a year and a half until reading is established; before that children are expected only to copy' (p. 12). This practice, which was common in Manitoba classrooms at the time, can be explained through a readiness theory (Sulzby and Teale, 2003). Teachers did not expect children to write until they were reading and as a result, young students were not given the opportunity to write. This created a 'narrow funneling of emergent literacy expertise' (McNaughton, 1999, p. 11) in which the activities provided for children were restricted by the beliefs and attitudes held about the teaching of literacy skills. Reading Recovery teachers began to question their assumptions about early writing and when it should begin. One of the teachers, Edwin Buettner, wrote in his article 'Lessons from Reading Recovery Lessons' (1996):

> I tended to give primacy to reading development, assuming that a solid basis in reading was almost sufficient for writing to 'happen'. I am now more convinced that reading and writing exist on a kind of a mutually scaffolding relationship and that one needs to support the other throughout various steps and stages of literacy growth and development. (p. 4)

If the lowest achieving students in Reading Recovery were able to write two or three long and complex sentences in lessons, why would we not expect the same from other children in the classroom?

The group of teachers continued to explore this concept by reading other works by Marie Clay: *Writing Begins at Home* (1987), *What Did I Write?*, (1975), *Becoming Literate: The Construction of Inner Control* (1991), *By Different Paths to Common Outcomes* (1998), and *Change over Time in Children's Literacy Development* (2001). The explanation of her theory of the contribution of early writing to literacy development and her examples of what to look for in early writing samples convinced the teachers that writing must be included as part of the literacy activities from the first days of schooling. In *What Did I Write?*, she included examples of young children's writing and 'looked beyond the forms to underlying principles such as linearity and recurrence and resisted treating the appearance of forms of writing alone as being indicative of development' (Sulzby & Teale, 2003, p. 306). Marie Clay provided a method for teachers to scrutinise the children's underlying conceptions and to make 'the children's difficulties a little more obvious' (Clay, 1975, p. 1). 'A guiding question to direct to sample of children's work is, "Which features of this extremely complex activity is this child attending to?" (Clay, 2001, p. 13). Armed with this knowledge, teachers could sharpen their observations and responses to children during writing events in the classroom.

Taking records of reading continuous texts

A second theoretical construct developed by Marie Clay that changed the education system in Manitoba was the idea that classroom teachers could and should be regularly monitoring the reading progress of young readers by taking records of reading continuous texts. Clay believed in the careful and systematic observation of children's literacy behaviours. She stated, 'What I like about observation is that I can watch the child at work, see something of the focus of his attention, watch him search for cues and confirmation. I can watch him solve a problem, sometimes showing his delight in a new discovery' (1993, p. 2). She went on to say, 'If we attend to individual children as they work, and if we focus on the progressions of learning that occur over time, such observations can provide feedback to our instruction' (Clay, 1993, p. 3).

Prior to the implementation of Reading Recovery in Manitoba, teachers of young children had to rely on standardised tests to assess young children's readiness to read or to assess learning. Occasionally, a few teachers administered informal reading inventories to assess children experiencing difficulty with reading or they asked the specialist teachers, resource teachers or reading clinicians to complete the assessments. The belief that the classroom teacher must carefully and systematically over time record and analyse the reading behaviours of students learning to read was an important concept.

With the introduction of the Running Records for classroom teachers, two aspects of reading instruction began to change. First, classroom teachers included little books as part of their reading instruction in place of the basal reading series. Second, the classroom teachers scheduled time to observe the students' reading of the little books in more systematic ways and they began to question their theories of reading.

During the analysis of the running records and the explanations of the information used and neglected in the reading, the teachers were forced to consider a theory of reading continuous text and they used their new theoretical understandings to inform their practice. This led to more reading and sharing of Clay's work. Teachers began reading and discussing *An Observation Survey of Early Literacy Achievement* (Clay, 1993), *Reading Begins at Home* (Butler and Clay, 1979), *Becoming Literate: The Construction of Inner Control* (Clay, 1991), and 'Introducing a New Storybook to Young Readers' (Clay, 1991).

Raising expectations

Marie Clay also introduced the teachers to the idea that they should expect accelerated progress for the lowest achieving students. 'In order to become an average-progress child, he will have to progress faster than his classmates for a time if he is to catch up to them. Acceleration refers to this increase in the rate of progress' (Clay, 2005, p. 22). The idea that the lowest achieving children could and must learn faster than their average peers was a radical concept. It was accepted practice at that time to either reduce the amount of content the low-achieving student had to learn or extend the amount of time required to master the tasks. This resulted in lower expectations for the students and ensured that they would not catch up with their peers. In addition, changes were made to the learning activities provided to these students. Instead of reading and writing texts, they often completed skill-based worksheets.

The Reading Recovery teachers in training had to learn that the lowest achieving students could learn faster than their average progress peers. This idea created the greatest dissonance for the Reading Recovery teachers. Buettner (1996), a reading clinician, talked about his challenges with this concept:

> I found it difficult to work with students without the explanatory concepts such as short-term memory, auditory blending, visual processing speed, and so on … I knew perfectly well why my Reading Recovery students were having difficulty, and I was most frustrated that I could not express it. I often wished I could refer the children to a reading clinician for confirmation of my diagnostic hunches. The most support I would get from my Teacher Leader and colleagues in training is the reassurance that the student will learn. (p. 2)

The students did learn, not with different methodology but by engaging in increased opportunities for reading and writing of continuous texts supported by an observant and informed teacher. Clay (2004) reported that:

> It has been one of the surprises of Reading Recovery that all kinds of children with all difficulties can be included, can learn, and can reach average-band performance for their class in both reading and writing achievement. Exceptions are not made for children of lower intelligence, for second language children, for children with low language skills, for children with poor motor coordination, for children who seem immature, for children who score poorly on readiness measures, or for children who have been categorised by someone else as learning disabled. (p. 8)

As these students began to improve their literacy skills in the Reading Recovery lessons, the classroom teachers observed changes in the students' achievement, confidence and independence. Many were becoming the most successful readers and writers in the class and classroom teachers wondered how they could increase the performance of the other students in the class. This relates to Marie's question, 'What is possible?', for children when we improve teaching and learning opportunities.

Conclusion
In the last 15 years, Reading Recovery has been implemented in more than 300 Manitoba schools, and teachers have been confronted with Clay's ideas. Learning and discussing these views has led improved learning opportunities for many students in the classroom and those included in Reading Recovery. Clay asked teachers to consider what was possible for the lowest achieving students and in the process changed educational opportunities for all. Her ideas were never presented in a prescriptive way, but rather in a style that showed her respect for the skills and

knowledge of teachers. She showed us if we ask the right questions, we can change the world. As Buettner said in the final words of his paper:

> I feel that my experience last year has opened my eyes to the ease with which one can become undisciplined in assisting learners who find the process of becoming literate a trying one that challenges their sense of competency and self-esteem. Reading Recovery teachers learn, just like their students, that learning to do something complex requires focused attention, clear and consistent guidelines, practice and the support of others. (1996, p. 5)

This is Marie Clay's legacy for Manitoba teachers and children. Her work will continue to challenge our thinking and practice for years to come. To those teachers who are not familiar with Clay's legacy, I challenge you to read and discuss her research and published works, and to consider what is possible for the children we teach.

Dianne Stuart, Marie and Irene Huggins.

References

Buettner, E. 1996. Lessons from Reading Recovery Lessons. *The Running Record*, Columbus, OH: Reading Recovery Council of North America.

Butler, D. and Clay, M. 1979. *Reading Begins at Home: Preparing Children for Reading Before They Go to School.* Portsmouth, NH: Heinemann.

Clay, M. M. 2005. *Literacy Lessons Designed for Individuals: Part One.* Auckland: Heinemann.

——. 1975. *What Did I Write?* Auckland: Heinemann.

——. 1987. *Writing Begins at Home: Preparing Children for Writing before They Go to School.* Auckland: Heinemann.

——. 1994. *Becoming Literate: The Construction of Inner Control.* Auckland: Heinemann.

——. 1991. Introducing a New Storybook to Young Readers in *The Reading Teacher* (1991), 45, 4:264–73.

——. (2004). Simply by sailing in a new direction you could enlarge the world. In C. Fairbanks, J. Worthy, B. Maloch, J. Hoffman, & D. Schallert. *53rd Yearbook of the National Reading Conference.* Oak Creek, WI: National Reading Conference, Inc.

——. 1993. *An Observation Survey of Early Literacy Achievement.* Portsmouth, NH: Heinemann.

——. 1998. *By Different Paths to Common Outcomes.* York, Maine: Stenhouse.

——. (2001). *Change over Time in Children's Literacy Development.* Portsmouth, NH: Heinemann.

Gaffney, J. and Askew, B. 1999. *Stirring the Waters: The Influence of Marie Clay.* Portsmouth, NH: Heinemann.

McNaughton, S. 1999. Developmental diversity and beginning literacy instruction at school. In J. Gaffney and B. Askew (eds), *Stirring the Waters: The Influence of Marie Clay.* (pp. 3–16). Portsmouth, NH: Heinemann.

Schmitt, M., Askew, B., Fountas, I., Lyons, C. and Pinnell, G. 2005. *Changing Futures: The Influence of Reading Recovery in the United States.* Worthington, OH: Reading Recovery Council of North America.

Sulzby, E. and Teale, W. 2003. The development of the young child and the emergence of literacy. In J. Flood, D. Lapp, J. Squire and J. Jensen (eds), *Handbook of Research on Teaching of English Language Arts* (pp. 300–13). Mahwah, NJ: Lawrence Erlbaum Associates Publishers.

Marie Clay: A Canadian Perspective

Dianne Stuart

Emeritus Trainer, President, Canadian Institute of Reading Recovery

'A leader takes people where they want to go. A great leader takes people where they don't necessarily want to go, but ought to be.' — Rosalynn Carter

Marie Clay was the consummate leader — brilliant, decisive, energetic, approachable, humble and inspiring. Marie had the courage to lead and the imagination to see new possibilities, She encouraged many educators to dream on a large scale about 'what could be possible', encouraging them to take on new learning, and to travel in new directions. Marie had a vision to make the world a better place and was able to encourage others to follow.

By being a good listener, Marie was a great problem-solver. Seeking to gain greater insights into what teachers and children were thinking and doing, Marie always took opportunities to talk with teachers, either individually or in a group. She felt that she learned more by listening than talking. People sought her company not only to extend their thinking and understandings but because she made everyone feel that they had something to offer her. In a conversation with a Canadian Teacher Leader, she demonstrated how greatly she valued others' opinions. Marie asked them how things were going. The Teacher Leader responded, 'You don't want to know', to which Marie replied, 'If I didn't want to know, I would not ask.' In the ensuing discussion Marie commented, 'As long as you continue in a state of enquiry, that is where you need to be.' For the Teacher Leader, those comments both reassured and reaffirmed the importance of their contribution.

Marie's dedication and commitment to others was evident in the number of times she left New Zealand to offer her support to Reading Recovery in Canada, as well as every other country with Reading Recovery. Since 1993 she made many trips to Canada, visiting Trainers, Teacher Leaders, teachers and children from coast to coast. A highlight was six weeks spent at the Ontario Institute for Studies in Education/University of Toronto where she was a visiting scholar, providing the class of Teacher Leaders in training that year with a very special opportunity. During that time, Marie co-taught a class with Dr Shelley Peterson, presented at the Toronto Reading Council inaugural meeting and worked with Reading Recovery, university and Ministry of Education personnel. An honorary founding member of the Toronto Reading Council, she selflessly refused an honorarium for presenting to the largest audience that has ever attended a conference hosted by this local council of the International Reading Association. Her talk swelled the initial membership and was instrumental in helping to launch the reading council.

Marie saw the importance of making Reading Recovery available for French-speaking children in Canada, a country with two official languages. With her invaluable guidance and support, Intervention preventive en ecture-ecriture/Reading Recovery is now available to French-speaking children in different provinces across the country.

Marie was a wonderful role model and mentor, always making herself available to us at meetings and conferences or by telephone. She had extraordinary faith in others and helped them believe they could do it! One could always count on her wise counsel. She had a wonderful way of eliciting information as she encouraged you to talk through the issues, providing constructive feedback, but letting you come to the final resolution. This was particularly helpful during the time of rapid expansion of Reading Recovery in Canada.

Always the scientist, Marie's acute observations were always enlightening. On one occasion while discussing the workings of the brain, she pointed out that she could observe from her house, cars entering a roundabout. In her notes for a talk in 2004, Marie wrote: 'I live in full view of a circular suburban roundabout. From my upstairs rooms I can look out at peak-hour traffic going to or coming from work. Four roads converge on a central circle, with eight lanes leaving the roundabout. In each vehicle the driver is making decisions that no other driver knows. The traffic flows based on road rules, courtesy, temper outbursts, cheeky me-first decisions; and occasionally metal crunches metal and police and ambulances arrive.' The complexity of the decision-making intrigued her. 'Somehow children entering school seem to get on a roundabout like this. At our bidding they drive quite well round and round the daily activities we provide. Some select the highway we want them to take. One or two take off in a strange direction but manage to rejoin the highway a little later [like a young reader who pauses] then goes back, reads again and says 'Oh! I see how it goes.' There are a few who slow down almost to a freeze position and refuse to make decisions.'

Marie decided that a driver had 12 different options when they entered the roundabout. How fascinated she was in trying to decide what 'led' to their ultimate decision. She had an inherent curiosity that drove her to ask questions and try new things. By asking these and other 'what if' questions, Marie has inspired the world.

On a personal level, all who got to know her enjoyed Marie's openness, friendliness and keen sense of humour. She liked being part of the group and was always a willing participant in any new adventure. While in Canada, Marie enjoyed travelling in the gondola to the top of the mountain in Whistler, British Columbia, a weekend at a lakeside cottage, searching for wildlife while being driven through Algonquin Park, walking under the falls at Niagara, enjoying the tides of Atlantic Canada or sitting in a Toronto pub with training Teacher Leaders after a class. Marie's enthusiasm for life was evident in her work and in her personal life. She always shared personal stories about family, a source of great pride.

Children were always Marie's priority. When a Canadian newspaper reporter told Marie that she must be so proud of what she had accomplished, Marie replied, 'You will be surprised by my answer: it is a start but not enough. There are still so many more children that need our support.'

Marie Clay was a truly remarkable person who touched and influenced more people than anyone will ever know. She was one of a kind. We are united in admiration, respect, and gratitude for what she has contributed to our lives and the world.

Personal Reflection about Marie M. Clay: Back Stories from Stirring the Waters

Janet S. Gaffney
University of Illinois at Urbana-Champaign

I will use some of the 'back stories' of the conceptualisation and development of *Stirring the Waters: The Influence of Marie Clay* as the backdrop of my reflection.

Marie's influence on the literacy learning and teaching of young children was legendary. Perhaps not so well known was her influence on literacy research. *Stirring the Waters* would be a festschrift, a collection of writings published in honour of a scholar, representing the breadth and depth of Marie's reach into the literacy research community. On hearing about the idea of a book in her honour for the first time, Marie's response was an emphatic 'No'. After some talk and time, however, Marie recanted. I would not characterise those early interactions as convincing Marie to let us move forward, as I do not believe Marie could be convinced to do anything that she did not want to do. Rather, I believe that she saw the potential value of the project to coalesce seemingly disparate researchers under a common umbrella.

Marie stipulated that the authors would present their research rather than writing about her. The international scope of the book was also important to Marie, as this was central to her professional mission. Finally, she requested not to be involved. Marie had a true sense of humility. As with *Stirring the Waters*, Marie was reluctant to be singled out for recognition. Over time I came to understand that Marie accepted her many prestigious awards and accolades as opportunities to forward the work for which she cared.

Every potential author that Billie Askew and I invited to write a chapter for *Stirring the Waters* responded with an emphatic and enthusiastic, 'Yes'. Each one understood Marie's request that they write about their own work and not about her, as they knew that Marie valued the influence of research above fame or personal influence. Billie and I felt enormously privileged to hear the stories of how each author's life and work intersected with Marie's, and, in some cases became the catalyst for the direction of their programmes of research. Billie and I wanted to find a way for authors to share the stories of their personal connection with Marie. We broke with the traditional brief biographies and invited each author to submit a brief (50–75 words) description of their connection with Marie. These personal nuggets in the Contributors' section convey the spirit of the book and I find myself rereading them to savour the acknowledgements of such cherished relationships.

We knew the book would not be complete without Marie's biography. We scoured websites and press releases and came up relatively empty-handed, except for a dated curriculum vitae. We turned to our friends at the National Reading

Recovery Training Centre in New Zealand, especially Ann Balintyne, and her colleagues, Christine Boocock, Blair Koefoed and Barbara Watson, to supply background information. We used the information to weave together Marie's professional journey. Knowing that nowhere previously had there been such a comprehensive history of Marie's career, we wanted Marie to have the opportunity to verify the information. The biographical tribute was nearly the undoing of the book. Marie's initial reaction was, 'No'. Billie and I, on the other hand, knew that a festschrift of Marie would not be complete without a review of her career. Given a few days of time and talk, Marie reluctantly relented. In retrospect, I think that her initial reaction was shock in seeing so much written about her life. Later, she understood the need for the piece to be in the book and with minor edits she allowed our tribute to move forward intact.

Interestingly, Marie talked very little about this publication with her family. Soon after her death her son, Alan, and daughter, Jenny, each took a paperback version from Marie's bookshelves. Jenny was not aware of the special leather-bound version until a few months later. She unearthed the leather version which Marie had carefully stowed away under a small side table in her lounge. It had been signed by every contributing author and was presented by Heinemann to Marie at the reception they sponsored for the 2000 National Reading Recovery Conference, which marked the fifteenth anniversary of Reading Recovery in North America.

The story of this book would not be complete without reference to Bill Varner, then an Acquisitions Editor at Heinemann. Bill listened to our 'quirky' ideas about author notes and worked with the title that to us represented what Marie most liked to do, *stir the waters*. He ran with our dreams of a cover that represented the expanding ripples of Marie's influence on literacy, learning, teaching and research.

Upon receipt, Marie sent a note that she read the book cover to cover and that she treasured each author's unique contribution. I did not know what she thought of our title until a few years later when she was invited to give a plenary speech at the 2003 National Reading Conference in honour of her Distinguished Scholar Lifetime Achievement Award and she quipped that she was 'stirring the waters, again' (Clay, 2004). In 2005, Marie presented the opening session at the National Reading Recovery and Classroom Literacy Conference in honour of the twentieth Anniversary of Reading Recovery in North America. Her talk was entitled *Stirring the Waters Yet Again* (Clay, 2005). As teachers, teacher educators and researchers continue to delve into Marie's body of work, she will stir the waters, again and again. Sometimes, one paragraph, one sentence or a phrase of Marie's has me see the world of literacy, teaching and learning in a whole new way. I am so, so grateful to have known Marie and to have her words to savour and challenge my thinking and teaching.

References

Clay, M.M. 2004. Simply by sailing in a new direction you could enlarge the world. In C.M. Fairbanks, J. Worthy, B. Maloch, J.V. Hoffman and D.L. Schallert (eds), *53rd Yearbook of the National Reading Conference* (pp. 60–66). Oak Creek, WI: National Reading Conference.

———. 2005. Stirring the Waters Yet Again. *Journal of Reading Recovery*, 4 (3): 1–10.

Reflections on Lessons Learned

Emily Rodgers

The Ohio State University, Associate Professor,
College of Education and Human Ecology

As I write this, it has only been about nine months since Marie Clay passed away so suddenly and unexpectedly in April 2007. With the passing of any cherished person, the longing to hear the person's voice only grows sharper as time goes on. Her email messages are still in my computer's inbox, turning up at unexpected moments usually when I'm in the middle of a search through my email, or when I reorder my sender list alphabetically to find a particular message. Now and then, when I come across one of Marie's emails, I open it and reread it to reconnect with Marie for a few moments.

This message, sent from Auckland in September 2006 just before her last visit to the US, charmed me when I read it:

> Dear Emily
> I've been to the hairdresser and I am almost ready to leave home at 4pm for my trip to USA. Thank you for all the arrangements — they look fine to me. I'll see you at the airport as you arranged.
>
> I do have a couple of personal requests. Do you think I might be able to visit Martha at some time — take her out for a meal perhaps like we did before? And I would like to buy some new reading glasses, no prescription required, just enlargement mimicking my current ones. Perhaps in Dublin if I go there early enough. Neither request is an imperative — don't go to any trouble over them.
> See you before long.
> Marie

Anyone who has met Marie Clay invariably came to comment on her humility. Her needs were as simple as the email message suggests: Can we pick up some new glasses if there's time? She did not want anyone to go out of their way, nor would she ever want to inconvenience anyone.

Marie preferred staying at someone's home rather than in a hotel room when she travelled. She could have commanded hefty speaking fees for the many keynote speeches that she gave at conferences but, as she told me once, she did not want to take money out of Reading Recovery. Nor did she receive payment when a school district implemented Reading Recovery, insisting instead that the licence to use Reading Recovery be made available on a royalty-free basis.

Her humility was obvious in other ways as well. I was a presenter at a conference in which the organisers invited each featured speaker to respond to the question, 'What are you most proud of?' Our responses were printed in the conference programme along with our photos and brief bios. I wrote something about bring proud that I had learned to ski, other people mentioned their children or a book they published. I chuckled out loud when I received my copy of the programme and I read Marie's response. Marie, who arguably had the most to be proud of, refrained from identifying anything, writing instead, 'My Presbyterian grandmother warned me that pride goeth before a fall.' Oh, I thought at the time, I wish I had thought of something like that! (Not the first time, I'm sure, that someone has wished that they had the same great idea that Marie did!)

Marie also asks in her email whether we can arrange a dinner with Martha. Martha King was a long-time friend of Marie's and professor emeritus at Ohio State. (Martha, as it turns out, passed away just three weeks before Marie.) Their relationship goes back to at least the early 1980s when Marie was at Ohio State working to implement Reading Recovery in the US, and it likely goes back even further than that. I know this because I was recently given a video of Marie Clay administering the Concepts About Print task to two six-year-olds for an education class at Ohio State in January 1976 — 32 years ago!

We exchanged many other messages over the eight-year period that I came to know Marie in my role as co-director of the Reading Recovery Center at Ohio State, and many more messages predate my arrival there. Her connection with Ohio State runs deep.

In 1990 she gave Ohio State the responsibility to uphold the trademark for Reading Recovery in the United States, and more recently, in 2007, the US licence for *Literacy Lessons*. In 1998, The Ohio State University awarded her an honorary doctorate in recognition of her scholarly contributions to the field of education. The degree was supposed to be conferred in the previous year but scheduling conflicts meant that Marie couldn't attend at that time. As a result, and to my delight, her degree was conferred in September 1998, which just happened to be the same ceremony in which I received my doctoral degree. That made us alumnae, I loved to remind Marie.

Over the years, when Marie came to Ohio State to work with us, I tried to ensure that she had time on her own to spend in the university library. In more recent years she accepted our offer to have a graduate student accompany her to help with photocopying articles. She did the research herself, telling me once that her method included reading 'adjacent journals', meaning that while she might be searching for a particular article in a certain journal, she would branch out and browse journals shelved alongside the targeted journal.

She always came back from the library with new information. Once she returned thoroughly upset because she learned that Helen Thelen had passed away — not because Marie knew her but because she had been eagerly awaiting Thelen's next publication.

She was such an amazing scholar. Marie didn't spend her time trying to defend her ideas, as some scholars do, but instead she was constantly looking for competing theories. She welcomed ideas about future directions for research from fair-minded critics. She focused on questions as much as answers, often starting out with 'I wonder why' or 'I wonder if ...'

Marie always had time to discuss a line of enquiry, to mull over puzzling data, and to help new scholars get under way with their research agendas. So often I have seen Marie heading off to a quiet corner after a meeting or even during a social event, not to be by herself but to give someone her undivided attention in order to discuss their research. I'm certain she never turned down anyone's request to think through their research no matter how or when the request came.

Even so, I was still surprised to receive this email message from her after she returned to Auckland following her September 2006 visit.

Dear Emily
I have located the name of the journal that Adrian and I discussed as a possible place for publication. It is *Interchange: A Quarterly Review of Education* with the following address in the year 2000.
    Education Tower, Room 1302
    University of Calgary.
Ian Winchester was the editor at the time I received some correspondence.
Just in case he's interested to follow-up the current situation.
Regards to you both
Marie

As it turns out, my husband Adrian, an education professor with a research interest in teacher education, asked Marie for advice on where to submit an article that he had written. The discussion took place at the end of a long day as Adrian drove Marie from Ohio State to Gay Pinnell's house where Marie was staying. During that brief time together, Marie listened to Adrian's questions, gave some advice about a possible outlet for the publication, and then, several weeks later after she returned home, followed up by sending the email with the name of the journal! She was always there to help with research no matter when questions came and she always followed through on her promises.

As a Marie Clay Literacy Trust Scholar I had the privilege of living in Auckland from June to August 2002, working alongside the Trainer team then at the Auckland College of Education and meeting regularly with Marie at her home in Hobson Circle to discuss my research. For many months afterwards I would talk to Marie about every detail of that wonderful experience. I missed everything about

Emily Rodgers in Auckland, 2002.

New Zealand right down to the delicious flat whites that I enjoyed every day. I told Marie that I could never figure out the right combination of espresso and milk to reproduce that coffee once home in Ohio.

One day out of the blue, an envelope addressed to me in Marie's unmistakable handwriting turned up in my mailbox. Inside I found a folded paper placemat with directions for flat whites, lattes and other coffees, along with the following note:

24/05/04

Dear Emily and Adrian

I stopped at a coffee café after a visit to the dentist today. This explanation of coffee making in N.Z. was on my tray. I thought it was a quick reference Emily might need to commit to memory before coming back to N.Z. There will be a test — if I can remember to provide it.

Marie

I imagine she had a good chuckle over that; I certainly did. As serious as she was about research, Marie had a fantastic sense of humour to match. I have heard her laugh so often that I can still hear her laughter today as easily and clearly as I can hear her voice.

Marie was a giant in the literacy field, but she never rested on her laurels. There was always a great sense of urgency in her work, particularly so in her recent publication, *Change over Time in Children's Literacy Development*, in

Emily Rodgers, and Mary Fried, an OSU Trainer, with Marie in the Martha King Center at OSU.

which she reviewed earlier and more recent publications in order to identify new questions and new directions for research. She communicated a sense of 'Let's get on with it, there's work to do' in everything she did, even her walking pace. I used to point out to her that whenever we walked together I had to adjust my pace to hers, sometimes walking at twice my usual speed to keep up with her in airports even though Marie was 40 years my senior!

Marie taught me about humility, about having an open mind to competing views, and she impressed upon me the urgency that surrounds our work to help young children having the greatest difficulty learning to read and write.

She has left us with a robust research agenda, a challenge to think about how Reading Recovery teaching procedures might be adapted to meet the learning needs of any individual student, and an organisational structure for Reading Recovery and Literacy Lessons around the world that will take us forward.

I have a feeling that we will be trying to catch up to Marie for a long time yet to come.

Language, Writings
and Translation

The Bermuda Connection

Elonda Stevens
Former Reading Recovery Teacher, Bermuda

So many wonderful accolades have been said and written about Marie Clay and her influence in the area of literacy and Reading Recovery. It is through a Reading Recovery connection that those of us who live in Bermuda have come to meet and know Marie. No matter how one approaches writing about Marie, one cannot get away from the Reading Recovery connection; however, there have been some very light-hearted moments that we have all had with her ...

How? Why? When? Where? What?

The diminutive lady with the sparkling blue eyes was always asking questions! We were in her presence to seek answers to our own burning questions about children and their learning and no sooner had she answered some of our questions, she was probing ... again. Who might this woman have been? None other than the indomitable Marie (rhymes with 'starry', as she once told me) Clay.

Marie's influence in Bermuda started when she was the president of the International Reading Association (IRA) in 1992. Juliette Harris, the president of the Bermuda Reading Association, invited Marie to be the keynote speaker at the annual reading conference. Marie spoke about Reading Recovery and its successes in New Zealand schools. She was so inspirational that senior officers at the Bermuda Ministry of Education invited her back several years later to confer with them regarding a system-wide implementation of Reading Recovery.

I attended that Reading Conference in 1992 as a classroom teacher. I was awed by this 'sprite' who challenged my thinking and made me think of my literacy teaching. Ten years later, in 2002, I was afforded the opportunity to leave my home in Bermuda for a year to train in Auckland as a Reading Recovery teacher/Teacher Leader. That year proved to be a year of new discoveries and experiences.

It was also the year that I met Marie Clay, in person, up front, person to person! The training I received in Auckland was rigorous. Marie met with our group on occasion, to discuss our understandings, to answer our questions, and ... to *ASK* us questions.

Elonda Stevens and Marie.

One of my Reading Recovery Trainers, Barbara Watson, invited my husband, Noel, and I to dinner at her home. Marie was also invited. She and Noel found that they were both born in the same year and soon established that they were kindred souls, discussing life in general and sharing interesting experiences with each other, fuelled by a 'nip of scotch'.

Halfway through a delicious dinner, Marie stopped, looked directly at me with those piercing eyes of hers and asked if I dreamt in Chinese. I was startled. That next bite of delicious salmon had to wait … I had never given it much thought and had to stop to reflect.

I told Marie that I actually thought that I only dreamt in Toysonese (a dialect of Cantonese) when I was dreaming about my parents. My mother speaks only Toysonese and that would mean that if we were to have any conversation at all, it would have to be in Toysonese. The rest of my dreams would be in English despite my dream of being able to speak a thousand different languages.

Not to be satisfied with that explanation, Marie then asked if I translated from Toysonese into English and vice versa when having a conversation. That got me thinking again. The answer was that there are moments when I had to seek 'translation' when speaking with my parents because my own Toysonese was functional and not philosophical. The evening progressed with more questions and, in retrospect, there were more questions from Marie than answers from me.

From that evening on, I made it a point to always ask questions of myself, of those with whom I work, and of those students whom I teach. The asking of questions does not always result in finite answers, but through the asking of questions we further our understandings which leads to something much more critical: a deeper understanding.

Marie has had a huge influence on the lives of teachers and children in Bermuda. Reading Recovery was implemented here over 10 years ago and it is still a robust intervention, assisting children to learn to read and write.

Reading Recovery in Bermuda was touched by her presence on many occasions. On one of her visits to Bermuda, Marie enjoyed an 'Ice-cream Social' with all the Reading Recovery children and teachers. She found great joy to be in the presence of the children. They answered her questions with great enthusiasm. For the teachers, it was an opportunity to share with Marie. It has been said, 'Awareness is the first step to positive change.' Marie was *always* seeking to be more aware. Teachers came to view her as a 'positive change' even on this little island of Bermuda, in the middle of the Atlantic Ocean. Marie asked so many questions on behalf of the children that it behoves us to continue to ask How?, Why?, When?, Where?, What? For Marie, there were no problems, simply challenges. It was up to us to find the solutions.

She challenged education systems, worldwide, to reflect and review their practices in preventing and recovering from literacy learning difficulties. Marie was a quiet voice of reason in a field frequently jarred by the conflicting cries of the marketplace. Charles Lauer stated, 'Leaders don't force people to follow; they invite them on a journey.' I am glad that she invited me on 'the journey'. Kia ora, Marie.

About Marie's Books

Marie Clay's first book, *Reading: The Patterning of Complex Behaviour,* was published by David Heap in 1972. David met Marie Clay soon after he became the Auckland Manager of Heinemann Educational Books. Professor Bob Chapman in the Political Studies department of the University of Auckland, who was a good friend of the Heinemann chairman Alan Hill in London, had suggested Marie as a potential author for Heinemann. David went to see her in 1969 because he was interested in the possibility of Marie editing a series of primary school level readers. Marie directed David away from primary readers to material that she was interested in having published. The idea developed for a small book on reading for teacher training college students.

David Heap was very impressed with the manuscript that Marie delivered. His colleague, Nick Hudson, the Managing Director of Heinemann Educational Books Australia, was even more convinced. He believed *Reading: The Patterning of Complex Behaviour* would become internationally recognised, and he was right. The first printing of the book sold out within months of publication in 1972. It was reprinted in 1973, and has been in print ever since. *Reading: The Patterning of Complex Behaviour,* now in a revised edition entitled *Becoming Literate: The Construction of Inner Control,* forms the basis of Marie Clay's theoretical description of young children developing control over literacy learning.

The Early Detection of Reading Difficulties: A Diagnostic Survey was a slim volume also published in 1972. This publication, also known as *The Diagnostic Survey,* came out of Marie's doctoral question 'Can we see the process of learning to read going astray close to the onset of reading instruction?' It described for teachers reliable observation tools for the assessment of changes over time in children's early literacy learning, including, running records, word and letter tests, and concepts about print.

The first *Concepts About Print (CAP)* test booklet *Sand* was published with *The Diagnostic Survey.* This *CAP* booklet was followed by *Stones* in 1979, and much later by *Follow Me Moon* and *No Shoes* in 2000. *The Diagnostic Survey* had expanded by 2002 to become *An Observation Survey of Early Literacy Achievement,* which is today widely used by teachers throughout the English-speaking world, and has been translated into several languages.

Marie Clay wrote many other books on literacy development for researchers, teachers, students and parents. These include *Change Over Time in Children's Literacy Development, Observing Young Readers: Selected Papers, What Did I Write?, Reading Begins at Home* (with Dorothy Butler), *Writing Begins at Home, Concepts About Print* and *Running Records for Classroom Teachers. Reading Recovery: A Guidebook for Teachers in Training* was the basic text for Reading Recovery, the international intervention designed to bring the lowest achieving children up to the average band of progress in their classrooms. *Literacy Lessons Designed for Individuals: Part One* and *Part Two*, published in 2005, developed from this book.

Marie's books relating to children's development included *Children of Parents Who Separate, Round about Twelve, Quadruplets and Higher Multiple Births, The Record of Oral Language and Biks and Gutches* and a collection of articles on taking children *By Different Paths to Common Outcomes*. In her final months, Marie was working on completing a small series of books designed to engage both parents and teachers of small children in being responsive to the codes of written and spoken language.

The Well-worn Book: The Continuing Legacy of *What Did I Write?*

Anne Haas Dyson

Professor of Education, University of Illinois at Urbana-Champaign

Six-year-olds Tionna and Mandisa are each holding a copy of a favourite book, which they are collaboratively reading. Mandisa stops suddenly and speaks her mind to her classmate Tionna about how she should be holding — and not holding — a book.

Anne Haas Dyson and Marie.

Mandisa: I don't want you to do that. *(She folds her own book so that only the page she is reading is visible; the book's covers almost, but not quite, lie flat against each other, face-to-face.)*

Tionna: Mrs Kay [her teacher] be like this. *(And she deliberately almost-but-not-quite folds her book's covers back.)*

Mandisa: That's just ripping a book up ...

Tionna: Ms Hache [the student teacher], all she do is like this. *(And Tionna holds her book so that one page is flat in her hands, the other page hanging down.)*

Sitting on my own shelf is a tattered book by Marie Clay, its back seam ripping apart. It has been opened many times over the years, its wide pages sometimes turned back in those offending ways Tionna and Mandisa discussed. The book and its textual sisters have helped me, and many others, learn how to analytically appreciate (not to mention enjoy) young children's first efforts to use written language in school.

That well-worn book is Marie Clay's (1975) *What Did I Write?* In this book, she serves as a kind of docent in a museum of children's writing. 'Oh look at this,' she seems to say. 'Did you notice the way this child has approximated written symbols, the way she solved the problem of how to arrange those letters, or the hopeful way she asks the more knowledgeable adult "What did I write?"'

At first glance, *What Did I Write?* may seem dated. In the current politics of school accountability in the US, written language is reduced to a set of sequential accomplishments, that is, to 'basics' like handwriting, alphabetic spelling, capitalisation, punctuation, and grammatical usage. In Tionna's urban school, supported by a federal grant for child literacy programmes, the teachers' guide book straightforwardly claims that children will become better writers if these '"lower level" skills are accurate and automatic'.

And yet, precisely because of such claims and expectations, educators and policy makers are in need of appreciating anew Marie Clay's fundamental message: If supported by others, young children can *actively* and *creatively* work to gain control over the writing task. In this short essay, I once again turn back the pages of *What Did I Write?*, this time to use her foundational message to respond to the current climate for children and literacy. As befits a book in her honour, I will draw on small children to help me do so — Tionna and her peer Ezekial, both six years old, and Alicia, just five. All three children lived in socio-economically distressed neighbourhoods and were children of colour (Tionna and Alicia identified as black, Ezekial as Mexican).

Children in worlds of literacy

Teachers who try to find out what children do not know ... are looking for initial points of contact in the wrong places ... Students who are active independent learners go on adding to their competencies in all their different environments, not just in school. (Clay, 1975, p. 3)

Write with complete sentences beginning with a capital letter and ending with a period, question mark or exclamation point. (First grade expectations in Tionna's state, 2003)

Into carefully graded lists of what children should (but might not) know, Marie Clay interjected an element of curricular disorder. Children bring to school what they have learned about language from their lives beyond school.

Consider, for example, Ezekial and his unusually alert eye for the visual display of written language in all his 'different environments'. His products suggested his attention to how letters and numbers were used in the sports activities so important to him; he knew how symbols were arranged and the purposes they served on scoreboards, playing fields, uniforms, and even on television screens displaying sports results. He noticed too the pervasive dialogue bubbles of cartoons and even the way letters were capitalised and sometimes repeated to capture stretched-out screams and shouts of joy and of defeat (a handy convention for portraying upset coaches in sports scenes).

These writing conventions were not included in the official first grade skill list. However, the visually attentive Ezekial was alert to them all, and they provided the repertoire against which he made sense of conventions taught in school.

One day, for example, Ezekial wrote that he and Jason 'got soccer. It will be fun. It is .C.O.O.L. P.L.A.I.N.G.'

'Why did you put all the periods?' I asked.

'Because I want'em all capitalised,' Ezekial replied.

Ezekial was trying to follow the rule that a capital letter follows a period. But written language is not a set of rules to be memorised; it is a symbol system that provides its users with a multi-layered communicative repertoire (message, encoding system, visual arrangement). As children gain experience using that system, they learn of its possibilities and constraints. Their efforts are worthy of our attention and response — and often quite ingenious, like Ezekial's .C.O.O.L work (discussed in Dyson, 2008).

Diverse paths into the system

> I doubt whether there is a fixed sequence of learning through which all children must pass, and this raises further doubts in my mind about the value of any sequenced programme which [does not proceed] … from an observation of what children are doing. (Clay, 1975, p. 7)

From the perspective of 'basic' writing skills, Ezekial's peer Tionna could be viewed as quite weak. She was not visually attentive like Ezekial. She showed little evidence of mastering the 'basics' of punctuation, capitalisation, and targeted elements of grammatical usage, yet Tionna was the most fluent writer in her class; she was aurally alert and attended to the voices surrounding her.

As just a sample, consider the feisty but affectionate voices Tionna appropriates in reporting on an encounter with her cousin (slashes indicate additional line breaks):

> Today I am going to Impression 5 [a children's science museum]
> my ant sue is going to take me
> I hope she bring … Miah … / … [Miah] is my firs cusin
> and the best cusint in the hole wide world
> … I bet she will won't [want] to do what I dow
> she all ways copycat me
> and I say aret you tier of copycatting me
> she say no am [I'm] not / that is my favord
> so plese stop ascking me mame [ma'am]
> I get tier of that / calling me mame
> so I will call her mame …

Despite the claims of the teacher guidebook, Tionna did not need automatic control of 'basic' skills in order to be a fluent writer.

Ezekial and Tionna would not end up identically skilled writers, but, in time, he would become more at ease in giving voice on paper, and she would become more attentive to visual conventions. They were following different paths, paying attention in different ways to the written language around them.

The consequences of adult-centric views of child writing

Just recently I met Alicia in a local kindergarten. In her school district, kindergarteners are to invent spellings and to write stories about personal experiences, but Alicia is drawn to telling imaginative stories and to writing in ways that would be at home in *What Did I Write?* She composes in cursive-like wavy lines, or, when pressed by her teacher, in strings of known letters, each line ending with a period.

Alicia is clearly learning about signs and messages, about directionality and page arrangement, just as Marie Clay would observe. But, against the backdrop of curricular expectations, Alicia is simply not 'writing'. She is in danger of failing kindergarten.

Marie Clay's life work was to counter the invisibility of child intelligence, and the rigidity of curricular space, by appreciating the diversity of children's early literacy actions. For me, as a young teacher (who discovered the brand new *What Did I Write?* on a bookstore shelf), Clay's work inspired a career. For all educators, though, her work is a living legacy for appreciating and supporting the potential of all our children.

References

Clay, M.M. 1975. *What Did I Write?* Auckland: Heinemann.

Dyson, A. Haas. 2008. Staying in the (Curricular) Lines: Practice Constraints and Possibilities in Childhood Writing. *Written Communication*, 25: 119–59.

EARLY WRITING FROM HATTIE

The following are examples of early writing and drawing for Marie by Hattie, Marie's grand-niece, around five years old.

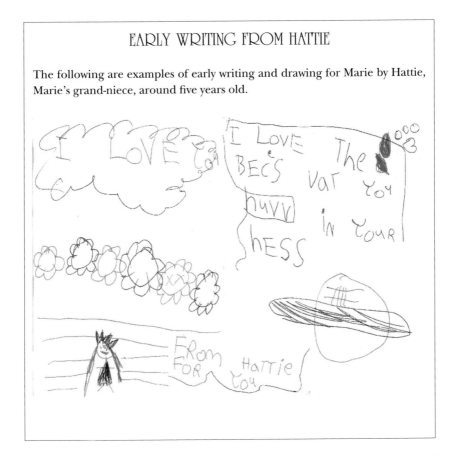

Quadruplets and Higher Multiple Births

M arie Clay's developmental studies of the Alexander quadruplets and the
Lawson quintuplets in New Zealand led to her further research on multiple
births in London in 1980 and to her book *Quadruplets and Higher Multiple Births*,
published in 1989. There is a dedication in the book to Jean Alexander, 'a mother
of quadruplets whose questions convinced me there was a need for it'. Jean, the
mother of four identical girls, had read all the information she could find about
multiples, mainly twins, and asked Marie about her challenge 'to bring up her
four daughters as normally as possible'. At the beginning of September 2007, the
Alexander quads gathered in Auckland, from different parts of the country, to
celebrate their fortieth birthday. I, Jenny Clay, took a tape-recorder along, with
their father Ron Alexander's permission, to their celebrations and talked with
Elizabeth, Delwyn, Kathryn and Louise about their memories of Marie.

Marie Clay first met the Alexander family when the quads were three years old.
The family consisted of the four identical girls, their two older brothers, Gavin
and Grant, and their parents, Jean and Ron Alexander. Marie did developmental
checks on the quads at the request of the paediatrician and their parents, and
these continued until they were seven. She initially administered intelligence
tests and took individual tape-recordings of their language. In her report to their
doctor she said 'they were friendly, co-operative and delightful to work with'.

The Alexander quadruplets were born in 1967, and were the first identical set
of four born in New Zealand. The first surviving non-identical set, the Johnson
quads, were born in 1935 in Dunedin. The Johnsons feature on the front of Marie's
book between the Morlok and Crawley quadruplets, two overseas sets. Louise met
Bruce Johnson, the only boy of this older generation, through a mutual workplace.
On his car he had a number plate 'Quad 1', as he was the first-born of the first set
of New Zealand quads. Louise thought of getting a number plate 'Quad 4', as the
Alexander sisters were the fourth set of quads born in New Zealand, and she was
the fourth one born.

Before the girls went to school, Louise said that they had their own language.
She remembers only two words they used. They called 'nor nor' the fluff off the
woolly blanket that they rubbed on their noses while sucking their thumbs; and
'bobos' the grain silos the family passed on Riverhead Road on the way to visit
the Alexander grandparents, Nana and Pop. About a year after starting school
and mixing with other children, they lost this shared language. Marie was very
interested in their private language and they discussed it with her. She asked them
what the words meant, and Louise said she was 'asking us … before we lost it'.

Marie looked at the interrelationships of language development and reading in a longitudinal study with the Alexander quads. She regarded this as a rare opportunity to look at the learning of a group of children who were born identical. Marie observed their approaches to print, as she had with other children during their first year of school in her study for her doctorate. She asked them to read the print in readers 'with their fingers' and observed where they started on the page, what direction they moved in, and where they would go on reaching the end of the line. She has accounts of the results in the chapter 'Directional Learning and Concepts About Print' in *Reading: The Patterning of Complex Behaviour* (Clay, 1979), and in *Observing Young Readers* (Clay, 1982).

In the chapter 'The Spatial Characteristics of the Open Book' in the latter book, Marie said, 'despite an unusual degree of similarity in hereditary and environmental histories, [the four identical girls] approached the problems of orientation to visible language on different time schedules and in different ways'. One of the quads was left-handed and the other three were right-handed during self-selected classroom activities. 'After two weeks at school, one right-handed subject B and one left-handed subject A were consistently using one hand for pointing to caption book texts' and the other two took four to five weeks to reach this stage. Later they would use either hand with flexibility, but also with accuracy not shown in the beginning of their approaches to print, the one making the most progress in reading reaching this point first.

Kathryn remembered that Marie was part of their lives before they went to school. She said their schoolbooks were saved for her high on a shelf at home in the early years, which was organised with their mother, Jean. Marie did comparisons of their writing. Delwyn is the only one of the girls who is left-handed. She said that they saw Marie 'every couple of weeks or months' and described her as 'a smiley grey-haired woman' who asked many questions. Marie always took notes, and Delwyn used to wonder whether she had a pen or a pencil, as 'we were only allowed pencils'. Louise thought it was exciting to be called away to go to see Marie. The quads met a lot of people, and were wary of some of them, but they were relaxed when meeting with her. Delwyn said she was 'interested in us and made us feel special'.

At Beachhaven Primary School they had a room on their own when they were talking with Marie. They would sit and look at readers in the room. Elizabeth was very impressed with one of the stories about the 'Little Green Elf', a cute elf who dressed in green with a belt, and curled-up shoes, and who had buck teeth. Elizabeth had buck teeth, and she said that 'Del and I had braces'. She told her family her name had changed from Elizabeth to 'Little Green Elf', and this lasted for a couple of weeks.

Marie had boxes and cards on some occasions. Elizabeth said that she asked questions about who does what in the house — Mum, Dad, one of the sisters, or Nobody — and they put the cards into the appropriate boxes. There were questions like, 'Who does the cooking?' and she would put card into the 'Mum' box. When she was asked, 'Who punishes you when you are naughty?', Elizabeth chose the 'Nobody' box, as she didn't think it was 'right to say that it was Dad'. Louise also remembers some of the questions: 'If we found a present on the table when we got home from school, would it be for me, a sister or Mr Nobody. I wanted it to be for me but said Mr Nobody.' Marie asked that if they had pocket money, 'whether we would buy for Mum, Dad or sisters or Mr Nobody'. Louise said 'it would have been Mum and Dad'. In *Quadruplets and Higher Multiple Births*, Marie stated, 'According to their responses to the Bene-Anthony Family Relations Test, they lived in a household of unusually positive interactions. Most exchanges between family were low-keyed but positive, and most of the negatively toned responses were placed in the "throw away" category not allocated to any family member'.

Marie took study leave from Auckland University in 1980 to follow up her multiple birth research through a survey of 'the developmental literature on children of higher multiple birth' in a wide range of libraries in London. According to Professor Marie Clay's report in the August 1981 *University News*, it took her two months through computer searches in the libraries of educational, psychological and medical literature to believe the answers she was getting. 'There had been no psychological studies of higher multiple groups reported since the early 1940s, and few before that … I revised my plan and turned to the medical records.' Marie was surprised that only geneticists had seen the value in studying multiple births and that psychologists 'had not seen them as of particular interest for the study of environmental factors'. Her research led to her book *Quadruplets and Higher Multiple Births* published in London by Mac Keith Press in 1989. The book was dedicated to Jean Alexander, who had died during that year. Louise is the house guardian of this book for the quads, and said she treasures the signed copy.

In October 1990 Marie spoke on her book at the New Zealand Adult Twins and Multiple Births Convention. In the description for this talk it said that once she had had the 'opportunity to monitor the normal development of two sets of higher multiples, the Alexander quads and the Lawson quins, she felt the need to bring together for other professionals all the information she could find about the special nature of growing up among a set of siblings of the same age'. Louise met Marie again at this convention. It was the first time Louise had seen so many identical people together in one place and understood, as an adult, the confusion that people have with telling multiples apart. Teachers and classmates had had this difficulty with the Alexander quads as they were often dressed alike. Elizabeth said the sisters had identical clothes, because it was easier for clothes to be made from the same material, or they were given sets by other people.

Marie had difficulty telling them apart in her visits with them and would search for the outgoing or independent one. She said in her book, 'After visits at regular intervals I came to recognise that on any one day I was probably sampling a mood or response in one child that was part of a common repertoire and might appear in another member of the set on another day'. Kathryn thinks the sisters all have distinctly different personalities, despite being born 'identical'. She regards herself as adventurous one, and planned to bungi jump off the Auckland Skytower as part of her fortieth-birthday celebration.

Jean Alexander gave Marie the address of Helen Kirk-Lauve, an American who collected extensive data on twins and on multiple births around the world. Helen was described as a supertwin statistician. She had kept track of twins through to sextuplets since the late 1930s, when she was the medical assistant to the doctor who delivered the Badgetts quadruplets in Galveston. She had contacted Jean Alexander shortly after the four identical girls were born, and they maintained a correspondence over the years. Louise remembers Jean sending things over to Helen in the States, such as a set of their identical clothes, and photographs of them. Helen Kirk-Lauve posted out a newsletter twice a year to the parents of multiples, and she would write notes to Jean at the bottom.

Marie sent Helen Kirk-Lauve a copy of her book. Helen was delighted and wrote to her in September 1990, 'We have got to meet in person!' She said the Morlok quads, who were on the cover of the book, 'and the Gemain quads are one and the same'. She added, 'I have personally met 43 sets of quads, some of whom are not on your list', but she was 'tremendously excited' with the book. Helen finished her letter, 'Please let me know when you'll be in Texas. I'll get my quad files up to date and we can have a fine time.'

In May 1996 Marie was taken by Billie Askew to where Helen Kirk-Lauve lived in Galveston. Helen was 80 and recovering from a stroke. In a letter Marie said, 'She knows more about twins and higher multiples than I do. [She] lives in a small house with no air-conditioning and has every room stacked with piles of papers, cuttings, books, boxes and photo albums, not to mention the trophies and memorabilia. She spent precious money adding a barn-like room out the back where she files all her treasures. She knows where everything is ... and can remember the names, dates of birth, places, histories, and deaths of almost every set I mentioned ... I am afraid that her collection will one day disappear, probably be burned by people who do not understand how remarkable it is.' Marie sent her photos of their meeting and Miss Helen said, 'We could almost pass for twins.' Helen Kirk-Lauve died in 2004. I am unsure what became of her collection, whether it disappeared as Marie feared or found a home elsewhere.

Delwyn was the first of the Alexander family to find out from the radio and TV3 news that Marie had died. She was upset and rang her father, Ron, in Auckland from Nelson where she lives with Geoff, to tell him.

The Alexander quads themselves are fit and well and are living, as their mother Jean would have wished, normal lives. At their fortieth celebration, their father looked after their children, his grandchildren, while I talked with the sisters. They seldom appear together, but a month later they were briefly on a 'Do You Remember' programme on television in New Zealand about the Lawson quintuplets. Louise told me their lives are too ordinary for a full-length feature, but they 'went on the programme to show what a great job Mum and Dad have done' and 'we hope we've made them proud'.

References

Clay, M.M. 1979. *Reading: The Patterning of Complex Behaviour*. Auckland: Heinemann.

———. 1982. *Observing Young Readers*. Selected Papers. Portsmouth, NH: Heinemann.

A Tribute to Dame Marie Clay, Whose Writing Changed My Life

Beverley Randell

Teacher, writer, editor

Reprinted, with permission, from *Reading Forum New Zealand,* Vol. 22, No. 3, 2007 published by the New Zealand Reading Association

Dame Marie Clay, who died in April 2007, was a meticulous, acutely intelligent observer of young children as they learned to talk, to read and to write. She shared her many insights with teachers, worldwide, and helped us all to improve our skills ... the debt teachers and children owe her is beyond measure.

Clay identified the conceptual problems children face in the emergent stage of reading and she knew that greater clarity and consistency in the layout of their first reading books could help them gain understanding. Her findings had an enduring influence on me, as a writer and publisher. I had once been a teacher, but after 1960 I was a full-time creator of books for beginners. I had been writing my graded *PM Story Books* (Price Milburn) for about 10 years before I met Clay, but after our first stimulating discussions at a reading conference in the early 1970s, I had a surer sense of direction.

Clay's personal spoken advice was precious, but her timeless written advice, available to all, was and is even more valuable, because written words are always there, and can be referred to again and again. My copies of *Reading: The Patterning of Complex Behaviour,* and *Becoming Literate: The Construction of Inner Control* became battered from frequent use. Because of the power of her books, I cannot think of Clay without recalling her written words. Over the years her ideas gave me both new insights and much needed encouragement, increasing my determination to write stories that would save children from frustration-level reading:

> When a graded sequence of reading is available, children must not be given a book that calls for too great a step forward ... the options are more often how many extra books the child will need at each level, rather than how many books he can skip. (Clay, 1972)

> Slow progress children need many more opportunities for independent reading than they usually get ... A wide selection of materials suited to the lower level of skills of slow readers should be available.

At the heart of the learning process there must be the opportunity for the child to use a gradient of difficulty in texts by which he can pull himself up by his bootstraps. (Clay, 1991)

A child who is on the way to independence needs as many books as possible at his level. Allow the child to learn to read by reading many books. (Clay, 1993)

[Teachers should take] … an accuracy check to find a book which the child can read with 95% accuracy. Above 95% accuracy represents pleasure reading, 90–95% accuracy represents teaching level (at completion of the learning task) and below this represents frustration level. (Clay, 1972)

This slow rate of new word introduction (no steeper than one unknown word in 20) was first recommended by Edward Dolch in the 1950s, and I had tried to follow it ever since my first graded stories, *Wake up, Dad* and *Honey for Baby Bear*, were published in 1963. Clay's similar belief in the need for levelled books gave me, and my colleagues, the courage to stick to our convictions.

We needed courage because, in the 1980s, the use of carefully levelled books became unfashionable. Pressure was put on teachers to make less use, not more, of graded readers, and many publishers, worldwide, decided not to produce them. The fashion in the 1980s swung towards 'shared' reading, using books that, because of their constant internal repetition, or use of rhythm and rhyme, could be easily learned by heart. The attractive theory was that children's oral memories could be the bridge that would let them learn high frequency words and add to their internal 'language storehouses'.

However, when the method was overused, a serious downside appeared. The vital job of attending to print was undervalued in many classrooms. As a result of this shift in classroom practice, many children developed the wrong concept about the nature of reading. One child proudly showed Clay that he could read his book when it was closed! He, and many other children, believed that reading was reciting from oral memory, and that close attention to printed words was not necessary. 'Memorising [lines of text],' wrote Clay, 'is *not* a place to begin because it gives the novice reader an incorrect impression of what the task is.' (Clay, 1993)

The fact that the *PM Story Books* (Nelson Cengage Learning) were revised and extended in 1993 was the direct result of widespread teacher dissatisfaction with the effects of memorising text. Teachers in mainstream classes had found that, to master high frequency words, little by little, children needed carefully graded stories. The growing worldwide reputation of Reading Recovery was an even more powerful indirect influence: if it had not been for Clay's work, our books would not be in print today. After the publication of *Becoming Literate: The Construction of Inner Control* (Clay, 1991), Annette Smith and Jenny Giles and I worked as a team to provide even wider platforms of books at each level, allowing… 'near-perfect reading [to be] fostered on many different texts of somewhat similar difficulty … New stories in new little books provide further practice of the same high frequency word in new settings and the near-perfect responding becomes correct responding.' (Clay, 1991)

I was thrilled by Marie Clay's personal warmth when we first met at an International Reading Association conference in the early 1970s, some years before Reading Recovery was founded. She asked if she might display, during her lecture, a page from *Baby*, one of our books for emergent reading. It had a dramatic black and white photograph of a baby in tears, taken by Penn McKay. Clay told me that this photo had produced the first response from an utterly silent child (one of a pair of twins) whose oral language she had not previously been able to assess: 'Baby crying,' said a small singsong voice at her side, responding with emotion.

It was good to know that my deliberate decision to produce books with illustrations that all children could understand and identify with was a sound one: the realism of this series of books was very different from the flippant stylised art of the 1960s.

At the same meeting, Clay pointed out something for which I was hugely grateful: she opened my eyes to the importance of wide word spacing. She showed me that when words were printed too close together, children at the emergent reading stage saw: 'Babycancry' and 'Babycanlaugh' instead of 'Baby can cry' and 'Baby can laugh.'

Of course! Now the fault was blindingly obvious — why hadn't I seen the need for wide word spacing before? But at that time, few publishers were sensitive to the problems of beginners who were struggling with the concept of what a 'word' was. The first line in the easiest *Ready to Read* (1963) book was just as closely set: 'Billisasleep'. Most publishers had been asleep, and it was Clay who woke us up.

After this reading conference, we widened the word spacing (and widened the line spacing to match) whenever a batch of *PM* books was reprinted. This work was labour intensive. Today, with computer typesetting and digital communication literally at our fingertips, print can be changed relatively easily, but back in the early 1970s most typesetters were still working with solid lead — resetting the type in lead, printing galley 'pulls', filming them, making aluminium photo-offset printing plates from the film, and printing on small offset machines, two colours at a time, was a long, slow, cumbersome process.

An unforeseen complication was that some schools suspected that a revised, re-spaced edition of a popular series was a deliberate plot to make existing books obsolete. Because the new books did not match the old, teachers had to replace whole sets, and some principals, who saw no good reason for our changes, wrote letters of complaint. It was no wonder Marie Clay told me, years later, that although she had given the same advice to several publishers, their response had been disappointing.

Clay shared more of her valuable practical advice about typesetting styles and page layouts in *Reading: The Patterning of Complex Behaviour*. This book had clear diagrams of page layouts labelled with the uncompromising words 'Good' and 'Bad'. For years these diagrams gave me the authority I needed to argue with professional designers who, naturally, disliked having rules imposed upon them. The last thing a good designer wanted to be associated with was sameness. Widely spaced words, always beginning in the same position at the top left of every page?

This request did not please innovative designers who wanted their pages to look modern and stylish.

Because of Clay's authority and admirably blunt printed advice, I managed to control the design of the inside pages of the *PM Story Books*, but then the battles continued with the covers. Clay explained that '[the child] should know what the story is about before he reads it' (Clay, 1993). That meant that the title and illustration printed on the cover should be as legible and meaningful as possible. Skilled designers of covers, however, were motivated to produce the attention grabbing, the subtle or the surprising. Over the years I had to reject, as tactfully as possible, a host of eye-catching design 'features': exaggerated condensed type, tightly kerned letters that touched each other, minimal line spacing, titles on a slant, hard-to-read fonts, type printed on top of busy background pictures, opposing colours such as red and green that danced before the eyes. Adding to the frustration of the designer was this often-repeated conversation:

Designer: Your suggestion for the cover will give the whole point of the book away.

Me: But I *want* to give it away. Marie Clay's research shows that children will read with so much more insight if they understand what the story is about before they begin.

'Marie Clay says', backed up every time by a quotation, was my catchcry. It says much for our long-suffering designers that, despite the limits that I tried to impose, they still created interesting covers.

Clarity of design was just one of our concerns. As my colleagues Annette Smith and Jenny Giles and I worked together to revise the *PM Story Books*, we greatly valued Clay's insights about children's control of oral language. In her *Record of Oral Language* (1983, 2007), Clay had made us more sensitive to the difficulties that young children have, orally, with handling two or more adjacent adjectives; in coping with negatives; with less usual tenses; with inversions of normal word order; with the addition of several phrases; with the position of adverbial phrases; with the introduction of extra clauses. We tried to avoid these challenges and complications in our texts for early reading, introducing them later only when we thought oral control was likely to have been achieved. The revised books, while retaining our original concern for meaning and story structure, now included (thanks to Clay's lectures and published books) a better understanding of children's language development.

We were honoured, when we launched our new edition at a reading conference in 1994, that Marie Clay appeared in the audience and, afterwards, found time to discuss our emergent level books with us. 'Whenever you introduce a variation of sentence structure, it helps children attend to print,' she said, and we were able to show her that we had small variations in some Level 1 books, many more in Level 2, and by Level 3, when storytelling shaped the books, the sentence structures changed on every page.

Clay always stressed that syntax and meaning were helpful decoding strategies from the very beginning. As she said, children use their prior experience to make sense of their reading: 'At first the child is producing a message from his oral language experience and a context of past associations. He verifies it as probable or improbable in terms of these past experiences, and changes the response if the check produces uncertainty' (Clay, 1972).

The progression of reading texts used in New Zealand 1900–63 reflected a long, slow battle to abandon distorted and idiotic texts that had no relationship to any child's prior experience of life or language (or any *adult's* prior experience!). It had taken almost a century of struggling with contrived language before teachers and writers realised that normal syntax and meaningful text would allow beginners to monitor their own reading, and self-correct:

1899   Is my ox to go in as I go by?   (*Imperial Readers*, Whitcombe & Tombs)

1908   Get the gum for Tim to gum the rim to the fan.
                                                             (*Phonic Primers*, Blackie)

1922   'Then,' said the door, 'I will jar.'
         So the door jarred.   (*Beacon Readers*, Ginn)

1928   hop to the can.
         hop to the bed.
         hop to the horse.   (*Progressive Readers*, Whitcombe & Tombs)

1949   Look, Janet.
         See my aeroplane.
         Down.   (*Janet and John*, Nisbet)

But in the 1960s there was a New Zealand breakthrough, spearheaded by the brilliant Pat Hattaway and Myrtle Simpson in School Publications Branch. They insisted that *Ready to Read* would be a set of natural 'language experience' stories reflecting the word order, syntax and vocabulary of familiar spoken English:

1963   Bill is asleep.
         'Wake up, Bill,' said Peter.
                   (*Ready to Read*, New Zealand Department of Education)

At long last, reality, story content, meaning and normal syntax were embedded in early reading texts. Meaning created the feedback that made self-monitoring and self-correction possible. Because of this fundamental change in the way texts for early reading were written, Clay was able to suggest that teachers prompt children with these words: 'Try that again, and think what would make sense (sound right)' (Clay, 1993).

This would have been a hopeless strategy before *Ready to Read* and other meaning-based books appeared in the 1950s and 1960s ('Hop to the horse.'??, 'I will jar.'??).

Clay wrote, 'For it is meaning which provides the context in which the word is embedded, the basis for anticipations of what comes next, and the signals of possible error that trigger a checking process.' (Clay, 1991) I had focused on writing and editing graded texts shaped by story content and clear meaning, texts that 'made sense and sounded right', for 10 years before I met Clay in 1972, and her endorsement of my respect for sense, and for story content, was heartening. As she said, 'independence in reading … is a cognitive exercise relating to thinking and understanding, and governed by feedback and self-correction processes' (Clay, 1991) and 'little children engage with books at the level of the story, not with isolated words. Children like to read stories, and they learn a great deal about print and texts as they do this (Clay, 1993). I was grateful when Clay, as one of a team of Reading Recovery people, encouraged me to offer my paper *Shaping the PM Story Books* to the Reading Recovery Council of North America for publication.

Clay remarked in *Becoming Literate* (1991) that 'all gradients of difficulty are inevitably fallible. They cannot be right for individual children, but a programme cannot work efficiently without them.' This is a paradox that writers and editors have to live with. To cater for children with widely different skills, experiences and interests, teachers have to make sure that the books selected for every level include a variety of subjects and styles. Clay always delighted in, and praised, many books from many publishers, provided that each was chosen to meet the needs of a particular child at a particular time. 'The teacher should know exactly what the child can read successfully at the 95% accuracy level' (Clay, 1972). No child should be asked to read a book that plunges him or her into frustration-level reading, where meaning crumbles, feedback disappears and self-correction is impossible. That is why 'authorities recommend that the child read with 95% accuracy' (Clay, 1991).

One of my most vivid memories of Marie Clay's encouragement and practical advice dates from the mid-nineties, when US editors were 'translating' the *PM Story Books* for an edition of their own. Of course they had to change 'Mum' to 'Mom', and switch our British/New Zealand idiom 'look after the baby' to 'take care of the baby' so that American children would not have to struggle with an unfamiliar usage. But the editors also wanted to remove every trace of repetition from the books, because the repetitive language that had been so much 'in' during the 1980s was now definitely 'out'. I needed Clay's authority to defend our stories from unnecessary changes, and we had a long session on the phone, looking at all the proposals. In my story *Tom is Brave*, one page has the emotion-packed line 'Tom cried and cried'. An editorial pen had reduced this to 'Tom cried' — a sentence with far less punch. She agreed with me that this change would reduce meaning and impact. 'There is another reason why the page should not be changed,' she said. 'Tell the editors that children need reading mileage. At Level 5, every word practised is an advantage — don't give them two words to read if you can give them four!' In the end, her recommendations on all the proposed changes were followed to the letter, and I was grateful that she gave me so much of her precious time when I needed her help.

I shall always be indebted to Dame Marie Clay for her advice, so freely given. New Zealand has lost the most sensitive observer and recorder of children's reading behaviours that we have ever known. Fortunately, because of her extensive writing, and because of her consummate efforts with Reading Recovery, her insights are there for all to share.

References

Clay, M.M. 1972. *Reading: The Patterning of Complex Behaviour.* Auckland: Heinemann.

———. 1983, 2007. *Record of Oral Language.* Auckland: Heinemann.

———. 1991. *Becoming Literate: The Construction of Inner Control.* Auckland: Heinemann.

———. 1993. *Reading Recovery: A Guidebook for Teachers in Training.* Auckland: Heinemann.

Randell, Beverley J. 2001. *Shaping the PM Story Books.* Wellington: Gondwanaland Press.

Marie Clay — Her Influence on My Work and Some Personal Memories

Ann Charlesworth
Reading Recovery Tutor, Victoria, Australia

It was late afternoon, school had finished for the day, the year I think was 1985, it was early autumn and I was driving in peak-hour traffic in Melbourne, Australia. My destination was St Kilda, a seaside suburb close to the city and the venue was a convent located across the road from a large, beautifully landscaped beach. An academic, Dr Marie Clay from Auckland, was the featured speaker and I was interested to hear what she had to say about teaching reading in the early years of schooling, and the success of Reading Recovery in New Zealand.

I attended this information session at the suggestion of our school principal, before training as a Reading Recovery teacher with the first training group in Melbourne the following year. I found the room and remember that there was a small group of educators, sitting in the dappled light in a room that opened out onto a sunny, leafy courtyard, waiting for the commencement of the session. As I remember, we didn't have time to enjoy this peaceful setting because when Marie Clay began, we were immediately fully focused on thinking and understanding what she was talking about! Little did I know at that stage in my life that I would experience listening to her in different places and for a variety of reasons, many times in the future. Furthermore that this lady would have a huge impact on me later in my life, both professionally and personally, until shortly before she passed away.

I remember Marie Clay at that first session as a petite, gently spoken woman who presented her theories of early reading and writing processing and, based upon her research, implications for teaching children who experience early literacy learning difficulties. I became fascinated because she was talking about basing teaching decisions on the things that individual children can do. In 1985 that was pretty radical because teaching from a deficit model at that time was common. I was motivated to continue to learn more because what she said made sense, so I was looking forward to my training as a Reading Recovery teacher. Later I undertook Tutor training in 1993.

In 1996 the first teacher of the deaf trained as a Reading Recovery teacher and, as her Tutor, I worked very closely with her. Marie became involved because our Reading Recovery Trainer, Heather Turpin, brought Marie to Furlong Park

School for Profoundly Deaf Children to see a lesson behind the one-way screen. I remember Marie saying as she arrived at the front door of the school that she had been taken to see lessons for children with hearing loss elsewhere in the world but, in her opinion, they weren't Reading Recovery lessons! You can imagine how tentative I felt as the lesson began and the teacher (profoundly deaf) began signing a conversation with the child. The lesson progressed and Marie, Heather and I sat and discussed what was happening — fortunately Marie declared that indeed she was seeing a Reading Recovery lesson and I remember heaving a huge sigh of relief. I remember the long conversation Marie had with Wendy, the (deaf) Reading Recovery teacher, following the lesson, she asked so many searching questions and was so lovely with her. Marie told us both to continue to design procedures that we could get to work with children with hearing loss and to do what we felt would work. We were thrilled with her endorsement of our efforts. When Marie left us at the end of the day, she had organised me into signing classes and then later the next year encouraged me to undertake PhD research focused upon Reading Recovery for children with hearing loss.

Following the completion of the PhD thesis eight years later, Marie 'strongly suggested' that I write academic papers discussing the implications for teaching Reading Recovery to children with hearing loss. I remember being so tired and made the mistake of saying that I felt I just could not write the papers. Marie became very calm and slowly said something like 'Then why did you do the research if you're not going to write about it in plain English? You have a responsibility to share the information ... Write the first by Christmas, write the next paper before the end of next year and keep ringing me to let me know how it's coming along!' I now have some very treasured memories in a professional and personal sense.

When I was at home writing the paper (thankfully co-written with my husband and my two university supervisors, Field Rickards and Bridie Raban), a letter arrived from America. Marie had been working in Boston and someone had asked her about deaf children and Reading Recovery. She organised the principal of Mill Neck of the School for the Deaf in Long Island to write to me (she wouldn't give them the phone number as 'Ann is busy writing a paper'), and thanks to Marie, I have since had two trips to work in New York, and Mill Neck has trained the first Reading Recovery teacher of the deaf in New York.

A couple of years ago Marie was back in Melbourne to provide professional development for her latest book. A large group of Reading Recovery Tutors (Teacher Leaders) participated in a full day of professional development and that day was just as motivating as the first time I heard her speak. As she explained various sections of the book *Literacy Lessons Designed for Individuals*, she referred to her original research that provided the rationale for some of the teaching procedures used by Reading Recovery teachers and where and why changes had been made. When I listened to her that day, I remembered the first time I had heard her speak, in the convent, and that it was just as challenging, and later on that day we enjoyed reminiscing about that first visit and other early visits she made to Melbourne.

Marie took a close interest in the teaching procedures I investigated in my research. We spent many hours having 'very expensive phone calls', as she often said, and often the conversation was related to using teaching procedures in a visual way and how signing, lip-reading and finger spelling could be used. For example, one challenge is to help teachers of the deaf to use visual approaches in Reading Recovery rather than those relying on oral language. In the year before Marie passed away, she made visits to a school of the deaf in Auckland, where she helped the training Reading Recovery teacher to use teaching procedures I had designed in Victoria with nine Reading Recovery teachers of the deaf. We had some hilarious phone calls, one in particular comes to mind with me trying to give her, step by step, the procedures for seeing and recording the letters in words rather than the hearing-and-recording-the-sounds-in-words approach used by hearing children in Reading Recovery.

One of the most memorable of many occasions I heard Marie speak was two or three years ago at the University of Melbourne, at a professional development session for Reading Recovery teachers. The Reading Recovery Trainers organised this session for about 500 teachers and Marie focused upon matters related to Reading Recovery teaching practice. It was in this familiar role, the gently spoken woman, that many of us will remember her. Later on the same evening, however, there was an insight into Dame Professor Marie Clay, the scholar and politician. There was a dinner at the university in Marie's honour, which was hosted by my two PhD supervisors, Dean of Education, Professor Field Rickards, and Professor Bridie Raban, a friend and colleague of Marie and Professor of Early Childhood Studies. There were about eight other academics there, as well as the Reading Recovery Trainers and myself. During the evening, at one stage there was intense discussion about various issues related to early literacy and it was on this occasion that Marie shone as an eminent scholar who could engage in dialogue with leaders in primary school education as well as those leading education faculties in universities, indeed, that she related to many different people in various roles.

I remember that Marie took over two years to recently write *Literacy Lessons Designed for Individuals* and during that time her commitment and focus was absolutely amazing. I was ringing her about once a month and she was frequently working on the manuscript for that book, consequently we had some interesting conversations. I observed that she spent hours sorting through and pondering about suggestions, information and research from the many people who contributed to the work at her invitation. This was a huge undertaking, which she did thoroughly. Marie wrote her book, and her gift to all in early literacy education in Reading Recovery is completed, published and being used.

I miss Marie very much but there is much to be thankful for in knowing her. She was a mentor, who helped to contribute to Reading Recovery for children with hearing loss. More importantly, Marie was a dear friend and a lovely person, who advised me about organising the needs of family and demands of research. She was very interested in music, family history and gardening. Marie could chat about lots of things other than things academic, she had a fantastic sense of humour and could even get angry, especially when her computer crashed! I frequently think of her, of what her advice would be. She has a special place in my memories — I will not forget her.

Conversations with Marie Clay

Yvonne Rodríguez

Reading Recovery/Descubriendo la Lectura Trainer, Texas Woman's University

'Two roads diverged in a yellow wood …
I took the one less travelled by,
And that has made all the difference.'
— Robert Frost

I find that Robert Frost's poem best describes the professional and personal relationship I had with Marie Clay. Conversations with Marie quite often led to exploring possibilities and travelling paths that I had possibly not explored before. I travelled many paths with Marie Clay. With each path, I found her to be my mentor, my beacon, and my friend.

Prior to my involvement with Reading Recovery, I had been a special education teacher for 13 years. Like many educators, I felt frustrated with not being able to help many of my students become literate. As I stood at this juncture of my professional life, I perceived I had two options: get out of education altogether, or accept the Reading Recovery teacher position my school system was offering me. I took the Reading Recovery path and that has made all the difference in the world for me and for the students I teach.

My relationship with Marie Clay began during one of the first Texas Woman's University Reading Recovery conferences. I found myself sitting beside her during the luncheon, worrying about what intelligent thing I could say to her. Obviously feeling my discomfort, Marie began the conversation. What I discovered about Marie that day was her boundless curiosity and ability to connect with people. More importantly, I discovered her ability to empower others with her genuineness.

During our luncheon conversation, Marie asked me, 'Are all your Spanish-speaking students from the southwest of the United States?' I informed her that Texas was experiencing a large influx of immigrants from Mexico, Central America and South America. She then asked me, 'Do all your students understand your Spanish dialect?' I quickly replied, 'Probably as easily as you understand my English dialect and I yours.' That quick response made her laugh. We proceeded to discuss how

Yvonne Rodríguez presents Marie with a collection of photographs from Texas Woman's University.

vocabulary, regional idiomatic expressions, and pronunciation were aspects of one's language that are often misunderstood. I have now come to realise how Marie's probing questions that day provided me with a venue to uncover and express my professional passions and beliefs. She also planted a seed for future enquiry.

Several years later, I again found myself beside Marie Clay. This time I was a doctoral student and lecturer for the Texas Woman's University Reading Recovery Center. Marie was coming to Texas Woman's University as a Scholar in Residence for an entire year. My office was to be next to hers and I was scheduled to take her classes for that year!

I treasure the opportunity I had to learn from Marie Clay that year. During her year-long research course, I explored *Instructional Conversations with Limited Language Children*. I shared with Marie numerous taped lessons and transcripts of my teaching. In turn, she provided me with a great deal of critical feedback that lead to deep theoretical conversations about language used by children and teachers during literacy lessons. I found my interest in finding out more about the role of language in literacy development mounting with each meeting I had with Marie.

It was also at this time that I began to look at Marie as my mentor. She encouraged me to take an active role in the reconstruction of Reading Recovery from English to Spanish, referred to as Descubriendo la Lectura (DLL). This path has had a major impact in my professional career and in the lives of struggling first-grade Spanish readers.

Conversations with Marie during Descubriendo la Lectura meetings always helped me and my colleagues to identify, articulate and address critical issues regarding the practice and implementation of DLL. Most conversations with Marie involved her asking questions such as, 'Why do you think that is?', 'How will you know?', 'What do you need to do?' and 'How will you go about finding out?' The genuine conversations that took place around these questions always led me and other bilingual educators to embark on some kind of research study or project involving English language learners and Spanish literacy practices.

What needed to be done and why it needed to be done came easily when talking with Marie. How to best answer our questions was the hard part. She once told me that knowing what needs to be done was not good enough; taking action, however, would make the difference. As our mentor, Marie inspired us to take action.

As our beacon, Marie ensured that we stay focused on our DLL projects. She was always asking for written accounts of our progress. The critical feedback she provided allowed us to refine the methods with which we originally started. In essence, she was actively involved with every DLL activity. Consequently, several Descubriendo la Lectura research projects were completed by the Descubriendo la Lectura Collaborative:

- Establishing the validity and reliability of the Spanish Observation Survey tasks

- Determining subsequent gains of former DLL students in third and fourth grade
- Revealing achievement differences among former DLL students based on when they were transitioned to all-English instruction
- Publishing a bilingual version of *An Observation Survey of Early Literacy Achievement* to be used within the United States
- Reconstructing and studying four sections of the Reading Recovery procedures to account for the linguistic differences between English and Spanish.

I will never forget the day Marie Clay and Billie Askew came into my office to have a conversation about what my doctoral dissertation course of study might be. I knew it was going to be a serious conversation since they came into my office together. As Marie sat down, she began by acknowledging she knew how interested I was in finding out more about the types of instructional interactions in bilingual classrooms that facilitate learning. However, she also needed someone to conduct a full Spanish translation of *An Observation Survey of Early Literacy Achievement* that could be used in any Spanish-speaking country. What Marie and Billie were proposing was that I consider taking on a full Spanish translation of *An Observation Survey of Early Literacy Achievement* as my doctoral dissertation. The choice was mine and, with trepidation, I accepted the challenge.

My exploration of measures needed to ensure that accurate meanings within an academic text are captured in a translation led me down yet another path. Now I needed to learn the art and craft of translation. Rather than conducting the translation myself, I chose to get a professional translator from Columbia to work with me. Obviously, Marie was going to be a major participant during this enquiry.

My conversations with Marie and the translator were the best part of my research process. Those conversations were analysed to ascertain the deeper meanings of terms that Marie used so that we could choose the best word or phrase to capture her intent. This applied translation process allowed me to determine whether my efforts had been successful in capturing Marie's meanings.

I believe the best part of the study for Marie was the back-translation. (A back-translation is a translation back into the original language from the second language, without sighting the original text.) For it was here that she could be confident that a solid Spanish translation of her work had been achieved. Consequently, Marie made the decision that any future translations of her work must be subjected to a back-translation to ensure her intended meanings were captured.

Deciding to make the translation of *An Observation Survey of Early Literacy Achievement* as part of my dissertation was one of the best decisions I have ever made. While it was not an easy process, it allowed me to walk a path with Marie. I will for ever treasure the moments I had with her. I will for ever remember the professional and personal talks we had over coffee and hearing her answer the phone with 'Marie here'.

The path I travelled with Marie Clay has indeed made all the difference.

Learning to Read and Write ... and Talk: The Wide Scope of Reading Recovery/Intervention Préventive en Lecture-écriture

Gisèle Bourque
French Canadian Reading Recovery Trainer

Reading Recovery is available in the United States and Canada in three languages: English, French and Spanish (Descrubriendro la Lectura). In the United States, Askew et al. (2003), using the National Reading Recovery Evaluation Data, found that children receiving Descrubriendro la Lectura, the Spanish version, achieved similar results to those who received Reading Recovery in English. In Canada, Reading Recovery implementation data is reported annually both nationally and provincially. This data indicates that Intervention préventive en lecture-écriture (the French version of Reading Recovery) is effective with students who received this support.

Reading Recovery has provided me, as a Trainer working in the French version, with opportunities to observe teachers working with Reading Recovery students, to work with students who started their schooling in French schools but who were not speaking French, and to work with students in the French immersion programme. It is interesting to note that in some cases, French may be the third or even fourth language spoken by a child.

French immersion programmes vary greatly across Canada. In some implementations almost all subjects are taught in French, while in other situations students will be taught to read and write in their first language, then gradually be exposed to French. Eventually they will all be expected to read and write in their second language. Over time, it has become evident there are huge differences between children in the lowest achieving group in the ways they express themselves in their second language. Marie Clay suggested that teachers 'listen for the longest, well-formed utterance or the most complex example the child constructs when talking'.

I have found that changes in the structure of language a child uses when talking can happen quickly. The following is an example of a child who is a French immersion student. After being in school a year and a half, he has been in

Intervention préventive en lecture-écriture (Reading Recovery) for 10 weeks. He is talking about what he might write.

Flocon est un cheval.
Flocon is a horse.

J'aime Flocon parce qu'il est Blanche [correct form is 'Blanc'].
I like Flocon because he is white.

J'aime des choses qui est (sont) blanches.
I like things which are white.

Finally, the story the child composes becomes:

J'aime Flocon parce qu'il est blanc. J'aime des choses qui sont blanches.
I like Flocon because he is white. I like things which are white.

Through my observations, it was evident that the way children express themselves, the way they understand what is said to them, how they read their books or comment about them, and how they compose stories varies greatly. This is where, as Reading Recovery professionals, Marie Clay reminds us that 'The complexity of language does not scare either the two-year-old talker or the eight-year-old reader who overnight moves from simple stories into chapter books.'

At each age, children handle complexity well. Researchers, linguists and curriculum designers develop theories about how fragments of language are learned and in what ways they are learned. Rarely do those educators stop to consider how the novice young learner might approach the task. Marie Clay suggested that 'there are no quick ways to extend language' but powerful conversations during Reading Recovery/Intervention préventive en lecture-écriture lessons will provide the child with wonderful opportunities to learn.

Here is an example of a conversation in French between a child and his teacher. Today the whole school is going skating.

Enseignante: C'est une journée très spéciale aujourd'hui. À quelle place allons-nous?
Teacher: It is a special day today. Where are we going?

Enfant: Ne semble pas se souvenir.
Child: I don't know.

Enseignante: Nous allons à la patinoire. As-tu apporté tes patins?
Teacher: We are going to the skating rink. Have you brought your skates?

Enseignante: Peux-tu patiner?
Teacher: Can you skate?

Enfant: Mon brother can skate [la prononciation de ce mot semble être entre ski and skate] like this et moi can skate like that.
(Nous avons droit à une très belle démonstration.)
Child: My brother can skate [the pronunciation of the word is between 'ski' and 'skate'] like this and I can skate like that.
(The child stood and made a wonderful demonstration.)

Enseignante: Ton frère va venir patiner aussi. À quelle place allons-nous?
Teacher: Your brother will also be skating. Where are we going?

Enfant: (*Cherche dans sa tête*) ... à la baignoire, ... à la piscine ...
Child: (*Thinking*) ... in the bath, ... at the swimming pool ...

Enseignante: Tu vas aller patiner à la patinoire.
Teacher: You will go skating at the skating rink.

This conversation happened at the beginning of the lesson.

At the writing time, the teacher began by saying:

Enseignante: Est-ce que tu as un bon message pour moi? (*Arrête quelques secondes et dit*) C'était très intéressant quand tu m'as dit que tu pouvais patiner.
Teacher: Do you have a good story for me? (*She stops for few seconds and says*) It was very interesting when you said that you can skate.

Enfant: Je peux patiner.
Child: I can skate.

Enseignante: Excellent! On peut écrire cela. Tu peux patiner comment ...bien ... et vite.
Teacher: Wonderful! We can write that. How can you skate ... well ... and fast?

Enfant: Vite *pense* ... et bien aussi.
Child: Fast ... and well also.

L'histoire de l'enfant est donc ce jour là:
The story of the child from that day :

Enfant: Je peux patiner vite et bien.
Child: I can skate fast and well.

At the end of the lesson, the child had another opportunity to use the new vocabulary and structure.

Enseignante: Maintenant, tu vas pouvoir aller patiner. Je vais voir si tu peux patiner vite.
Teacher: Now, you can skate. I will see if you can skate fast.

Enfant: Je ne sars pas si (*arrête et réfléchit*) je peux (*arrête*) patiner vite à la (*arrête*) patinoire because je patine sur le pond.
Child: I don't know if (*stops to think*) I can (*pause*) skate fast at the (*pause*) skating rink because I skate on the pond.

Enseignante: Tu vas voir ça va être encore plus facile à la patinoire.
Teacher: You will see it is even easier at the skating rink.

These examples illustrate the different levels of proficiency between the two children who have been in school for the same amount of time and how teacher interactions can make a difference in providing rich opportunities.

Teachers are building a wide range of expertise to better serve the children according to their needs. They have expressed their appreciation of Marie Clay's work in helping them build such expertise.

We are so fortunate to have in written form the treasures of her theories and research.

References

Askew, B., Fountas, I., Lyons, C., Pinnell, G., and Schmitt, M. (2003). *Reading Recovery Review: Understandings, Outcomes and Implications.* Coumbus, OH: Reading Recovery Council of North America.

Marie Clay's Work in Irish

Gabrielle Nig Uidhir

Lecturer in Irish-medium Education, St Mary's University College, Belfast

Reprinted from the Fall 2007 *Journal of Reading Recovery* with permission of the Reading Recovery Council of North America

Since my first contact with Professor Marie Clay in the spring of 2001, I have been quite overwhelmed by the honour of being permitted to work on her brilliant *An Observation Survey of Early Literacy Achievement*. Not only did Marie grant me permission to redevelop her work in Irish but she provided me with support, guidance, wisdom and inspiration at many critical moments. I was amused and appropriately jolted on several occasions by the sharp observations that she made in red ink on some of the early drafts that I sent to her. Until the work was finally published in April 2007, I was always very sensitive to the onerous responsibility involved in this task. Marie had designed a literacy assessment tool that had been used internationally for over 30 years. It was truly excellent and reflected so many of Marie's own qualities — her direct, precise focus on detail and accuracy, and there at its centre — a noble aim, empowering teachers to intervene in a really meaningful way on the behalf of children.

Marie believed in the dynamics of the support that people can give to one another. It was appropriate, therefore, that this redevelopment of Marie's work for Irish-medium teachers was carried out within a context of a support network. Firstly, participation in the Reading Recovery training programme in Belfast ensured that the work could draw upon the expertise and insights into early literacy development that Marie had shaped and shared with her Trainers. Secondly, partnership with Angela Hobsbaum at the Institute of Education, University of London, and the international members of the Comenius project provided many stimulating, enjoyable and colourful opportunities for interacting and discussing the challenges involved in redeveloping the Observation Survey into Irish, Spanish, Danish and Slovak.

When Marie visited the group in London, she impressed me with her clear understanding of issues involved in a language with which she was unfamiliar (though maybe not entirely unfamiliar, as she was of Irish descent herself). I asked her a specific question relating to the Letter Identification task. Marie responded by asking me a series of detailed questions about the Irish linguistic system and then gave her answer with decisiveness and certainty. I wanted to be like that! Indeed, I think that I will always aspire to emulate the fine qualities that I came to recognise in Dame Marie Clay.

On behalf of Irish-medium teachers and the thousands of children learning to read and write in Irish in their primary schools, I feel a sense of deep gratitude to Marie. Prior to the publication of the *Áis Mheasúnaithe sa Luathliteartacht: Treoir Do Theagasc na Litearthachta* (ÁML = An Observation Survey), there had been no literacy assessment tool available to teachers that offered them a standard, well-tested means to profile children's early literacy achievement. Her contribution to the Irish-medium sector will only become fully appreciated as this resource is introduced into schools throughout Ireland. It also paves the way for the introduction of Reading Recovery in Irish.

Marie's letters to me during the years of collaborating on the ÁML redevelopment project provided me with her commentary on the progress of the work. Her last letter remains truly precious. Here, she gave her final approval. Her generous words have meant more to me than any praise that I have ever received from anyone. I was pleased to have met the daunting responsibility, mentioned above. Marie asked her publishers to cite me as a co-author in this work. What an honour! It has been a real privilege to have been given the chance to work alongside Marie for this short while. She made a difference in the lives of so many people, influencing their views and sharpening their skills and understanding. As a role model, Marie will remain very much present among teachers, Trainers, parents and others who safeguard the interests of children.

Danish Concepts About Print: A Return Journey 1982–2005

Kirsten Wangebo
Danish Reading Recovery Trainer

A personal account of the first and second introduction to Denmark of the Concepts about Print task, devised by Marie Clay.

In front of me on my writing desk lies a modest-looking little grey booklet. The text is typewritten and graphs and curves are handmade. The booklet is titled *Early Learning about Written Language: A Comparison of United States and Danish Children* (Schmidt, 1982). This booklet is the result of Marie Clay's visits to Denmark in the late 1960s before I entered the educational arena. Marie Clay gave me this booklet, which I didn't know about, when I came to see her in Auckland in 2004. I'd come to discuss the final steps of my work on the redevelopment of the Concepts About Print (CAP) task (Clay, 2000) into the Danish language. Mine wasn't the first attempt to introduce the CAP tasks into the Danish educational culture. I will recount the work and challenges of this earlier attempt, and of my final redevelopment of the CAP tasks for children and the manual for teachers, after a pause of some 20 years.

Marie Clay and the 'Danish project'
Marie Clay visited Denmark in 1968 as an invited speaker at the 2nd World Congress on Reading in Copenhagen. This was her first major international speaking engagement. The conference introduced her to educational contacts in Scandinavia. During her Fulbright year in the early fifties, Marie had made Norwegian and Dutch friends, and during the eighties, family ties through a Swedish daughter-in-law also brought her to Scandinavia. In 1971 she met Eve Malmquist of Sweden, and they subsequently worked on cross-national proposals and research designs together, and were both involved in the International Reading Association.

Marie had a professional curiosity about the educational system in Scandinavia. Denmark is well known for its child-centred, democratic values based on the philosophy of Grundtvig and Kold exemplified by a teacher autonomy based on trust and aimed at meeting the needs of all children throughout their school career. Marie Clay undoubtedly found the late school entry of Danish children at the age of seven interesting too, in contrast to the New Zealand entry of around five years old.

Marie met with Danish educational psychologist Mogens Jansen, a member of the International Reading Organisation's Reading Hall of Fame. Over a private dinner, Marie Clay introduced her first test book, *Sand* (1972), and discussed its role in assessing the very early conceptual understandings necessary for reading. Mogens Jansen still remembers their discussions around issues such as directionality, the concepts of first and last, and the front page. As a result of this meeting, it was decided to trial the CAP tasks with older children in Denmark and USA.

In the 1980s, children received formal instruction in reading in the United States at the age of six, although trends extended formal instruction downward to the five year olds in kindergarten. In contrast, beginning reading instruction was given to seven year olds in Year One in Denmark (Schmidt 1982). It was believed that once in school, most Danish children would learn to read. The early years and approximately the first six months of Year One were devoted to developing oral language skills as a prerequisite to reading, and formal instruction was given later. Jansen (1984) explained that:

> ... reading skills are thought to be developed through real-life experiences in a social context and related to natural language, not by the artificially segmented training provided by formal pencil and paper tasks. Without these foundations, the teaching of reading would be based on 'sand'. The reading would serve no purpose for the child, and hence he might learn, albeit by accident, that reading is non-functional (cited in Schmidt, 1984, page 23).

A United States–Danish comparative study
A cross-cultural, cross-lingual study was set up by Dr Eunice Schmidt of Seattle Pacific University (Schmidt 1984). Danish speech therapist Knud Hare was responsible for collecting and interpreting the Danish data.

The purpose of the study was to examine the contrast in the age of when formal instruction occurs. The knowledge of early print awareness of 80 randomly selected young Danish children was compared with 80 United States children using the Concept About Print tasks and *Sand* booklet (Clay, 1972). Furthermore, each national sample was divided into four age groups, with 10 boys and 10 girls in each. The samples were socio-economically matched (middle-class, suburban).

Age	USA	Denmark
5	Preschool class (K)	Kindergarten/home
6	Year 1	Kindergarten class (not compulsory)
7	Year 2	Year 1
8	Year 3	Year 2

A Danish version of *Sand* was constructed around the same print concepts as the originals, and the original teacher questions were translated into Danish. Each group of children was assessed 9–12 weeks after the start of the school year.

- The researchers looked for differences in age groups, sex and nationality based on mean scores. No standard deviations to indicate spread of scores were reported. The results indicated that there were no significant differences between boys and girls, neither between the two countries nor within the individual country.

- At the age of five, the USA children and the Danish children did not demonstrate any significant differences.
- At the ages of six and seven, the USA children had significantly higher scores in the CAP Sand test.
- At the age of eight, no significant differences were found between USA children and Danish children. Both Year Two groups had almost the same mean scores in each individual item.

Although the data demonstrated that the Danish cohort had little knowledge of the concepts of written language at school entry, the majority of Danish children at the beginning of Year Two, having had little formal instruction (Hare, 1982), caught up with their peers in the USA study. In other words, this evidence did not support the conclusion that, based on consideration of literacy progress alone, Danish children should start formal schooling at an earlier age. The report failed to discuss issues around the children who did not develop an understanding of the Concepts About Print tasks during Year One. After this first attempt to trial the CAP tasks in Denmark, Marie Clay did not pursue the 'Danish project' any further.

A rude awakening
Thus in Danish eyes, the study confirmed their beliefs 'that the Danes had maybe the world's best school system'. Many years went by without any questioning of the reading competencies of Danish pupils. Towards the end of the 1980s, however, new political and educational agendas emerged, and the then Minister of Education wanted evidence collected on the reading skills of Danish children, and thus came a rude awakening.

In the 1990s, Denmark participated for the first time in the comparative international literacy study. Denmark was placed as the third-lowest nation for nine year olds' reading skills of accuracy and speed. Additionally, *Project Danread* (Nielsen, 2000) identified that 25 per cent of Danish pupils, acknowledged as poor readers in the first form, remain as the 25 per cent lowest achieving children in literacy throughout their school career. Suddenly Denmark found herself in the position of an 'ugly duckling' left back on the shore not being able to fly, seeing his Scandinavian brothers and sisters (Finland, Sweden, Iceland and Norway) fly away as 'swans'. And another swan joined the flock: the New Zealand one.

Immense interest in the New Zealand system of early literacy learning grew. Danish administrators and educators on all levels flocked to New Zealand to study the school system. I had the opportunity to visit New Zealand in 1999 as well, and on that occasion I was introduced to Reading Recovery, which was entirely new to me. Three years later, in 2002, I started my Reading Recovery Trainer training at the Institute of Education, University of London. Thirty-four years after Marie Clay's first visit to Denmark, I finally met her. Marie Clay's research was to re-emerge in Denmark.

The Danish Concept About Print tasks

As the Danish Reading Recovery Trainer it is my task to facilitate the redevelopment and transformation of Reading Recovery into the Danish educational system on all levels including translating the Reading Recovery core texts and material. Translation of texts involves meaning reconstruction. Translation is not just about replacing words at a literal level; it is about interpreting the text and constructing meaning within the culture and knowledge in an accessible form (Bassnett and Lefevre, 1998; Eco, 2003; Tymoczko and Gentzler, 2002). The main issues are loyalty to the author's text, the translator's knowledgeable interpretation of the message, the transformation of the message into the target culture and, finally, the acceptance of the message in the target culture. The literature on translation concludes that if the imported message does not 'go native', the job of transformation has not been successfully completed. So, during my training year I met with Marie Clay several times to discuss the redevelopment of Reading Recovery in Denmark. The CAP tasks were decided to be the first core text to be translated. Marie Clay had constructed two more test booklets for the child: *Follow Me Moon* and *No Shoes* (2000). We estimated that these texts and the illustrations would fit well with the Danish context, so no new texts needed to be constructed. Much time, however, was spent in analysing the details of each individual task to be able to construct a task matching the original ones. No new tasks were devised. Minor changes were made to the font: curved j's and curved l's replaced the original font of these letters. Most of the core text was negotiated either face to face with Marie Clay or on email, and parts of the teacher's manual were back-translated. A few sections were recomposed; a new section describing the redevelopment was inserted along with two examples of entry and exit scores in one average kindergarten class (age 6.0–7.6 years) and one Year 1 class (age 6.9–8.7 years). The tasks were trialled on 1246 children by 60 teachers specially trained to conduct the CAP tests.

The final decisions about the Danish title of the CAP tasks proved to be a major challenge. Since the label for 'print' does not exist in the Danish language, the original title could not be literally translated. Marie Clay reminds us of the value and importance of acknowledging the child's implicit knowledge before it becomes explicit. Inspired by the title of Danish author Peter Hoeg's novel *Smilla's Feeling for Snow* (*Froeken, Smillas fornemmelse for sne*, 1992) which Marie Clay had read, we found a way out; however, Marie argued 'feelings' did not quite capture the concept of implicit knowledge, instead she suggested 'sensations'. So the literal back-translation of the Danish title is: *Children's Sensations of Written Language: What to Do When Reading?* (*Børns fornemmelse for skriftsprog: Huad gør man når man laeser?*, Clay and Wangebo, 2005).

Times are changing again

Since the early 1990s, the Danish educational system has undergone major changes. By August 2008, kindergarten class will be compulsory for all six year olds. Because of the attendant change of curriculum, the kindergarten teachers are now expected to teach early literacy and numeracy skills without losing the Danish traditions of a creative learning environment.

Currently (2008) 114 Reading Recovery teachers and three Reading Recovery Tutors are trained in Denmark and the Danish CAP tasks are well implemented in all the schools which have Reading Recovery. We also run courses for class teachers and special needs teachers. However, we don't yet know if CAP has 'gone native'. Reading Recovery is still in its early phases of redevelopment and I am involved in translating and transforming the remaining Reading Recovery core texts into Danish as part of the redevelopment. We are close to making the final decisions before they go to print, this time sadly without Marie Clay to consult. However, I am leaning on the International Reading Recovery Trainers Organisation (IRRTO) and my European team colleagues as an ongoing source of support for the redevelopment. Marie Clay was wise and careful to put this in place some years before her death, while she was still here to inspire and shape its goal of ensuring that Reading Recovery would continue its high standards, remain sensitive to new research, and ensure continuation of outstanding outcomes for children at risk, including those becoming literate in many differing home languages.

Today I cannot help wondering what would have happened if the Concept About Print tasks had been adopted in the Danish schooling context of early literacy learning in the eighties. We do not know, and we can never have the answer. We have to accept that with the patterns of change which are well described elsewhere in the literature, the Danes were not ready to take this knowledge on board in 1982. But as Marie Clay said, there is always a second chance. We have that chance now.

References

Bassnett, S. and Lefevre, A. 1998. *Constructing Cultures. Essays on Literary Translation. Topics in Translation.* Clevedon, UK: Multilingual Matters.

Clay, M.M. 1972. *Sand,* Auckland: Heinemann.

———. 1979. *Stones,* Auckland: Heinemann.

———. 2000. *Follow Me Moon,* Auckland: Heinemann.

———. 2000. *No Shoes.* Auckland: Heinemann.

———. 2000. *Concepts About Print: What Have Children Learned about the Way We Print Language?* USA: Heinemann.

Clay, M.M. and Wangebo, K. 2005. *Børns fornemmelse for skriftsprog. Hvad gør man når man laeser?* Copenhagen: Alinea.

Eco, U. 2003. *Mouse or Rat? Translation as Negotiation.* London: Weidenfeld & Nicholson.

Hare, K. 1982. Early Learnings about Written Language: A Comparison of United States and Danish Children. In *International Research in Reading,* Vol 1, No. 1, 1984. The International Reading Association.

Hoeg, P. 1992. *Froeken Smillas fornemmelse for sne.* Koebenhavn: Rosinante.

Jansen, M. 1984. Language and Concepts: Play or Work? Seriousness or Fun? Basics or Creativity? In *International Research in Reading,* Vol. 1, No. 1, 1984. The International Reading Association.

Meiding, J. 1994. *Den grimme aelling og svanerne.* Koebenhavn: Hans Reizels Forlag.

Nielsen. J.C. 2000. *Project Danlaes. Undersoegelse og paedagisk evaluering af danske boerns laesning. Dialogoplaeg 3. Elever med vanskeligheder (P25-eleverne).* Koebenhavn: Danmarks Paedagigiske Institut.

Schmidt, E. 1984. Early Learning About Written Language: A Comparison of United States and Danish Children. In *International Research in Reading,* Vol. 1, No. 1, 1984. The International Reading Association. (Translation in Danish: 'Hvad ved skolebegyndere om bøgernes sprog? — En sammenligning mellem børn fra USA og Danmark' in Schmidt 1982: *Læsning: Læserapport 6: København.*

Tymoczco, M. and Gentzler, E. 2002. *Translation and Power.* Amherst: University of Massachusetts Press.

Marie Clay's Influence in Greece: The Development of Concepts About Print in Greek

Eufimia Tafa

Associate Professor, Department of Preschool Education, University of Crete

Marie Clay's work is well known in Greece as it is around the world. Her writings on emergent literacy have inspired all of us who are working in the field of literacy education to help Greek kindergarten teachers understand the concept of emergent literacy and implement instructional methods that will help young children become literate. This is the reason why, during the 2001–02 academic year, the Laboratory of Educational Research and Applications at the Department of Preschool Education at the University of Crete launched an effort to standardise Concepts About Print for Greek teachers to use as an assessment tool in order to find out what young children know about print and what they still need to learn.

In the spring of 2004, while I was on a three-month Fulbright grant at Rutgers University working with Professor Lesley Mandel Morrow, who was IRA president at the time, I contacted Marie to ask for guidance and to discuss with her several issues regarding the translation and development of Concepts About Print in Greece. It was during the 49th Annual IRA Convention in Reno, Nevada, in May 2004, when I met Marie Clay for the first time. She had just delivered a keynote address, which had been attended, as always, by a large audience of educators from around the world.

During our meeting, I presented her with the results of the pilot project of the development of Concepts About Print in Greece. She seemed satisfied and enthusiastic that one of her assessments was going to be translated into another language (in addition to Spanish, French, Maori, Portuguese, Irish, Slovakian, Welsh, Danish, German and Hebrew) and was going to help Greek educators to observe young children and find out what they know about print. At that time, Marie asked me to contact Eva Konstantellou, who is a native of Greece and an associate professor and Reading Recovery Trainer at Lesley University in Cambridge, Massachusetts, in order to discuss the details of the project, the translation of the CAP manual into Greek and the publication of two special booklets for this observation task. Since then, Eva and I have been in constant communication about the development of the project. Marie's work became the catalyst that marked the beginning of a collegial relationship and a friendship that have enriched us both professionally and personally.

The task of CAP was standardised to 2744 children aged 4 years 4 months to 7 years 6 months from all over Greece. For the purpose of this project, two new booklets titled *The Moon Has Gone* and *A Sunny Day* were written in Greek since the original stories were not appropriate for the Greek linguistic and cultural context. The standardisation was successful. The data analysis showed that the Greek CAP is a reliable (Cronbach's alpha reliability coefficient 0.91 for the total sample) and valid task for Greek beginning readers. The analysis also showed that the Greek children's knowledge of Concepts About Print does not differ from that of English-speaking children, since the stanine scores of the Greek children are similar to those of the English-speaking children.

During the course of the research project, Marie's advice and comments encouraged and supported us. Eva and I were in frequent communication through telephone, email and face-to-face contact during Eva's summer visits to Greece. In September 2006, during the International Reading Recovery Trainers Organisation meeting in Columbus, Ohio, Eva presented Marie with the completed Greek materials and sought her input into the arrangements for publication. Marie was very pleased to see the final results from the administration and to find out that the project was carried out successfully. She explained further the protocol that has been established for translating her work into other languages, namely translation into Greek followed by back-translation of the text to English to be studied by her for final approval.

During her last communication with me, Marie gave her final approval for the publication of CAP in Greek. On 13 February 2007, Graham McEwan (chairman of the Marie Clay Literacy Trust) wrote on her behalf: 'Everything is approved — Marie is very pleased with your scores.' It seems that she had already been experiencing health problems, which prevented her from responding to my letter herself, as she had always done in our previous communications.

She had shared with us that she had enjoyed visiting Greece many years ago. She was very excited when she was invited to be the keynote speaker at the international conference that was to be held in Crete in October 2007 entitled 'Emergent Literacy: Research and Applications' and when she was told that the University of Crete, following the proposal of the Department of Preschool Education, was planning to bestow upon her an honorary doctorate. She responded: 'I am sure that I would enjoy sitting back and hearing what today's researchers are saying at the international conference you are planning, and seeing as much of your country as I can.' However, her health problems made her hesitant to accept the invitation and attempt the long trip. Her words were prophetic: 'It would be an honour to have an honorary doctorate conferred by your university but because of my health problems that would be the most risky part of your suggestions. I am just not so sure that I could promise to be there for such an important event.'

Jenny Clay and Eufimia Tafa at the 2007 Emergent Literacy Conference in Crete.

The conference was dedicated to her memory. Even though she was not there, the 250 participants had the opportunity to celebrate her contributions

Attending the 2007 Emergent Literacy Conference in Crete, (left to right) Linda Gambrell, Graham McEwan, Mary Anne Doyle, Peter Hannon and Jenny Clay, by the Iraklio fountain.

to children's literacy worldwide. Marie's daughter, Jenny Clay, Graham McEwan, and Mary Anne Doyle, Reading Recovery Trainer and chair of the Executive Board of the International Reading Recovery Trainers Organisation, travelled to Crete, participated in the conference and spoke about Marie's life and work.

The translation of Marie's work in different languages has contributed to greater understanding about emergent literacy and literacy teaching and learning around the world. I am honoured that I have been able to introduce one of Marie's assessments to Greek educators. Its administration will deepen our understandings and inform our teaching of young children.

Thank you, Marie.

Tāu Mahi, E Iti Kahurangi — Well Done, Oh Little Treasure

Cath Rau

Kia Ata Mai Educational Trust, New Zealand

I had the privilege of working with Marie on developing the Māori version of *An Observation Survey* on behalf of a cluster of Māori-medium educators in New Zealand. It was to be a journey that would traverse more than 15 years, a journey where together with Marie, our large team of developers would come to experience many challenges, periods of steep learning, moments of frustration and the highs of exhilaration and satisfaction when the project was finally completed.

In the early 1980s, bilingual (Māori/English) programmes were just becoming established in New Zealand. Part of our development included searching for any procedures, instruments and support that might enable us to positively transform learning for Māori learners in newly established bilingual programmes. Certainly for me as a recently trained teacher along with my colleagues, Marie Clay was the definitive, undisputed authority in early literacy English language programmes here in New Zealand. Every conversation around early literacy achievement began and finished with her work. Period!

We set about the ambitious task of 'translating' *An Observation Survey* into Māori, which required we navigate around full-time teaching commitments, family responsibilities, geographical distance, dialectal differences and a lack of expertise in test construction. There was no denying our determination and Marie's patience with us.

The following proverbial saying, which appears in the manual we reconstructed from English to Māori, provided a source of inspiration as we struggled with seemingly endless rewrites over several years:

Te ohonga ake i taku moemoeā ko te puāwaitanga o ngā whakaaro.
Dreams become reality when we take action.

Marie also contributed the following commentary in the foreword of that manual in acknowledgment of the effort expended.

This project has truly been a cooperative enterprise, bringing together several early attempts to launch this project, nurtured in a climate of consultation and careful consideration of cultural and linguistic issues, funded from here and there through the generosity of those who felt it was a cause to be supported, and carried to completion by very dedicated people.

The fact that the Spanish version of *An Observation Survey* was published during our own development work provided further impetus and encouragement to persevere and see the project through to completion.

Every change we wanted to make to her original work in the Māori version we had to be able to carefully

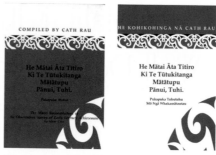

The manuals produced for the Māori reconstruction of An Observation Survey.

justify and, as a result, some lively debates ensued. Sometimes we would have to post our drafts overseas to her during her many stints working in other countries and we would wait with bated breath for the next 'instalment' from her. She was always direct, sometimes abrupt and also very economic with her pencilled written comments — she let us know in no uncertain terms when we were getting it wrong! She was certainly far more forgiving and accommodating when we met her face to face to discuss these issues.

The effect of all of this was that we got truly invaluable insights into the workings of her intellect, which was overwhelming at times but also highly stimulating. She was fiercely protective of her work and rightfully so. Safeguarding the integrity of the original assessment became as important to us as it was to her — it was certainly one of our drivers. It was therefore no small feat to achieve some concessions in the reconstruction process.

One of the phrases she often repeated to me as we reviewed our work was 'Yes, but what is the actual purpose of the task?' This had the immediate effect of

keeping us tightly focused and removed the temptation to take creative liberties that characterised our earlier attempts. We came to appreciate that these 'creative liberties' in fact reduced the effectiveness of the assessment procedure. There was no questioning the academic rigour of her work, but I also learned that there was a very practical reason for the things that she did. She was a unique teacher.

We recently commissioned one of our local Māori artists to produce a piece of artwork based on the symbols used to record reading behaviours for the Māori reconstruction of running records, one of the six tasks in Marie's *Observation Survey*. One of the designs

he incorporated into the artwork is *te mangopare,* or the hammerhead shark, a much admired creature sometimes associated with fierce determination. He explained that this symbolised the expectation that administrators of this task adhere to the instructions and not deviate from them. With these characteristics in mind, we think *te mangopare* therefore also symbolises Marie herself. Much like the hammerhead, with grit and a clear direction in mind, she forged a way through and left an indelible mark in education for young children.

We often expect people who have a super-sized reputation to also in real life be physically super-sized. I remember the first time I met her, I couldn't help thinking that should I find myself standing next to her at a pedestrian crossing, I'd be tempted to ask if she wanted a hand to cross the road. It did not take me long to realise that Marie would not have appreciated that gesture very much at all.

There was no arguing that she had a super-sized reputation that came from having a super-sized intellect and a super-sized dedication to improving literacy for children at home and around the world.

She also had this air of humility. We asked her once how we should refer to her, as she was, after all, an iconic figure on the educational scene both here and abroad — Professor Marie Clay, Dame Marie Clay, Dame Professor Marie Clay. Her quick response to us was 'Marie will be fine', and so from that point on, 'Marie' was how we always came to address her.

On occasion, we would meet at her home in Auckland to talk through, or rather rigorously debate, our way through the development. I have vivid memories of the time when I had little choice but to bring my then two-year-old daughter along to a meeting with her together with my husband who was also working on the project. When I reflect back on it, my daughter had every right to be there too — I was pregnant with her at the time we would get together in the holidays and weekends with teachers from other areas to work on our Māori version. More importantly, the maternity leave I had to take after she was born gave everyone in the group the excuse to argue that I was in the best position to write up the two manuals we had decided upon — after all, I was at home doing nothing!

Two or three years later and I found myself stepping across the threshold of Marie's residence, this time with daughter in tow. I looked around her personal space and immediately had a major mother panic episode: all I could see was white carpet everywhere, treasures from all over the world on display and stairs that led up to her bedroom — all highly attractive to an inquisitive toddler eager to explore and touch everything within reach and also out of reach.

My daughter managed to sit with us for a good five minutes. Naturally, a conversation about how we might go about representing all phonemes in the Māori language in the dictation task and, if possible, the two digraphs and vowel blends as well had little appeal to her, and it wasn't long before her patience had been exhausted. Before we knew it, she had managed to escape the grasp of her father and was gleefully exploring this exciting new place. Marie didn't appear to even notice. I, however, just couldn't concentrate, worried that those little fingers would damage or destroy some of those treasures. Marie, of course, eventually noticed — not my daughter so much — but the unease I was feeling and clearly showing. Eventually, she leaned across and said, 'Cath, it's all right. She's fine.' Despite her reassurance, I really only felt fine once we had concluded our business and exited out of her home.

We were privileged by her attending our launch for the project where we were joined by a great friend of hers who happened to be in the country at the time, Courtney Cazden. This was certainly a night of celebration. Regretfully I'm not sure that we ever articulated to Marie the huge impact that that piece of work had on literacy development for Māori-medium education, which became the foundation for other developments and certainly shaped our thinking about literacy learning for our students.

I have had reason to meet with Marie intermittently since that project and continued to be in awe of her focus and energy.

Māori-medium education thanks Marie for being so generous with her time, her energy, her knowledge. Education for children in literacy programmes where they are receiving their instruction in Māori is certainly richer and better off for it.

I went in search of a *whakatauki,* or Māori proverbial saying, for Marie and I came across this one, which I think is testament to the legacy she has left us with:

Tāu mahi, e iti kahurangi.
Well done, oh little treasure.

Marie's Legacy

International Acumen and the Triumph of Communication

Mary Anne Doyle

Professor of Education and Reading Recovery Trainer, University of Connecticut;
Chair of the Executive Board of the International Reading Recovery Trainers Organisation

Marie M. Clay's rich legacy of scholarship and influence transcends academic fields and international settings. She was a citizen of the world, concerned to understand others and willing to share her expertise and perspectives in caring and intelligent ways. We observe this in her approach to the expansion of Reading Recovery around the world, and others in this volume illustrate her wisdom and success by sharing

Marie and Mary Anne Doyle.

wonderful stories of their collaborations with her, including work in redeveloping Reading Recovery, and its related assessments, in multiple languages.

We find her unique and special acumen in addressing international challenges by her responses to wide-reaching global issues. Many such demands were presented to her as she travelled the world to support Reading Recovery implementations. Other instances arose from her tenure as president of the International Reading Association and a member of their Board of Directors. But that is certainly not all, as Marie was a force in many academic circles and was well respected by scientists and educators of diverse backgrounds in international settings. To each of these experiences, she brought good judgement and a keen interest in learning about others and understanding diverse perspectives.

In my work with Marie, developing and supporting the International Reading Recovery Trainers Organisation (IRRTO), I had the opportunity to talk with her about working across international settings and to observe her in a range of contexts. IRRTO board members and I often asked her about how she approached various international requests, and we sought her guidance in our decision-making. In one conversation, we kidded with her about becoming as sharp as expert card players who sense 'when to hold and when to fold'. From our many conversations, I learned that she evaluated each situation according to its unique circumstances, and she considered communication key to the process.

Marie's problem-solving seemed to begin with careful listening, and she was astute at asking the 'just-right' questions. Finally, she gave us insight into the importance of both holding to standards and our convictions while also evaluating when and how to compromise. Compromise was considered if judged both appropriate for the circumstances and not in conflict with ideals and understandings, most often supported by research evidence.

Marie offered sage advice and supported our fledgling efforts to establish IRRTO with patience, sensitivity and success. To share my experiences and reflections, I share brief details of two accounts that I consider compelling examples of her unique abilities to problem solve, communicate, and lead on an international stage.

My first example is documented in a speech presented by Marie to the Auckland Council of the New Zealand Reading Association in 1994 and revised and published in 1997. In this talk, Marie relates that in 1992 she was asked by an acquaintance in UNESCO to provide perspective on the concept of reading readiness/school readiness that could be used to guide the development of a project in Africa. She seized this invitation as the one opportunity she would have to make an important statement about the concept of readiness and an important contribution to literacy efforts in Africa. In reflecting on her response, she shared that 'My reply was bold and emphatic … I wrote that the concept was outdated, highly problematic and not to be perpetuated in any new UNESCO project' (Clay, 1997, p. 16). Marie supported her assertion with alternative considerations. She explained that:

> … children learn much in their preschool years which they bring to literacy learning in school — oral language, a liking for stories, and some primitive ideas about written messages in their environment. They enter school with vast individual differences in what they have already learned. Different homes and communities have taught them different things. Every child is ready for school if the teachers take the programme to where the child is. The challenge to teachers is to do that. I asserted that there is no need to pre-teach children a basic vocabulary of spoken or printed words to ensure success in literacy learning, because in the simple speech which children use there are high frequency words which occur again and again. Therefore to read texts orally composed by children, and written down by teachers and children, is to practise the words which occur often in the language.
>
> (Clay, 1997, p. 16)

We recognise the appropriate theory and related practices offered by Marie, and yet, the compelling impact of her response did not become clear to her for several years. She was working in London at the time, and I am quite sure this was at the Institute of Education at the University of London, the home of the Reading Recovery Centre of the UK. She related that she was delighted to receive a visit from an African scholar, a lawyer who was directing the African literacy initiative for UNESCO. This lady had come to Marie's office to thank her for the letter and direction regarding readiness and to share that they had indeed taken her advice.

Marie wrote that the woman said: 'We are working in four different countries and we are documenting what the communities help their children to learn about themselves and their environment before they come to school and we will build our first schools and our beginning literacy materials out of what we find.' Marie revealed her delight by writing: 'That seemed like a triumph of communication' (Clay, 1997, p. 17). It appears that Marie was successful in impacting literacy instruction for thousands of African children by responding to the request directly, honestly and without compromise. Marie's wisdom was in knowing she could not compromise, and this appears to have made an important difference.

The recommendation of an early intervention, like Reading Recovery, was not in Marie's set of suggestions for the newly emerging educational systems in African nations, and this was intentional. We discussed such requests with her, and Marie shared that she advised supporting the development of strong educational systems and effective school-wide literacy programmes initially before introducing the challenges of an early intervention in any emerging countries.

A second example of Marie's unique influence as an international educator and researcher is her participation in a meeting that occurred at the White House in Washington, DC in April 2001. This meeting was held during a North American Leadership Academy organised by Trainers and the Reading Recovery Council of North America (RRCNA).

In planning the academy programme, I had invited Marie to keynote the opening session. She declined, explaining that while she was glad to attend, she felt it was time for US Trainers to take centre stage and assume the role ascribed to her for setting the tone for the opening day. Trika Smith-Burke graciously assumed this responsibility and delivered a motivating address. Marie offered her special support by being present to talk with participants and answer questions.

Our conference location prompted our RRCNA and Trainer leadership to pursue advocacy opportunities with President Bush's education advisers, and yes, Marie was amenable to any meetings arranged with government officials. Lucy Getman, RRCNA's Director of Advocacy, pursued contacts and was able to arrange an historic meeting.

It was very timely. The Bush administration was new and literacy was a prominent focus of the president's proposed education initiative entitled No Child Left Behind (NCLB). A National Reading Panel (NRP) report had been completed and was foremost in discussions of federal policy and funding (for example, the Reading First legislation), and scientifically based reading research was demanded of programmes and interventions proposed by local and state entities seeking federal support.

When word was received that Marie, with RRCNA and Trainer representatives, was to meet with education officials at the White House, everyone was impressed and excited. Those accompanying Marie included Clifford Johnson, Trainer from Georgia State University and President of RRCNA; Jean Bussell, Executive Director of RRCNA; and Lucy Gettman, Director of Advocacy for RRCNA. This was one time that I know of that Marie wanted a picture! I'm not sure if that happened, as the meeting, as described by Marie, was involved and intense.

Our Reading Recovery delegation and Marie met with representatives of President Bush's Department of Education and the National Institute of Health (NIH), an entity engaged in critical decisions regarding literacy research and policy decisions of the new administration. Both Marie and Cliff shared that the representatives had interesting questions about Reading Recovery and Reading Recovery teachers. However, they were not particularly focused on Marie's theoretical perspectives, extensive study or research evidence. I have wondered if this might have been due to their strong commitment to the recommendations of the NRP report. It appeared that they considered themselves well informed about literacy instruction and were interested in seeking, or testing, Marie's support of their plans and initiatives for beginning reading instruction.

Marie knew immediately that collaboration would not be possible; however, she listened intently and responded graciously. She was decisive in her remarks and targeted the apparent differences between their perspective and hers by posing a few key, or just-right, questions:

- What instructional attention have you planned regarding the development of early writing proficiency?
- What instructional recommendations have you planned for those children for whom English is a second language?
- What research informs your decisions and discussion of how to teach the essential skills identified as important by the NRP report?
- What research supports the use of 'decodable texts' for beginning readers?

There may have been additional questions, but these were the essential ones. Discussion of these gave Marie sufficient opportunity to demonstrate her concern for both theoretical considerations and scientifically based research evidence supporting the proposed approaches. Reading Recovery educators will recognise that her questions reflect the hallmark of her work: meticulous testing of one's assumptions regarding instructional practices, instruction informed by research, and an understanding of the reciprocity between reading and writing for beginning readers.

In summary, Marie was uncompromising in this conversation, adhering to her convictions and important research-based theory and evidence. She was not distracted, and she offered challenges to the assumptions she had heard promoted by the Department of Education and National Institute of Health leaders. They had to agree that the evidence supporting some of their basic assumptions was equivocal, and they shared that related research had been planned.

Initially, Marie did not consider this meeting a 'triumph of communication' in the sense of establishing common understandings that would be mutually beneficial. She was, however, successful and insightful in communicating her perspective and in judging that there could be no compromise in this situation. There were positive aspects. Cliff reported that our team felt confident that Reading Recovery would not be excluded from federal funding even if it was not specifically named. Furthermore, Marie's leadership and example motivated

Trainers to continue efforts to engage in dialogue with the wide range of educators and policymakers in order to promote understanding and mutual respect. This advocacy continues.

In light of this experience, I was very pleased to share with Marie the report of the What Works Clearinghouse (WWC), a branch of the United States Department of Education and the Institute of Education Sciences, in March 2007. This review of the experimental research of Reading Recovery established that Reading Recovery is a highly effective intervention based on scientific evidence. Furthermore, of all beginning reading programmes reviewed by the WWC, Reading Recovery was the only one to demonstrate positive and/or potentially positive effects on all four domains examined (that is, alphabetics, fluency, comprehension, general reading ability). Marie was pleased with this report and expressed her conviction in the potential of these findings to impact Reading Recovery positively in the United States and around the world, and that would be a triumph of communication.

I have profound respect for Marie and deep appreciation for her kind guidance in many ventures. As an international educator and leader, she was superb in her ability to communicate and problem solve. With her sensitivity to cultural differences, she demonstrated respect for others and was able to offer insights based on keen observations while remaining true to her convictions and beliefs. Her advice and model remain with me and serve as exemplars and triumphs of communication and judgement.

Marie with Reading Recovery Trainers affiliated with all trademark implementations from around the world, and several international colleagues.

Reference:

Clay, M. M. 1997. Future directions and challenges: A talk to the Auckland Council of the New Zealand Reading Association. Auckland: Auckland Reading Association.

READING RECOVERY TRADEMARK HOLDERS

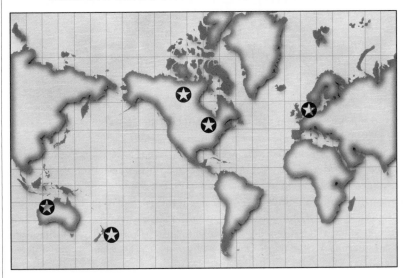

The current Reading Recovery trademark holders are:

Australia – The Marie Clay Literacy Trust, Auckland
New Zealand – The Marie Clay Literacy Trust, Auckland
United States – The Ohio State University, Ohio
Canada – The Canadian Institute of Reading Recovery (a body established jointly
    by the Scarborough Board of Education and the University of Toronto)
United Kingdom – Institute of Education, London

Several of these trademark holders support and represent implementations beyond their borders:

Bermuda – affiliated with United States trademark
Department of Defense Schools on Overseas Bases – affiliated with United
    States trademark
Denmark – affiliated with United Kingdom trademark
Republic of Ireland – affiliated with United Kingdom trademark

Also affiliated with these national trademark holders are implementations of redevelopments of Reading Recovery in other languages:

Danish – affiliated with United Kingdom trademark
French (for French Canada) – affiliated with Canadian trademark
Spanish (for United States) – affiliated with United States trademark

Sailing Sampler for Marie Clay

Patricia R. Kelly
Reading Recovery Trainer, California

I was trained as a Reading Recovery Trainer in the 1992–93 academic year by Gay Su Pinnell when she came to California to train a cohort of Trainers and Teacher Leaders. During that year, Marie visited us in California. We were studying her theory and the practice associated with it, so it was an honour to meet her. Over the years, Marie came to our Trainers' meetings and our conferences, so I had many opportunities to talk with her informally. Despite her stature as a distinguished scholar, she was always approachable, warm and engaging.

When she was awarded the National Reading Conference's Distinguished Scholar Lifetime Achievement Award (2003) in the United States — and only four people to date have received this award — Marie gave her address at the National Reading Conference Annual Meeting and I was in the audience. I was struck by the title and content of her remarks. The line 'Simply by sailing in a new direction you could enlarge the world' (from New Zealand poet Allen Curnow) resonated with me. It seemed the perfect description of Marie's journey and impact in the field of literacy.

I am also a stitcher who has studied the history of stitching. I have been particularly interested in samplers from an historic perspective and as a record of events at various times. The term sampler comes from the Latin *exemplum*, meaning an example (to be followed). In a way, Marie Clay herself represented an example to be followed.

As the twentieth anniversary of Reading Recovery in the United States approached, I decided to stitch the sampler to honour Marie. The sampler was simply a token of my gratitude to her. The design is done in counted cross-stitch and it evolved over time as I worked on the design first on paper, then in stitches. I began the design in a traditional way with an alphabet, perhaps classifying this as an alphabet sampler; but with the quote from the poem and the sailing ships, I think of it more as a commemorative sampler. The sailboats represent the quote from the poem: four are moving towards the right, while one — Marie Clay — is sailing to the left, in the new direction that Marie took in her thinking, research and design of Reading Recovery. I used wave patterns between lines to represent the sea. I wanted the colours to be subtle rather than primary colours, and I kept the border simple.

On a personal note, the lovely thing about designing and stitching a sampler for someone is that you think about that person all the while you are working on it. I had a lot of time to think about Marie as I made the sampler. I guess it goes without saying that I held her in the highest regard. She made a difference in the lives of so many children and teachers alike. For those of us lucky enough to be acquainted with her and her work, and especially those trained in Reading Recovery, she made a difference in the way we viewed teaching and learning. She helped us to enlarge our thinking and to be successful with even the hardest to teach children.

She is missed by many of us across the Pacific but she sails with us every day in our work.

Sailing sampler for Marie Clay by Patricia Kelly.

Marie's Legacy in Pictures

Marie after her arrival in Minnesota in 1951, reading a colour London Illustrated *magazine in her bedroom in the Weldon household.*

At Rotoiti, January 1956, Marie holds her young son, Alan.

Marie and Eve Malmquist of Sweden attending an International Reading Association Convention in 1990 in Stockholm.

Marie in a classroom around 1992 in the USA.

Planning for an International Reading Association meeting at Newark, Delaware, the IRA headquarters: Marie, Vince Greaney (Ireland) and Carl Braun (Canada), when Carl was the President of the IRA.

Jenny receiving the New Zealander of the Year award in 1994 on Marie's behalf, in her absence, from Dame Catherine Tizard while Sir Edmund Hillary looks on.

Terry Walbran and Marie at the opening of the Auckland Reading Recovery Tutors centre at Epsom, Auckland.

Marie being given advice on her sled ride by the young daughter of the musher in Alaska.

Christmas at Marie's home in 1997. Marie with her son, Alan, and her grandson, Michael, standing, and Ida, one of Marie's grand-daughters, sitting on the couch. Ida's mother, Kerstin, and Kerstin's husband, Ary, are in the foreground.

Martha King, Gay Su Pinnell, Marie, Barbara Watson and Charlotte Huck at Ohio State University.

Rose Spicola, Marie and Billie Askew in Texas.

Marie with two of her grandchildren, Manuka and Michael, and her son, Alan, in the Auckland Domain in 2002 after a family picnic celebrating her 76th birthday.

Barbara MacGilchrist and Teresa Kourdoulus, the administrator for the European Centre for Reading Recovery, with Marie Clay after Marie received an honorary doctorate from the Institute of Education, University of London in 2002 at their Centenary Degree ceremony.

The presentation of an Honorary Doctorate in Humane Letters to Marie at Ohio State University in June 1998 by OSU President William E. Kirwin.

Mary Rosser (Maine), Lyne Legault (Canada), Jackie Heinz (Wisconsin) and Mary Fritz (Illinois) knitted a scarf for Marie after they were all snowbound in Maine. It was presented to her at the 20th anniversary of Reading Recovery in the United States conference in Columbus in 2005.

Marie receiving a plaque, acknowledging the establishment of the Marie M. Clay Endowed Chair of Reading Recovery and Early Literacy at The Ohio State University, from Gay Su Pinnell at the 2005 National Reading Recovery Conference in Ohio.

Peter Johnston, Professor at Albany State University of New York, and Marie at the 2006 National Reading Recovery Conference in Ohio.

Marie and Ida, her grand-daughter, at Marie's home.

Marie signing copies of the newly released Literacy Lessons Designed for Individuals *at the 2006 National Reading Recovery Conference, with Rose Mary Estice, one of the original Reading Recovery Trainers in Ohio.*

Book ladies: Margaret Mahy, Joy Cowley, Marie and Dorothy Butler during a Storylines Festival event held at the Music Auditorium of Epsom campus in Auckland.

Book Ladies: Margaret Mahy, Marie Clay and Joy Cowley

An email from Marie to Jenny after she attended Margaret Mahy's 70th birthday celebration

Sunday, 12 March 2006

I went to the Margaret Mahy dinner last night: a stellar event. Compered by Michael Hurst decked out in cream brocade and singing a Mahy take-off of a Gilbert and Sullivan song — 'I am the very model of a modern major general', but this was about a Christchurch festival. This morning as I finished the last fifty pages of the book you gave me for Christmas [*Margaret Mahy: A Writer's Life* by Tessa Duder] I found the 'patter-song' again.

It was held at the Heritage Hotel which used to be the old Farmer's Trading Company and we were wined and dined in the old tearoom where many of us remembered we took our children to play in the Farmer's rooftop playground while we drank tea!

Our eating was interspersed with dramatic renderings of *The Lion in the Meadow*, a child's reading of a book about a little pig who wanted to shed his 'piggish ways', and Margaret's history presented in ten minutes by young actors mingling among tables of eaters.

Marie was also invited to a congratulatory party a month later to celebrate Margaret Mahy receiving the world-renowned Hans Christian Andersen Award.

Letter from Joy Cowley

8 August 2007

I've just come back from a trip to the States, writing workshops in Pennsylvania and Chautauqua and an early literacy conference in Texas. In each place Marie's name was a part of conversation and I felt that my greatest achievement was to say, 'Yes!' to the question, 'Do you know Marie Clay?'

Few people in New Zealand know how Marie was, and is, revered in the United States … her methods of rescuing at-risk readers are the safety nets in many schools there. 'I'm Reading Recovery trained', teachers say with pride and confidence.

It was a joke between Marie and me that we never seemed to meet in New Zealand. It was over a bowl of noodles in Singapore, at an IRA conference in the States, or some function in Hong Kong. But she was in Auckland with Margaret Mahy, Dorothy Butler and I at a Storylines celebration when this photo was taken.

Marie Clay — A Tribute to an Enduring Scholar

Bridie Raban

*Professorial Fellow, Melbourne Graduate School of Education,
University of Melbourne*

I began my teaching career in 1965 as a peripatetic remedial reading teacher, working in three UK primary schools in the north of England. I was engaged to work with small groups of children who were falling behind with their reading and writing after two years in school. They were in their third year of school experience. These young children were dejected and demoralised and I argued frequently that we should be supporting them earlier in their school careers. However, the position then was that they could not have been deemed to have failed so soon in their school experience, and it would be damaging to label them as failures so early in their school experience.

It wasn't until a decade later that the groundbreaking work of Marie Clay began to invade those northern shores, from New Zealand. Here we were introduced to an intervention that worked with children intensively (not in small groups), after one year of school experience. The idea was not to label them as failures but rather to offer extra assistance to keep them up with their peers, to support them positively before poor habits became ingrained and difficult to change. What an impact this had on our practice with these children. It was slow to take off, but soon to be researched and acknowledged as a positive and practical intervention for these young children, offsetting the potential negative experiences which followed from leaving them to struggle in regular classrooms for too long.

Dame Professor Marie Clay devoted her working life to understanding early reading development. Her PhD (1966) was focused on young learners' self-correcting behaviours while reading continuous text, and her observations gave shape to a unique set of descriptors. Across the world she was one of the first to indicate the complex nature of young children's processing activity as they used multiple cueing systems to reach resolutions to text challenges. She illuminated the ways in which young children draw on a range of strategies to solve text problems. Marie was one of the first people to identify this range of activity more than 40 years ago. She identified and distinguished visual from linguistic strategies and further differentiated syntactic and semantic processes. These powerful foci enabled scholars across the world to raise awareness of the sophistication of young learners and to take notice of their endeavours. Error analysis from this time became a positive arena for study, with Running Records a cornerstone of Reading Recovery practice.

Let me share a guiding quotation from Marie's work:

Observation of children suggests that they do not learn about language on any one level of organisation *before* they manipulate units at higher levels. (Many teaching schemes imply that this is so.) When they know a few letters they can produce several words, and with several words they can make a variety of sentences … A simplification achieved by dealing firstly with letters, then with words, and finally with word groups may be easy for teachers to understand but children learn on all levels at once. (Clay, 1975, p. 19)

What Marie has to say here, more than 30 years ago, is profound. What she is identifying is the complexity of children's learning about language on all levels at once. Immediately, we see the powerful way in which she has translated theory into practice. Her Reading Recovery procedures take every opportunity to work at all levels 'at once', giving teachers and children the opportunity to interact across the linguistic and visual strategies to solve the challenges of both known and unknown texts.

Here we see the brilliance of Marie's devotion to her work. Her theoretical insights have always been profound. What has made them world class is the ways in which she has turned them into practice, a practice that has crossed international boundaries and boundaries of language. The translation of her theoretical insights into a powerful and enduring set of practices is a tribute to Marie's ability to identify theoretical perspectives and translate them into practical procedures that support young learners.

Reading Recovery is an immense tribute to Marie's work across decades of theoretical considerations. Reading Recovery captures every aspect of Marie's work and makes available to Reading Recovery teachers a manageable set of activities to support young literacy learners. She has put in place a whole training and support programme to ensure that young learners are initiated appropriately. Internationally, Reading Recovery speaks with one voice and continues to share a perspective across nations.

My own scholarship owes much to that of Marie Clay.

Her insights into the processes of young literacy learners have illuminated my understandings, and my appreciation of practice. I am profoundly indebted for Marie's ability to translate theory into sound practice. She has created a network of international practice that has influenced the lives of millions of children across the world. This is truly an accomplishment at the highest level. Being an academic is one thing; being a change agent for positive outcomes as well is a great gift.

Marie, your great good humour, your patience with book signing and photos, your ability to continue to explain complex processes, and your determination to keep young literacy learners in focus is a tribute to you as a scholar of the highest order.

Thank you, Marie Clay, for all you have done and all your work will do. Your work will endure because it is sound, it is powerful, and it is transcendent. Your life's memory will be supported and continued by those who acclaim your worth and value. Reading Recovery will support thousands of children and, through you, their memories will persist and succeed in ways that are remarkable.

Marie Clay, we value your insights, your ability to process theory into practice, and your support across nations for young literacy learners.

Marie, your life will never be forgotten. Your genius and your legacy will live on.

Reference

Clay, M.M. 1975. *What Did I Write?* Auckland: Heinemann.

Marie and New Zealand Reading Recovery

Christine Boocock

*Reading Recovery Trainer, National Reading Recovery
Faculty of Education, The University of Auckland*

Attempting to capture the breadth of Marie's contribution to Reading Recovery in New Zealand is a challenging task. Every person who knew her has unique memories of Marie presenting at conferences, participating in meetings, working with teachers, speaking to administrators or answering the countless questions each of us asked.

Christine Boocock, Dianne Stuart (Canada) and Marie in 1994.

We greatly valued the special place Marie always kept for New Zealanders in Reading Recovery. We thought of her as 'our Marie' who always returned to New Zealand, like the amazing godwits that fly back to this country after journeying to the other side of the world. From the very beginnings of Reading Recovery while a busy professor at the University of Auckland, Marie made herself continuously available to listen to and support Reading Recovery practitioners. On retiring from the Faculty of Education at the University of Auckland, in 1991, she turned her attention full-time to assisting Reading Recovery in New Zealand as well as throughout the world, providing unstinting assistance and guidance.

In her writings, Marie likened effective teaching to a conversation where the teacher must take responsibility at different times to be both a speaker and a listener. In these terms Marie was always an outstanding teacher. Her defining characteristic over all the years was her ability to *listen* to people and to respond. She loved meeting and talking with Reading Recovery people and all others engaged and interested in education: children, parents, teachers, researchers, Tutors and Trainers across New Zealand and the world. Marie always made herself available to talk. She kept a listed phone number so that people could contact her directly. No one's questions were too trivial; whether a teacher puzzled about children's writing development, a Tutor's enquiry about research design, or a Trainer with an issue regarding future developments. Marie revelled in the challenge of every problem to solve and the chance to guide. She did this in a sometimes firm but always humble way. That's why everyone felt so very comfortable calling her simply 'Marie'.

On a personal note, when I was one of her students I remember being overwhelmed with the willingness with which Marie gave of her time. As I was working to a tight deadline, Marie agreed to meet with me regularly during the public holidays between Christmas and New Year to discuss my thesis. I was not alone in receiving this attention. Countless other students over her long career reaped the benefit of Marie's sharp intellect, wide scholarship and personal time.

Emily Rodgers (Ohio) and Mary K. Lose (Michigan) were Marie Clay Literacy Trust scholars in 2002.

Marie created opportunities to make things happen. Her forward thinking, as well as her generosity, in setting up the Marie Clay Literacy Trust meant there was a source of funding for varied research and development purposes related to literacy that continues to benefit many New Zealand and overseas teachers, Tutors and Trainers. Grants available to overseas Trainers to visit New Zealand for an extended period to undertake research in the educational context in which Reading Recovery began are an example of this assistance.

Marie was also instrumental in the formation of an advisory committee for New Zealand Reading Recovery comprising representatives of educational sectors who provide valuable advice, connections and support for the work of the national centre.

Since Reading Recovery began, hundreds of visitors from overseas, both Reading Recovery professionals and interested educators, have come to New Zealand from every part of the world to deepen their understandings. Marie played an integral part in the success of these visits, always showing a keen interest in the planning, and sharing and relishing the professional discussions in both formal and informal settings.

Many times in the latter part of her life Marie said, 'I do not need to study history, I am history', but her astute mind was always on the future, never looking backwards, except at times to remark on how cyclical trends in educational practices and movements are over time. Always the astute political thinker, Marie guided Reading Recovery through many challenging times, demonstrating along the journey crucial guiding principles for the effective management of an intervention in a changing educational world. Her foresight was demonstrated in her insistence that the international Reading Recovery Trainer body create an International Trainers Organisation (IRRTO) so that all countries involved in Reading Recovery, small and large, had an equal voice in any possible changes needed in the future.

Marie was there for New Zealand Reading Recovery on many special occasions, both professional and social. Whether a main speaker or an observer at our annual Tutor professional development week or at one of the many celebrations of milestones in Reading Recovery, Marie's presence was always confirming and

New Zealand Tutors and Trainers with Marie at the study forum for Literacy Lessons Designed for Individuals *in 2006.*

hugely encouraging. She made it a particular priority, if she were available, to acknowledge the future professionals in Reading Recovery by attending the graduation ceremonies of each new group of Tutors and Trainers.

Her last professional outing was to an Auckland Reading Recovery end-of-year event. Marie spoke briefly to teachers gathered to celebrate the completion of the 2006 teacher training course, talking about the future of the global enterprise of Reading Recovery.

We celebrate the opportunity to have known and worked with an extraordinary New Zealander. As we read her words, we will continue to hear her voice guiding us.

In a poem by one of Marie's favourite New Zealand poets, Allen Curnow, written near the end of his life, called *When and Where,* there are lines that Marie might have spoken:

Gently as I stroke
this child's head, I'm thinking, 'Goodbye!
It's all yours now, the season's crop —
your time to bud, and bloom ...'

Letter from a Former Student, Maris O'Rourke

Maris O'Rourke was the first CEO of the Ministry of Education in New Zealand, and Marie had been on the selection panel. Maris later worked as the Director of Education for the World Bank and is currently an Education Consultant to the World Bank, working on a project, Primary Education for Disadvantaged Children in Vietnam, until 2011. Maris wrote this letter on 3 April 2007 to Marie in the hospice after she found out how ill Marie was from another former student and friend of Marie's, Dee Twiss.

My Dear Marie

How lucky I was to have you giving a lecture on Developmental Psychology in the first month of the first year of my university life in 1970. Everything you said resonated with me and I knew I had found my thing.

As you know, I took Education 1 because it was on at a time I could attend University. We were living in Grafton and I had a small child. I had always wanted to go to University but somehow never thought I could do it — so Education 1 was my first try and it was with nervous fear and lots of excitement that I went off to my first week of lectures. To be honest, I had no idea what this subject 'Education' might even entail. And then I met you — and my future was decided.

I carried on taking Education and/or Psychology every year plus some other interesting stuff here and there like Sociolinguistics with Anne Salmond. I always enrolled in your courses — they were tough, uncompromising, relevant — there was nothing easy about them. A lot like you, really. When I succeeded, I would feel the most amazing and satisfying sense of real accomplishment. It was like a wonderful gift and I knew my mind was improving and that I was growing not just intellectually but in every way. I was able to bring my natural curiosity and love of learning to a higher and more useful level.

I still remember when a whole group of us enrolled in Changing Deviant Development with you for our Masters. After the first class, Tony Pine and I were walking back along Wynyard Street and talking about how much we had enjoyed the class and you. We were both saying how much better you were now; that the teaching was clearer; the subject matter more relevant etc. Suddenly we both started laughing and realised you hadn't changed — but we certainly had! You had never compromised and we had finally caught up with you (well, to some extent).

I'd like to be able to tell you I was the same sort of teacher you were but I wasn't — for all that I was good and many of the things I learned from you like setting standards, the need for intellectual rigour and using a wide body of knowledge were there. From you I learned that there is nothing as practical as a good theory and I learned to love research and use it well. I still use those skills every day, albeit in very different ways, for example my family history that I wrote last year was better for the rigorous research skills I applied to it.

Someone wise once said that the purpose of life is to matter — to count, to stand for something, to have it make some difference that we lived at all. I believe that. You can feel a quiet and deep sense of real satisfaction that you meet all those criteria.

At every level, from global to local, what you have done has mattered — and still does. Children too many to number can read because of you. Parents too many to number have had the lives of their families improved and their fears allayed because of you. Teachers too many to number are more skilled because of you. I have seen them taking individual differences into account and using a common methodology in a specific way to get uncommon results. It's amazing stuff and I know from recent feedback that the Reading Recovery teachers rate you as tops; love it when you speak to them; love the revised books; and continue to be passionate about the programme. What you have done is basic, fundamental and has therefore lasted; and will continue to do so.

I have always appreciated the way you have supported me and helped me further my career and dreams as a student, research assistant, lecturer and public servant. Whenever I asked you to be a referee you would say, 'No, I can do more for you in other ways.' And you were so right. You have been on the interview panel for so many significant events in my life — and it was always good to see you there. I knew the interview would be hard, challenging, probing and worthwhile and, interestingly enough, that I would come away knowing more, and less, than when I went in. You are very good at making people think and going away feeling appropriately uncomfortable; that there is more to know; that there is 'unfinished business'; and that there is a great deal more to do.

I think one of my proudest moments was when you wrote about my Masters thesis in *Research in Education in New Zealand: The State of the Art*. I still treasure what you wrote and it was because of that I felt confident enough to enrol in a PhD. You also gave me 9½ once for an essay — an unheard of event. There was a lot of oohing and aahing and I had a brief period of fame and glory in the MA class for that one!

Another thing that affected me was when you gave up being HOD of Education, saying, 'There are more interesting things to be doing.' I've used that too and moved on despite the status, power, money etc when there were 'more interesting things to be doing'. In the 70s and 80s there weren't many women around as models and mentors — you were one of the few. I count myself fortunate that you have been in my life.

Finally, of course, who could forget that wonderful, magical day at the Eden Gardens where the sun shone, flowers were blooming, perfume was everywhere, birds were singing and Dee Twiss, you and I sat outside and lunched, laughed, talked, shared stories and appreciated each other until the sun went down. We added another ex-student, Marie Cameron, to the group and continued to meet regularly for 'fun lunches' — those were special times that we will miss. Dee and Marie have read this and 'agree with every word'.

Know that we will treasure the memories.

Letter from Connie Briggs

This is one of the letters received after Marie's death. The letter, dated 18 April 2007, is from Connie Briggs, Reading Recovery Trainer Emeritus and Professor of Reading at Texas Woman's University.

Dear Family of Marie Clay

Marie was a very special person. I'm sure you all knew that as members of her family. However, as most family, you loved her as a sister, mother, or grandmother, and maybe were unaware of just how much her work was respected and how much she was treasured around the world. The letters, cards and memorials will be testament to this fact.

Marie was extraordinary for many reasons. Her intellect was incredible. In education it is rare for someone to be a researcher, theorist and practitioner and do them all so well. Her research and theoretical work were groundbreaking and will continue to be important into the future. Marie left us with important research questions that will continue to guide our work in Reading Recovery and in literacy in general.

Marie showed the world what was possible for the lowest achieving children. Her work not only touched the thousands of teachers, Teacher Leaders, and Trainers who were trained in Reading Recovery, but made a lifelong difference to millions of children around the world. What a legacy! Her work was far reaching beyond Reading Recovery. Last year she published our new teaching manuals and challenged international Trainers to reach out to other professionals who teach special populations of students to share what we have learned through our work in Reading Recovery. Her work will continue to influence teaching and learning around the world.

By rights, Marie should have had a huge ego, but she didn't. Her focus was always on the children. We would often miss her at meetings to find her sitting at a table in the corner talking to teachers. She was interested in what they were thinking and how their teaching was going. She saw more value in working with a group of Teacher Leaders or teachers than at speaking at a large conference. I will for ever be reminded by her example that the work that I do is in the service of the children that we teach.

Marie was a mentor and friend to many, many people. We felt she cared about us and our work. She made herself available to consult with many of us on our research and writing projects. She supported our attempts, always challenging us to do our best. She was a person who walked her talk and led by example.

The highlight of my professional career is that I was able to personally know Marie as a friend and a mentor. She will be truly missed. She will remain in our hearts and our work as we try to fulfil the challenges that she set for us and her vision that all children will learn to be literate.

Epilogue

On their card of sympathy, the Southland branch of the New Zealand Reading Association included the quote 'To teach is to touch tomorrow.'

Marie liked the story of the star-thrower that Loren Eiseley saw and wrote about in *The Unexpected Universe*, the man who threw stranded starfish back into the sea: 'I turned as I neared the bend in the coast and saw him toss another star, skimming it skilfully over the ravening and tumultuous water.' He picked up a 'still-living star' himself, he spun it far out into the waves and thought, 'After us, there will be others.' In typed notes, Marie Clay said, 'I spent a great deal of my 'retirement' helping others to become starfish throwers … teachers across the world are working … with amazing dedication to bring young children who were straying away from success back to a sense of self-efficacy in literacy learning.'

In 2007, I heard the poem *What the Living Do* by Marie Howe on the car radio. It tells of the ordinary things we continue to do even after someone important to us has died.

> For weeks now, driving, or dropping a bag of groceries in the street,
>   the bag breaking,

> I've been thinking: This is what the living do.

We will continue to do ordinary and not so ordinary things. The living will think about Marie Clay, talk about her, write about the influence of her ideas, read her books, and use the tools she developed to help others into literacy.

We are living. We will remember you, Marie.

We will remember you.